EverQuest®

The Shadows of Luclin

Prima's Official Strategy Guide

An Incan Monkey God Studios Production

Prima Games

A Division of Random House, Inc.

3000 Lava Ridge Court

Roseville, CA 95661

(916) 787-7000

www.primagames.com

Credits

IMGS Writers Beth Loubet (managing editor), Melissa Tyler, Tuesday Frase, Chris McCubbin

Co-Writer Alan VanCouvering of Sony Online Entertainment

Additional Writers Eugen "Ellegon" Weber and our irreplaceable panel of experts

Statistics David Ladyman

Interior Graphic Design Sharon Freilich, Raini Madden

Interior Layout Sharon Freilich (lead), Raini Madden, Tuesday Frase, Melissa Tyler

Cover Art Keith Parkinson

Fact-Checking Alan VanCouvering and our fantastic panel

EQ Atlas Maps Portions © 2001 Mike Swiernik and EQAtlas; used here by permission, all rights reserved.

Newbie FAQ From The *EverQuest* Newbie Zone, http://newbiezone.freewebspace.com or http://pub57.ezboard.com/btheeverquestnewbiezone used here by permission. Newbie Zone writers: Eugen "Ellegon" Weber (Druid, Antonius Bayle) with DwWarrior, Balkin_Ironfist, Balkor Ironfist, CorwinH, Lost-INNer, Mara, Naked-Newbie, Nevat, Nusabrecat, Pand, Sinda, Sysop-Vinria, Sysop-Wendelius, Sysop-Elbrop, Tielle, T. Henmant, Zandar, Ashara, Cyranith, Wadin, Yumon, Zernan and others on the Newbie Board

Many Thanks to SOE team members Jeff Butler, Gordon Wrinn, Lawrence Poe, Scott McDaniel (lead artist), Ronnie Ashlock, Milo D. Cooper, Adam McMahon, Ken Meyer, Jr., Cory Rohlfs, Rick Schmitz, Robert Collier, Sabrina Fox, Daniel MacGibbon, David Nevala, Vu Nguyen, Bob Painter, Tim Petty, James Romedy, Ranjeet Singhal, Patrick Ho, Rick Johnson, Shaun Johnston, Ben Lazzaro, Evan Sampson, Julius Willis, Bill Yeatts

Special Thanks to Arch Mage Alex "Zandar" Harkness for recruiting the Companions from Bristlebane (www.cotg.net).

Our Undying Gratitude to our Expert *EverQuest* Panel

Airik Wolfe (Vonairik of Bristlebane); Brian Wishnousky (Zzrod); Alex "Zandar" Harkness (Arch Mage, Bristlebane); Chris Skinner; Andrea Silva (Cryth Thistledown, Bristlebane); James "Ronaldor Vladimir" Lewis; Brandon de la Cruz (http://www.seventenmusic.com); Jason "Tennier" Claxton; Brian L. Beagle (Gnish, Mage of Death/Jietoh); Jason "Reijas" Reisz; Dador Caduceus (Realm of Valor, Mithaniel Marr); Ken White; Dave Harrod (Sslithiss Elghinn 'Faer); Kevin "Skoriksis" Freet; Falaanla Marr (Human Magician of Fennin Ro); Mike Swiernik; Monica Wishnousky (Moonshadow Litherial, Luneshadow, Lunemew Gernawl); Stephen "Tarthug" Reinsborough and Gilles "Barawin" André for his help with the Firiona Vie section

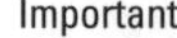

ISBN: 7615-3678-7
Library of Congress Catalog Card Number: 2001097716
Printed in the United States of America
01 02 03 04 BB 10 9 8 7 6 5 4 3 2 1

Table of Contents

Table of Contents

Now Hear This!

The information in this book was correct at the time of printing. However, EverQuest is an ever-changing world and all of this information is subject to change at any time.

Newbie focus. This book is mostly intended for newer players — the most experienced players already know most of the advice in it, although the maps and lists may prove useful. Therefore, the advice here is more directed to newer characters.

Details, but limits. Similarly, only spells through level 25 are fully detailed, the mapped areas only include the starting cities and nearby zones available to lower level characters, and the creatures described are only those found near these cities. Nearly all of these creatures have more powerful relatives living further from the cities, whose stats are not included here.

So, what does this book include?

Experienced *EverQuest* players may recognize two things about this book right off the bat. The first is that much of this information is available on the web, and some of it is available from various screens in the game, but some of it could only come from the *EQ* designers at Sony Online Entertainment. In this book, everything is in one place and at your fingertips while playing. The second thing is that not quite everything is included. This is a no-spoiler strategy guide, which avoids revealing things that might give a few players an unfair advantage over the rest. SOE has gone to a great deal of trouble to create a world where people must work together, and it doesn't seem quite fair for every last secret to be revealed in such an impersonal format as a book. So, for instance, there are no descriptions of the deepest, darkest dungeons, or explanations of quests in which many have died trying to unravel their secrets.

PLAYER CHARACTERS (p. 6). This chapter begins with race, class and deity **tables** (pp. 10-17), useful for quick comparisons. It goes on to describe the races and classes on Luclin, including the new Vah Shir race and Beastlord class, skills, and the new alternative advancement schemes for upper-level characters.

ALTERNATIVE SERVERS (p. 78). Your choice of which server to play on is important, and this chapter gives a description of the new role-playing server, Firiona Vie, and the new type of PvP server, Sullon Zek, with advice on how to survive and have fun playing PvP.

EXPLORING LUCLIN (p. 98). We give you a quick tour of all of the main zones of Luclin, including maps, with detailed keys, of the cities of Shar Vahl and Shadow Haven and the nearby zones of Shadeweaver's Thicket, Hollowshade Moor and Grimling Forest (where new characters can gain their first few levels of experience).

CREATURES (p. 120). Stats for the monsters and critters found near the starting cities.

SPELLS (p. 142). Complete info on all new spells through level 25, including the new Beastlord spells, plus lesser information on all other new spells.

WORDS TO THE WISE (p. 174). Strategies, tips, advice, websites, commands and emotes, new items stats, a newbie FAQ – all arranged for easy access. It's not a substitute for getting out there, talking to other players and joining a guild, but is full of advice to point you in the right directions.

And a reminder, the information in this book was correct at the time of printing. However, EverQuest is an ever-changing world and all of this information is subject to change at any time.

Player Characters

primagames.com

Toshizo's First Quest

by Airik Wolfe (Vonairik of Bristlebane)

Bright and sunny was the day and Toshizo was almost too happy, for today was his last day of youth. The day when all young ones become citizens and take up a skill or trade. He was already on his first quest, having spent the morning in the Palace with his family getting sworn into his father's profession. For now, he was a Beastlord in training, and he had to make his father proud.

Looking at the map his mother gave him, Toshizo made his way from the Palace to the south gate. The pure excitement was almost too much, and young Toshizo made many wrong turns along the way, leaving him with no choice but to constantly ask for directions. He had never been to see the Registrar before, and his excitement from walking the bright streets alone made this one of the best days in his life. Daydreaming of things yet to come, he at last stumbled into the proper office and walked shyly up to the front counter. Almost embarrassed, he called out.

"Hail, Registrar Bindarah, I am here to become a citizen."

Registrar Bindarah replied, "Sorry friend, no time to talk right now. Busy, busy, busy!"

Almost turning to leave, Toshizo stood his ground, coughed, and handed the note Elder Animist Sahdi had given him over to the Registrar.

Registrar Bindarah examined it, then finally spoke. "Young Toshizo, I will be happy to process your registration for you. While I etch your name on our people's book of records, I will require you to run a couple of errands. Take this certificate to the tax collector and obtain his seal. While you're away, have Mignah create your personal acrylia slate for you. Bring both the seal and the slate to me as soon as you can."

Thanking Registrar Bindarah and scampering off, Toshizo almost forgot the certificate for the tax collector. Within minutes, Toshizo knew he was lost and had to stop again and ask directions.

"Hail, Welfyr Bristlewind. Can you direct me to the Tax Collector?"

Welfyr Bristlewind answered, "You can find Tax Collector Khugra in the bank. It's in the south-eastern end of the merchant's quarter."

Thanking Welfyr, Toshizo ran off to the bank in the merchant's quarter. He had been to the bank with his mother once before and made his way there without any trouble at all. Opening the door and stepping into the darkened interior, Toshizo watched with amazement as money was handled right before his very eyes. Spying the Tax Collector sign above a desk in the back, Toshizo made his way over to it and handed in his paperwork.

"Hail, Tax Collector Khugra. I am here to request your seal on my citizen certificate, please."

Tax Collector Khugra placed his seal on the certificate before returning it. "Ahh, a new taxpayer, wonderful! You must always remember that it is a distinct privilege to contribute to the upkeep of our noble society, and not merely a duty or a burden. I look forward to collecting your honorable taxes in the future. May the spirits prosper you, Toshizo."

Almost returning to the Registrar without his slate, Toshizo remembered it at the last moment and headed off in search of Mignah. It took no time at all to find Mignah by asking for directions at every turn.

"Hail, Mignah Cahru, I am in need of a personal acrylia slate."

Mignah Cahru pulled a smoldering piece of forged acrylia from a nearby oven and, before Toshizo could react, pressed his hand into the still-soft metal. "This may hurt a bit, but it'll heal." He etched Toshizo's name and the date into the slate and plunged it into a bucket before placing it into Toshizo's stinging palm.

Shaking his still-stinging hand as he walked out the door, Toshizo wondered what just happened and held the slate up to take a look. He made his way back to the Registrar's office and got there just as she was locking up for lunch.

"Hail, Registrar Bindarah, here are the items you requested I bring to you!"

Registrar Bindarah said, "Ahh, there you are. I was about to send someone looking for you. Everything seems to be in order here, only one task remains. You must gain audience with the king and swear fealty to his highness by handing him this document. Return to me when this is done."

Toshizo turned and headed back to the Palace, wondering if all this running around was really worth it, then remembered his father's pride, and quickened his pace. As Toshizo neared the Palace, the guards requested his papers and teased him because of his youth. After showing all the guards his citizenship papers and explaining why he was there, Toshizo soon found himself among the crowd of other young ones waiting to see the King for the same reasons. An hour passed before they called his name, and Toshizo walked up to the king without showing any of the fear he was really feeling. Bowing deeply, he handed over his paperwork and mustered his deepest, most formal-sounding voice.

"Hail, Raja Kerrath. I am here to offer my services to the King and his people!"

Raja Kerrath accepted his pledge, then gave Toshizo his next task. "Your humility and willingness to serve shall not be wasted. There is much to be done, Toshizo, and our people thank you in advance for your selfless service. Take this form back to the Registrar and you will be one of our new citizens."

Toshizo left the Palace at a galloping run, for he knew he was almost finished with his first quest. He reached the Registrar's office in record time and tossed his paperwork onto her desk.

"Hail, Registrar Bindarah! My completed paper work. I hope everything is in order."

Registrar Bindarah glanced over the paperwork and made some marks on her personal slate.

Registrar Bindarah said, "Well done, Toshizo. I am honored to be the first to welcome you to citizenship of Shar Vahl! May you serve our society as well as it serves you. Return to your guildmaster and present these to him. The acrylia slate shall henceforth serve as proof of your citizenship."

Registrar Bindarah handed Toshizo back his slate and his hard-earned Note of Citizenship.

Returning yet again to the Palace to find his new guildmaster, Toshizo wondered at his day-long adventure and hoped that every coming day would be as exciting. Upon arriving at the palace, the guards remembered Toshizo and congratulated him on his Citizenship, directing him to his guildmaster with no problems.

"Hail, Elder Animist Sahdi. I have returned a Citizen and I am ready to go forth and prove myself like my father before me."

Elder Animist Sahdi replied warmly, "Greetings, Toshizo. Nice to see you."

Toshizo handed Elder Animist Sahdi his paperwork and slate.

Elder Animist Sahdi spoke again. "'Allow me to be the first to welcome you to the Khati Sha, lords of the beasts. Accept this cloak, young initiate. It is a symbol of your loyalty to our noble people. May it serve you as you serve us all. Present your acrylia slate to Animist Poren and he will give you instruction. May the spirits of the beasts guide you and keep you safe."

Toshizo walked over to Animist Poren. "Hail, Animist Poren."

Animist Poren said, "Greetings, Toshizo. It is good to see you. If you have come for the first stage of Khati Sha training, please show me your acrylia slate."

His heart nearly bursting with anticipation, Toshizo handed his slate over to Poren, wondering what his next task would be.

Animist Poren waved and said, "I have much for you to do, Toshizo. There is great need for capable Khati Sha in this new land. It is important that you progress speedily. We need to outfit you with the equipment that defines our chosen path. We'll start with your battleclaws ..."

Figuring out what you want to be in the game is an integral part of your playing experience. From the tough Barbarian Warrior to the gentle Vah Shir Beastlord, EverQuest: The Shadows of Luclin *offers many alternatives through which to bring your online character to life.*

Even though you select race before class in the Character Creation screens, you should plan out your character in advance. Pick the class you want to play first, then select a race based on the most desirable skills and abilities out of the races able to play that class. Remember, the race and class that you choose should reflect your playing style and overall goals. Some combinations, notably with regard to the spellcasting classes, are more difficult to master. Every race and class has its own strengths and weaknesses, and what one player perceives as a drawback might actually be an advantage in your eyes.

Another aspect of character creation you should consider before investing a lot of time and effort is how you plan to develop your character. As you progress in level, you'll be able to spend your points on acquiring and improving skills. Check out the Skill tables (p. 57) and Advanced Ability charts (p. 12) to figure out what abilities you want your character to attain later in life.

Tables

Race and Class Combinations

	BRD	BST	CLR	DRU	ENC	MAG	MNK	NEC	PAL	RNG	ROG	SHD	SHM	WAR	WIZ
Barbarian		√									√		√	√	
Dark Elf			√		√	√		√			√	√		√	√
Dwarf			√						√		√			√	
Erudite			√		√	√		√	√			√			√
Gnome			√		√	√		√			√			√	√
Half Elf	√			√					√	√	√			√	
Halfling			√	√							√			√	
High Elf			√		√	√			√						√
Human	√		√	√	√	√	√	√	√	√	√	√		√	√
Iksar		√					√	√				√	√	√	
Ogre		√										√	√	√	
Troll		√										√	√	√	
Vah Shir	√	√									√		√	√	
Wood Elf	√			√						√	√			√	

Starting Cities and Racial Tensions

Race	Abbrev.	Starting Cities	Racial Tensions With ...												
Barbarian	*(Br)*	Halas		DE								Ik	Og	Tr	
Dark Elf	*(DE)*	Neriak	Br		Dw	Er	Gn	1/2	Hg	HE	Hm	Ik			WE
Dwarf	*(Dw)*	Kaladim		DE								Ik	Og	Tr	
Erudite	*(Er)*	Erudin Paineel (Nec, ShKn) [1]		DE								Ik	Og	Tr	
Gnome	*(Gn)*	Ak'Anon		DE								Ik	Og	Tr	
Half-Elf	*(1/2)*	Felwithe, Freeport, Kelethin, Qeynos [2]		DE								Ik	Og	Tr	
Halfling	*(Hg)*	Rivervale		DE								Ik	Og	Tr	
High Elf	*(HE)*	Felwithe		DE								Ik	Og	Tr	
Human	*(Hm)*	Qeynos [2], Freeport		DE								Ik	Og	Tr	
Iksar	*(Ik)*	Cabilis	Br	DE	Dw	Er	Gn	1/2	Hg	HE	Hm		Og	Tr	WE
Ogre	*(Og)*	Oggok	Br		Dw	Er	Gn	1/2	Hg	HE	Hm	Ik			WE
Troll	*(Tr)*	Grobb	Br		Dw	Er	Gn	1/2	Hg	HE	Hm	Ik			WE
Vah Shir	*(VS)*	Shar Vahl	None exist												
Wood Elf	*(WE)*	Kelethin		DE								Ik	Og	Tr	

1 Erudite Necromancers and Shadow Knights start in Paineel, even though the Starting City map screen only lists Erudin.

2 Human and Half Elf Rangers and Druids who pick Qeynos actually start just outside Qeynos, in Surefall Glade.

Basic Race Abilities

	STR	STA	AGI	DEX	WIS	INT	CHA	Bonus	Total
Barbarian	103	95	82	70	70	60	55	50	585
Dark Elf	60	65	90	75	83	99	60	50	582
Dwarf	90	90	70	90	83	60	45	50	578
Erudite	60	70	70	70	83	107	70	50	580
Gnome	60	70	85	85	67	98	60	50	575
Half Elf	70	70	90	85	60	75	75	50	575
Halfling	70	75	95	90	80	67	50	50	577
High Elf	55	65	85	70	95	92	80	50	592
Human	75	75	75	75	75	75	75	50	575
Iksar	70	70	90	85	80	75	55	50	575
Ogre	130	122	70	70	67	60	37	50	606
Troll	108	109	83	75	60	52	40	50	577
Vah Shir	90	75	90	70	70	65	65	50	575
Wood Elf	65	65	95	80	80	75	75	50	585

Class Ability Modifiers

	STR	STA	AGI	DEX	WIS	INT	CHA	Bonus Ability Points
Bard	+5	–	–	+10	–	–	+10	25
Beastlord	–	+10	+5	–	+10	–	+5	20
Cleric	+5	+5	–	–	+10	–	–	30
Druid	–	+10	–	–	+10	–	–	30
Enchanter	–	–	–	–	–	+10	+10	30
Magician	–	+10	–	–	–	+10	–	30
Monk	+5	+5	+10	+10	–	–	–	20
Necromancer	–	–	–	+10	–	+10	–	30
Paladin	+10	+5	–	–	+5	–	+10	20
Ranger	+5	+10	+10	–	+5	–	–	20
Rogue	–	–	+10	+10	–	–	–	30
Shadow Knight	+10	+5	–	–	–	+10	+5	20
Shaman	–	+5	–	–	+10	–	+5	30
Warrior	+10	+10	+5	–	–	–	–	25
Wizard	–	+10	–	–	–	+10	–	30

Alternative Advancement Abilities

As you gain levels, you can set aside some earned experience to accrue training points. You can then spend these points on advanced abilities – minor permanent attribute and resistance boosts, unique skills based on your class (Warrior, Magician, etc.) or archetype (fighter, magic user, and priest), plus general skills available to everyone. The following two tables show general, archetype and class skills. *See p. 61 for details on alternative advancement.*

Advanced General and Archetype Abilities

General Abilities

First Aid
Improved Natural Agility
Improved Natural Charisma
Improved Natural Cold Protection
Improved Natural Dexterity
Improved Natural Disease Protection
Improved Natural Fire Protection
Improved Natural Intelligence
Improved Natural Lung Capacity
Improved Natural Magic Protection
Improved Natural Metabolism
Improved Natural Poison Protection
Improved Natural Regeneration
Improved Natural Run Speed
Improved Natural Stamina
Improved Natural Strength
Improved Natural Wisdom

Archetype Abilities

Caster

Channeling Focus
Mental Clarity
Spell Casting Deftness
Spell Casting Expertise
Spell Casting Fury
Spell Casting Mastery
Spell Casting Subtlety

Melee

Combat Agility
Combat Fury
Combat Stability
Fear Resistance
Finishing Blow
Improved Natural Durability
Improved Natural Healing

Priest

Channeling Focus
Healing Adept
Healing Gift
Mental Clarity
Spell Casting Fury
Spell Casting Mastery
Spell Casting Reinforcement

Advanced Class Abilities

Class Abilities

Bard

Archetype

Caster, Melee Abilities

Class

Acrobatics
Adv. Trap Negotiation
Body and Mind Rejuvenation
Extended Notes
Instrument Mastery
Jam Fest
Physical Enhancement
Scribble Notes
Singing Mastery

Beastlord

Archetype

Melee, Priest Abilities

Class

Body and Mind Rejuvenation
Double Riposte
Pet Discipline
Physical Enhancement

Cleric

Archetype

Priest Abilities

Class

Bestow Divine Aura
Celestial Regeneration
Divine Resurrection
Innate Invisibility to Undead
Mass Group Buff
Purify Soul
Spell Casting Reinforcement Mastery
Turn Undead

Druid

Archetype

Priest Abilities

Class

Dire Charm
Enhanced Root
Exodus
Innate Camouflage
Mass Group Buff
Quick Direct Damage
Quick Evacuation
Spell Casting Reinf. Mastery

Enchanter

Archetype

Caster Abilities

Class

Dire Charm
Gather Mana
Jewel Craft Mastery
Mass Group Buff
Permanent Illusion
Quick Buff
Spell Casting Reinf. Mastery

Magician

Archetype

Caster Abilities

Class

Elemental Form Air/Earth/Fire/Water
Elemental Pact
Frenzied Burnout
Improved Reclaim Energy
Mass Group Buff
Mend Companion
Pet Discipline
Quick Summoning
Turn Summoned

Monk

Archetype

Melee Abilities

Class

Acrobatics
Critical Mend
Double Riposte
Dragon Punch
Purify Body
Rapid Feign
Return Kick

Necromancer

Archetype

Caster Abilities

Class

Call to Corpse
Dead Mesmerization
Dire Charm
Fearstorm
Flesh to Bone
Innate Invisibility to Undead
Life Burn
Mass Group Buff
Mend Companion
Pet Discipline

Paladin

Archetype

Melee, Priest Abilities

Class

Act of Valor
Body and Mind Rejuvenation
Divine Stun
Double Riposte
Fearless
Holy Steed
Improved Lay of Hands
Mass Group Buff
Physical Enhancement
Slay Undead
Two-Hand Bash

Ranger

Archetype

Melee, Priest Abilities

Class

Ambidexterity
Archery Mastery
Body and Mind Rejuvenation
Double Riposte
Endless Quiver
Innate Camouflage
Mass Group Buff
Physical Enhancement

Rogue

Archetype

Melee Abilities

Class

Acrobatics
Adv. Trap Negotiation
Chaotic Stab
Double Riposte
Escape
Poison Mastery
Purge Poison

Shaman

Archetype

Priest Abilities

Class

Alchemy Mastery
Cannibalization
Mass Group Buff
Pet Discipline
Quick Buff
Rabid Bear
Spell Casting Reinf. Mastery

Shadow Knight

Archetype

Caster, Melee Abilities

Class

Body and Mind Rejuvenation
Double Riposte
Fearless
Leech Touch
Pet Discipline
Physical Enhancement
Soul Abrasion
Super Harm Touch
Two-Hand Bash
Unholy Steed

Warrior

Archetype

Melee Abilities

Class

Area Taunt
Bandage Wound
Double Riposte
Flurry
Rampage
Warcry

Wizard

Archetype

Caster Abilities

Class

Exodus
Improved Familiar
Mana Burn
Nexus Gate
Quick Direct Damage
Quick Evacuation
Spell Casting Fury Mastery
Strong Root

Deities Table

(Ag) Agnostic
(PB) Bertoxxulous, the Plaguebringer
(KT) Bristlebane Fizzlethorpe, the King of Thieves
(FL) Cazic-Thule, the Faceless
(PHt) Innoruuk, the Prince of Hate
(RK) Karana, the Rainkeeper
(QL) Erollisi Marr, the Queen of Love
(LB) Mithaniel Marr, the Lightbringer
(PHl) Rodcet Nife, the Prime Healer
(OL) Prexus, the Oceanlord
(TQ) Quellious, the Tranquil
(BP) Solusek Ro, the Burning Prince
(DB) Brell Serilis, the Duke of Below
(SH) The Tribunal, the Six Hammers
(MA) Tunare, the Mother of All
(WQ) Veeshan, the Wurmqueen
(WL) Rallos Zek, the Warlord

Deity Table

	Ag	*PB*	*KT*	*FL*	*PHt*	*RK*	*QL*	*LB*	*PHl*	*OL*	*TQ*	*BP*	*DB*	*SH*	*MA*	*WQ*	*WL*
Barbarian All start in Halas.																	
Beastlord														SH			
Rogue	Ag		KT											SH			
Shaman														SH			
Warrior	Ag													SH			WL
Dark Elf All start in Neriak.																	
Cleric					PHt												
Enchanter	Ag				PHt												
Magician	Ag				PHt												
Necromancer					PHt												
Rogue	Ag		KT		PHt												
Shadow Knight					PHt												
Warrior	Ag				PHt												WL
Wizard	Ag				PHt							BP					
Dwarf All start in Kaladim.																	
Cleric													DB				
Paladin													DB				
Rogue	Ag		KT										DB				
Warrior	Ag												DB				
Erudite All start in Erudin, except Necromancers and Shadow Knights, who start in Paineel.																	
Cleric										OL	TQ						
Enchanter	Ag									OL	TQ						
Magician	Ag									OL	TQ						
Necromancer				FL													
Paladin										OL	TQ						
Shadow Knight				FL													
Wizard	Ag									OL	TQ	BP					

	Ag	PB	KT	FL	PHt	RK	QL	LB	PHI	OL	TQ	BP	DB	SH	MA	WQ	WL
Gnome All start in Ak'Anon																	
Cleric		PB	KT										DB				
Enchanter	Ag	PB											DB				
Magician	Ag	PB											DB				
Necromancer		PB															
Rogue	Ag	PB	KT										DB				
Warrior	Ag	PB											DB				WL
Wizard	Ag	PB										BP	DB				
Human O = Oeynos, F = Freeport																	
Bard	Ag (FQ)		KT (FQ)			RK (Q)	QL (F)	LB (F)	PHI (Q)	OL (FQ)	TQ (FQ)	BP (FQ)	DB (FQ)	SH (FQ)	MA (FQ)	WQ (FQ)	WL (FQ)
Cleric		PB (Q)			PHt (F)	RK (Q)	QL (F)	LB (F)	PHI (Q)								
Druid						RK (Q)									MA (Q)		
Enchanter	Ag (FQ)	PB (Q)			PHt (F)	RK (Q)	QL (F)	LB (F)	PHI (Q)								
Magician	Ag (FQ)	PB (Q)			PHt (F)	RK (Q)	QL (F)	LB (F)	PHI (Q)								
Monk	Ag (Q)										TQ (F)						
Necromancer		PB (Q)				PHt (F)											
Paladin						RK (Q)	QL (F)	LB (F)	PHI (Q)								
Ranger						RK (Q)									MA (Q)		
Rogue	Ag (FQ)	PB (Q)	KT (FQ)		PHt (F)	RK (Q)	QL (F)		PHI (Q)								
Shadow Knight		PB (Q)			PHt (F)												
Warrior	Ag (FQ)	PB (Q)			PHt (F)	RK (Q)	QL (F)	LB (F)	PHI (Q)								WL (FQ)
Wizard	Ag (FQ)	PB (Q)			PHt (F)	RK (Q)	QL (F)	LB (F)	PHI (Q)			BP (FQ)					
Half Elves O = Oeynos, F = Freeport, K = Kelethin, 3 = Oeynos, Freeport & Kelethin, Fw = Felwithe																	
Bard	Ag (3)		KT (3)			RK (Q)	QL (F)	LB (F)	PHI (Q)	OL (3)	TQ (3)	BP (3)	DB (3)	SH (3)	MA (3)	WQ (3)	WL (3)
Druid						RK (Q)									MA (QK)		
Paladin						RK (Q)	QL (F)	LB (F)	PHI (Q)						MA (Fw)		
Ranger						RK (Q)									MA (QK)		
Rogue	Ag (3)	PB (Q)	KT (3)			RK (Q)	QL (F)		PHI (Q)						MA (K)		
Warrior	Ag (3)	PB (Q)			PHt (F)	RK (Q)	QL (F)	LB (F)	PHI (Q)	OL (3)				SH (3)	MA (K)		WL (3)

	Ag	PB	KT	FL	PHt	RK	QL	LB	PHl	OL	TQ	BP	DB	SH	MA	WQ	WL
Halfling All start in Rivervale																	
Cleric			KT														
Druid						RK											
Rogue	Ag		KT										DB				
Warrior	Ag												DB				WL
High Elf All start in Felwithe																	
Cleric															MA		
Enchanter	Ag					RK	QL	LB							MA		
Magician	Ag					RK	QL	LB							MA		
Paladin															MA		
Wizard	Ag					RK	QL	LB				BP			MA		
Iksar All start in Cabilis																	
Beastlord	Ag																
Monk				FL													
Necromancer				FL													
Shadow Knight				FL													
Shaman				FL													
Warrior				FL													
Ogre All start in Oggok																	
Beastlord																	WL
Shadow Knight				FL													WL
Shaman																	WL
Warrior	Ag			FL													WL
Troll All start in Grobb																	
Beastlord				FL	PHt												
Shadow Knight				FL	PHt												
Shaman				FL	PHt												
Warrior	Ag			FL	PHt												WL
Wood Elf All start in Kelethin																	
Bard	Ag		KT			RK	QL	LB	PHl	OL	TQ	BP	DB	SH	MA	WQ	WL
Druid															MA		
Ranger															MA		
Rogue	Ag		KT			RK									MA		
Warrior	Ag					RK									MA		
Vah Shir All start in Shar Vahl																	
Bard	Ag																
Beastlord	Ag																
Rogue	Ag																
Shaman	Ag																
Warrior	Ag																

Racial Abilities and Armor

Races with an innate ability that is otherwise a skill (such as the Dark Elves' Hide ability) automatically get that skill as though they had improved it to level 50. (The Iksar can swim as though they have the Swimming skill at level 100.) If a character with an innate ability wants to train further in that skill, he may do so once his innate ability is lower than the skill's level limit (assuming the skill is available to his chosen class). In most cases, that means he can start training in the skill when he reaches experience level 10.

Racial Abilities and Armor

Race	Vision	Armor	Abilities
Barbarian	Unenhanced	Medium or Large	Slam, +10 Cold Resistance
Dark Elf	Ultravision	Small or Medium	Hide (50)
Dwarf	Infravision	Small	Sense Direction (50) +5 Poison, Magic Resistance
Erudite	Unenhanced	Medium	+5 Magic Resistance -5 Disease Resistance
Gnome	Infravision	Small	Tinkering at level 16
Half Elf	Infravision	Medium	
Halfling	Infravision	Small	Sneak (50), Hide (50) +5 Poison, Disease Resistance
High Elf	Infravision	Small or Medium	
Human	Unenhanced	Medium	
Iksar	Infravision	Medium	+5 Heat Resistance -10 Cold Resistance, AC +12 Swim (100), Forage (50) Enhanced Regeneration [1]
Ogre	Infravision	Large	Slam
Troll	Infravision	Large	Slam, -20 Heat Resistance Enhanced Regeneration [1]
Wood Elf	Infravision	Small or Medium	Forage (50), Hide (50)
Vah Shir	Infravision	Medium or Large	Sneak (50), Safe Fall (50)

[1] Two points every 6 seconds when standing, 4 when sitting (others regenerate no more than half that quickly)

Class & Race

The Shadows of Luclin brings a new dimension to the realm of *EverQuest* — the addition of a new race (Vah Shir) and class (Beastlord). Additionally, the existing classes have seen a few changes since the release of *Ruins of Kunark* and the last *EverQuest* strategy guide. This section covers all races and classes in the game. Within each description for spell-casting classes, you'll also see a set of new spells. These are not a cumulative list; they only list spells that have been added since the *Ruins of Kunark* was released.

You may note that some classes have more new spells than other classes, but don't worry — this was part of the team's effort to balance magical abilities between classes.

Finally, the end of this chapter gives an overview of the game's alternative advancement system, a new way to expand your character. By shunting some of your experience into an advancement pool, you can earn extra abilities.

The following abbreviations are commonly used by players, both in the game and in Internet posts. It's a good idea to be familiar with them when discussing your character. (In the book, however, we've used shorter, two-character descriptions to save space.)

Race Abbreviations

BAR	Barbarian
DEF	Dark Elf
DWF	Dwarf
ELF	Wood Elf
ERU	Erudite
GNM	Gnome
HEF	Half Elf
HFL	Halfling
HIE	High Elf
HUM	Human
IKS	Iksar
OGR	Ogre
TRL	Troll
VAH	Vah Shir

Class Abbreviations

BRD	Bard
BST	Beastlord
CLR	Cleric
DRU	Druid
ENC	Enchanter
MAG	Magician
MNK	Monk
NEC	Necromancer
PAL	Paladin
RNG	Ranger
ROG	Rogue
SHD	Shadow Knight
SHM	Shaman
WAR	Warrior
WIZ	Wizard

Classes

Beastlord

Beastlords are a unique class bound to nature and combat. For the first few years of their career, they must wander the land and hone their natural-born ability to navigate and communicate with animals. Much of this time is spent hunting and questing in order to acquire food, armor and knowledge. With these tools in place, the adult Beastlord is then ready to progress to the next stage of his career — the adoption of a lifelong companion.

While other classes with critters tend to select different pets based on their current situation, Beastlords have a natural affinity for a single type of animal. They also call their summoned pets "warders," or beasts that watch over their owners. Barbarian Beastlords convoke wolves, Iksar use scaled wolves, and Vah Shir adopt tigers. Ogres team up with bears from the nearby Rathe Mountains, and Trolls call alligators from Innothule Swamp. Raised from a tender age by their master, these beasts grow up with undying loyalty for their owners, and the feeling is usually quite mutual. A warder does not assume a persistent stance beside its owner. Instead, it lurks nearby and will appear at a moment's notice when summoned.

A lifelong pledge of protection and unspoken friendship bonds the Beastlord with his or her warder and remains unbroken through death. It is said that upon its owner's death, the warder of a Beastlord will assume a steadfast post by his or her owner's side until resurrection can be managed. Also, unlike the pets available to other casting classes, warders are not limited to your current zone and can travel freely about the world.

Capable of swift blows and buffing spells, Beastlords are naturally drawn to fighting — with their warder close by, of course. It's not uncommon to see a Beastlord casting spells on a warder in between blows against an enemy. What the Beastlord lacks in armor and weaponry is paltry compared to the combined abilities of Beastlord and warder. Together, they make a fierce, formidable fighting team.

Beastlord Skills

Beastlords are part mystical Warriors, more in tune with nature than an everyday fighter, and part wild medicine men. They're similar to Monks in that they're most dangerous when their hands are empty, but Beastlords are also skilled in the use of smaller blunt or piercing weapons. The most dangerous tool at the Beastlord's disposal, however, is his ability to summon a warder at level 9.

At lower levels, the Beastlord is without a warder and closely resembles a Monk fighter. Combat will be difficult, and it's best to stay with a group to ensure that you safely make it to the next level. Later, with more levels and a warder, the Beastlord assumes the role of a Shaman, buffing friends and pets while debuffing enemies. As the Beastlord grows in power and level, so does the warder. Therein lies the real advantage to playing a Beastlord – with buffing spells, the warder pet is one of the most powerful pets in the game.

Every good Beastlord has a respectable repertoire of spells. The majority of a Beastlord's spells are intended to buff, heal or hasten a warder, although this class also has access to a number of other self-buffing and target de-buffing spells (see p. 22).

Even without a warder, young Beastlords can maintain a presence on the battlefield. Month upon month of wandering during the adolescent years gives the Beastlord a high resistance to disease and frostbite and allows him time to build upon certain innate skills, including Kick, Dodge, Dual Wield and Riposte.

Beastlord Races

Members of the Barbarian, Iksar, Ogre, Troll and Vah Shir races can train as a Beastlord, though as an agnostic race, Vah Shir is probably the most neutrally aligned.

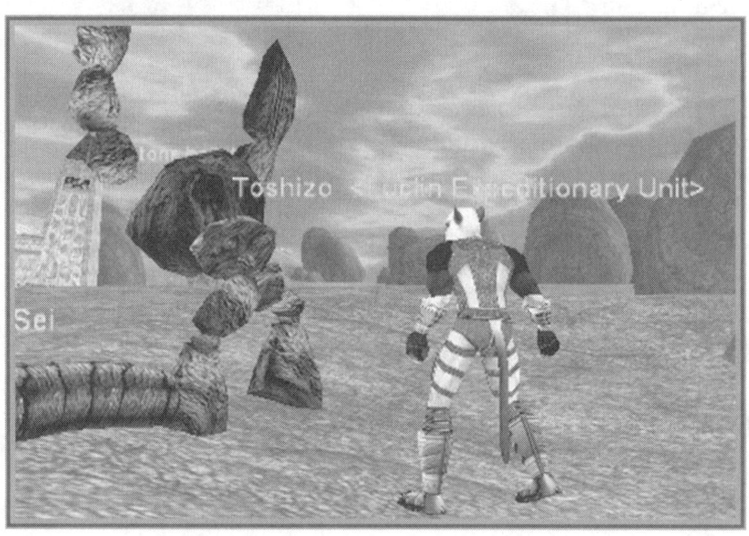

Beastlord Attributes

The Beastlord is a hybrid class, blessed with the fighting ability of a Monk and the spellcasting ability of a Shaman. On the whole, Beastlord-capable races are geared more toward fighting than spellcasting and do not possess a particularly high Intelligence or Wisdom. In the case of the Vah Shir and Iksar, Strength is also slightly lower. Beastlords tend to be limited to chain armor (at least until Beast Tamer's armor can be earned) and smaller hand weapons – but only because they need to stay light on their feet as they silently stalk prey in the wilderness.

Stamina, Agility, Wisdom and **Charisma** are the primary attributes for a Beastlord, and you should pay special attention to these attributes throughout your career. Given that spellcasting is a large part of a Beastlord's existence at level 9 and higher, it's a good idea to put most, if not all, of your 20 starting points into Wisdom to boost casting ability as early as possible. A little Charisma may not hurt, either, if you're planning on traveling.

If you're a Vah Shir Beastlord, keep in mind that many of your early quests require hand fighting and the assistance of other classes. Traveling in parties can help you accomplish them. At higher levels, you'll get a defensive boost by earning Beast Tamer armor.

Most players choose to develop an Ogre or Barbarian Beastlord in order to take advantage of slightly higher starting attributes, specifically Strength. While those race-class combinations work well in combat, the stronger races tend to sacrifice Charisma and Agility, areas in which the Vah Shir score high.

Ultimately, choosing which race you want for a Beastlord character depends on where you want to start (Vah Shir are limited to one starting city, for example), what deity you want to follow, and your playing style. Go for high Strength and Stamina if you enjoy melee combat, or at least pump a lot of starting points into it. Concentrate on high Wisdom and Charisma if you plan to use a warder and spells for the bulk of your combat.

Beastlord Starting Attributes

	Start Pts.	STR	STA*	AGI*	DEX	WIS*	INT	CHA*
Barbarian	20	103	105	87	70	80	60	60
Iksar	20	70	80	95	85	90	75	60
Ogre	20	130	132	75	70	77	60	42
Troll	20	108	119	88	75	70	52	45
Vah Shir	20	90	85	95	70	80	65	70

* Primary Beastlord attributes

Beastlord Spells

Beastlord spell descriptions begin on pg. 145.

Level	Spell	Skill
9	Cure Disease	Alteration
9	Endure Cold	Abjuration
9	Flash of Light	Divination
9	Inner Fire	Abjuration
9	Minor Healing	Alteration
9	Sharik's Replenishing	Alteration
9	Spirit of Sharik	Alteration
15	Cure Poison	Alteration
15	Endure Fire	Abjuration
15	Fleeting Fury	Abjuration
15	Keshuval's Rejuvenation	Alteration
15	Scale Skin	Abjuration
15	Sense Animals	Divination
15	Sicken	Conjuration
15	Spirit of Khaliz	Alteration
15	Spirit of Lightning	Alteration
15	Strengthen	Alteration
22	Drowsy	Alteration
22	Endure Poison	Abjuration
22	Light Healing	Alteration
22	Spirit of Bear	Abjuration
22	Spirit of Keshuval	Alteration
22	Spirit of the Blizzard	Alteration
22	Summon Drink	Conjuration
22	Tainted Breath	Conjuration
30	Herikol's Soothing	Alteration
30	Shrink	Alteration
30	Spirit of Herikol	Alteration
30	Spirit of Inferno	Alteration
30	Spirit of Wolf	Alteration
30	Spirit Sight	Divination
30	Spirit Strength	Alteration
30	Spirit Strike	Evocation
30	Summon Food	Conjuration
30	Turtle Skin	Abjuration
39	Endure Magic	Abjuration
39	Envenomed Breath	Conjuration
39	Healing	Alteration
39	Spirit of Monkey	Alteration
39	Spirit of Ox	Alteration
39	Spirit of the Scorpion	Alteration
39	Spirit of Yekan	Alteration
39	Summon Companion	Conjuration
39	Yekan's Quickening	Alteration
39	Yekan's Recovery	Alteration
49	Counteract Disease	Alteration
49	Frenzy	Abjuration
49	Invigor	Alteration
49	Invisibility	Divination
49	Listless Power	Alteration
49	Protect	Abjuration
49	Raging Strength	Alteration
49	Spirit of Kashek	Alteration
49	Spirit of Vermin	Alteration
49	Vigor of Zehkes	Alteration
50	Sha's Lethargy	Alteration
51	Ultravision	Divination
52	Aid of Khurenz	Alteration
52	Health	Alteration
52	Spirit of Wind	Alteration
52	Venom of the Snake	Conjuration
53	Deftness	Alteration
54	Resist Poison	Abjuration
54	Spirit of Omakin	Alteration
54	Spirit of the Storm	Alteration
54	Strength of Stone	Alteration
55	Chloroplast	Alteration
55	Omakin's Alacrity	Alteration
55	Sha's Restoration	Alteration
56	Incapacitate	Alteration
56	Shifting Shield	Abjuration
56	Spirit of Zehkes	Alteration
57	Greater Healing	Alteration
58	Nullify Magic	Abjuration
58	Spirit of Khurenz	Alteration
58	Talisman of Altuna	Alteration
59	Blizzard Blast	Evocation
59	Sha's Ferocity	Alteration
59	Spiritual Purity	Alteration
60	Alacrity	Alteration
60	Spirit of Kati Sha	Alteration
60	Spiritual Strength	Alteration

Suggested Organization for Beastlord Spellbook

by Gnish, Mage of Death

Practicing good spellbook organization is a critical part of playing a Beastlord. By keeping similar types of spells on a page and putting the main spells at the top of your spellbook, you have quick access to them as needed. You can relegate all of your old (upgraded) spells to page 30 or later.

Pages 1-2

Type	Healing, Regeneration, Shield, Travel spells
Examples	Healing, Inner Fire, Talisman of Altuna, SoW, Shrink, etc.
Exclusions	Resistance buffs, pet buffs

Page 3

Type	Self-buff spells
Examples	Attribute-enhancing spells (those that boost Strength, Agility, etc.)
Exclusions	—

Page 4

Type	Pet-buff spells
Examples	Pet healing spells, Beastlord Pet Haste, Spirit of _____ (level buff spell)
Exclusions	Pet procs

Pages 5-6

Type	Pet proc buffs
Examples	Spirit of Lightning through Spirit of Storm
Exclusions	—

Page 7

Type	Resistance spells
Examples	Endure Poison/Cold/Magic/Fire
Exclusions	—

Page 8

Type	Cure spells
Examples	Cure Poison/Disease
Exclusions	—

Page 9-10

Type	Utility spells
Examples	Summon Food/Drink, Invigor, Sense Animals, Spirit Sight
Exclusions	—

Page 11

Type	Direct damage, damage-over-time spells
Examples	Spirit Strike, Sicken, Tainted Breath, etc.
Exclusions	—

Page 12

Type	De-buff spells
Examples	Sha's Lethargy, Incapacitate, Drowsy, Nullify Magic
Exclusions	—

Suggested Spells to Purchase

You aren't going to automatically get every spell that comes in handy. Some of them must be bought. In the Vah Shir's home city, look for the Royal Palace. Go through the door to the right of the Raja, turn right and go to the end of the hall. Turn left, then proceed down the steps. You'll find yourself in an area with a few spell merchants.

If you can afford it, buy the following spells to add to your book. You'll be glad you did later.

Yekan's Quickening	Endure Magic
Envenomed Breath	Healing
Spirit of Monkey	Spirit of Ox
Spirit of Scorpion	Spirit of Yekan
Yekan's Recovery	

Bard

by Brandon de la Cruz

What can a Bard do? Perhaps it is easier to ask, "What *can't* a Bard do?" Bards make a good substitute for almost any other class, as well as having a host of unique skills and songs that make them vital to any party. You will find that Bards are in demand most often for their ability to boost the effectiveness of the party by raising attributes and regenerating Hit Points and mana. They are also sought after for their crowd control skills, in the form of *Charm* and *Mesmerize*, derived from the lore of Enchanters. Well-played, a Bard can do just about anything he pleases – travel quickly and secretly, explore unknown places without fear, or attract monsters for the party to kill. Despite all of these characteristics, the Bard class is a difficult one to master, and because of their rarity, a good Bard is always welcome.

As Kunark and Velious have shown, the discovery of new lands stirs a passion in the hearts of Bards. As masters of travel, song, legend and lore, the prospect of having new songs to sing and stories to tell will surely attract many of them to sign on with the first expedition teams. Bards are excellent traveling companions, as their songs can help the party avoid dangerous situations while exploring. Additionally, most Bards have excellent night vision, either naturally or through song. They have songs that quicken, songs that heal both body and mind, songs that levitate, and songs that conceal. These songs are extremely versatile; they are quicker than spells and harder to interrupt. But more important than any skill or ability, Bards have an honest desire to *know*. They will persevere, acting quickly and effectively in the face of danger in order to secure victory for their party.

New Bard Spells (since Kunark)

Bard spell descriptions begin on page 144.

Level	Spell	Skill
9	Magical Monologue	Singing
15	Song of Sustenance	Stringed Instruments
20	Cassindra`s Chant of Clarity	Singing
30	Amplification	Singing
34	Cantata of Soothing	Stringed Instruments
39	Katta's Song of Sword Dancing	Percussion Instruments
49	Selo`s Accelerating Chorus	Percussion Instruments
49	Shield of Songs	Stringed Instruments
50	Melody of Ervaj	Brass Instruments
52	Battlecry of the Vah Shir	Brass Instruments
54	Elemental Chorus	Percussion Instruments
55	Occlusion of Sound	Percussion Instruments
56	Purifying Chorus	Percussion Instruments
58	Chorus of Replenishment	Stringed Instruments
60	Composition of Ervaj	Brass Instruments
60	Warsong of the Vah Shir	Brass Instruments

Cleric

by Zzrod

Clerics fall into the support group of classes, and they are the principal force that keeps a party alive. Clerical spells fall into two categories — healing and buffing (character enhancement). Buff spells can be further divided into three categories — Hit Point upgrades, armor class upgrades, and a combination of the two. As you can imagine, as a Cleric increases in level, so does the power of his or her buffs. No class has better Hit Point or armor class buffs than the Cleric, though the Druid does have an equivalent line of spells.

Healing, though it sounds quite easy, actually poses quite a challenge for a Cleric. It's not only a matter of making sure that the group does not perish at the hands of evildoers, but also making sure that you do not receive too much attention from the monster being fought by the group. Say that in battle, your tank (Warrior) is taking damage. The monster is beating him to a pulp, but you (the Cleric) heal him. Each time he loses 20% of his health, you heal him again. The monster, though not too bright, realizes that his dinner is not dying as quickly as it should. He looks around and sees you, the Cleric, keeping dinner off the table! He doesn't like this and starts attacking you. This is called an "aggro," and if you play a Cleric, you need to learn how to not aggro a monster.

So, there are the two main functions of a Cleric. But, to break up the monotony of combat, the Cleric is given other spells — root spells that glue a monster in place, damage spells that can hit various types of creatures (undead, living, summoned), and stun spells that stop all creature actions. On the darker side of Clericdom, you're charged with keeping people alive, and you may feel bad when people die. Fortunately, when people die, you also have the ability to bring them back to life. And let's face it, everyone wants a Cleric around when they enter a dungeon!

New Cleric Spells (since Kunark)

Cleric spell descriptions begin on page 155.

Level	Spell	Skill
9	Sanctuary	Divination
19	Celestial Remedy	Alteration
29	Imbue Amber	Alteration
29	Imbue Black Pearl	Alteration
29	Imbue Black Sapphire	Alteration
29	Imbue Diamond	Alteration
29	Imbue Emerald	Alteration
29	Imbue Opal	Alteration
29	Imbue Peridot	Alteration
29	Imbue Plains Pebble	Alteration
29	Imbue Rose Quartz	Alteration
29	Imbue Ruby	Alteration
29	Imbue Sapphire	Alteration
29	Imbue Topaz	Alteration
29	Sermon of the Righteous	Evocation
34	Armor of Protection	Abjuration
39	Sacred Word	Evocation
44	Celestial Healing	Alteration
49	Armor of the Faithful	Abjuration
50	Improved Invisibility to Undead	Divination
52	Epitaph of Life	Evocation
52	Heroic Bond	Abjuration
54	Mark of Retribution	Abjuration
55	Stun Command	Evocation
56	Judgement	Evocation
58	Blessed Armor of the Risen	Abjuration
58	Naltron's Mark	Abjuration
60	Aegolism	Abjuration
60	Blessing of Aegolism	Abjuration

Druid

by Andrea Silva (Cryth Thistledown, Bristlebane)

Druids are one of the priest classes, healers and nurturers who have the ability to cast some damaging spells as well. They are aligned with good deities and are generally welcome everywhere in Norrath. Druids are limited to leather armor, and they are not renowned for their ability to melee or take hits. They do, however, have a wide variety of spells and skills that make them well-rounded characters.

You'll find that as a Druid, you're an invaluable addition to adventuring groups headed to Luclin. Druids have the ability to teleport themselves and their groups to various locations throughout the world. They can buff their party with enhancements, such as *Spirit of the Wolf* (movement rate increase), a line of strength buffs, a protective skin buff which raises a character's Hit Points and armor class, thorn shields, and regenerative spells.

Druids can also charm animals and cast fire-based direct-damage spells. Gifted with the ability to track and forage, Druids are also very self-sufficient when far away from a city. That's just the tip of the iceberg when it comes to the many skills a Druid has in his or her possession. Overall, Druids are a very versatile class and can fill many roles in a group, making them a desired class for many adventuring parties.

New Druid Spells (since Kunark)

Druid spell descriptions begin on pg. 157.

Level	Spell	Skill
1	Tangling Weeds	Alteration
9	Protection of Wood	Abjuration
19	Protection of Rock	Abjuration
19	Ring of Surefall Glade	Alteration
24	Ring of the Combines	Alteration
29	Imbue Emerald	Alteration
29	Imbue Plains Pebble	Alteration
29	Circle of Surefall Glade	Alteration
29	Protection of Steel	Abjuration
34	Circle of Iceclad	Alteration
34	Fury of Air	Evocation
34	Ring of Great Divide	Alteration
34	Ring of Iceclad	Alteration
39	Circle of Great Divide	Alteration
39	Protection of Diamond	Abjuration
39	Ring of Cobalt Scar	Alteration
39	Ring of Wakening Lands	Alteration
39	Ro`s Fiery Sundering	Evocation
44	Circle of Cobalt Scar	Alteration
44	Circle of Wakening Lands	Alteration
44	Fixation of Ro	Alteration
49	Protection of Nature	Abjuration
50	Improved Superior Camouflage	Divination
52	Foliage Shield	Divination
54	Life Shield	Conjuration
54	Spirit of Eagle	Alteration
55	Chloroblast	Alteration
55	Nature Walkers Behest	Conjuration
56	Ro's Smoldering Disjunction	Alteration
58	Circle of Seasons	Abjuration
60	Nature's Recovery	Alteration
60	Nature's Touch	Alteration
60	Protection of the Glades	Abjuration

Enchanter

by Zzrod

The support role in a group often falls to Enchanters. They don't do damage (usually), but they direct the action and make the whole group much more effective. To use an analogy, the Enchanter is the "quarterback."

Spells available to members of this class vary widely. Enchanters are able to make monsters sit around and do nothing, no matter who walks by (often called "mezzing"). They can also make the monster hit slower than normal, as well as make the group hit faster than normal with more damage. Enchanters can also make the monster forget the group was ever there (*Memory Blur*), suck the mana from the monster so it cannot heal (*Mana Sieve, Theft of Thought*), cast four different area of effect stun spells, and ensure that other casters don't run out of mana (*Clarity, Gift of ...*).

As if that were not enough, Enchanters can enchant metals and clay that can then be used to create wondrous magical items, and have the ability to temporarily disguise themselves as any other race, including Werewolves and Elementals. The abilities granted to this class are only limited by imagination.

Imagine this ... your group is attacked. The Warrior tanks jump on the monsters, the Cleric roots one over in the corner. Everything is great. One resist later, you discover that a runaway monster has called in reinforcements, and the group is now fighting four monsters! Here's where the Enchanter can shine. The Enchanter casts a mesmerizing spell on three of the new arrivals to slow them down, and then stuns the caster monster as it tries to throw a spell off at the tanks. Once again, all is well.

Transforming a situation of probable death into a situation under complete control – that is what an Enchanter does. What a rush, being the Boss! On the down side, Enchanters very seldom have time for idle chitchat, as there is always a spell to cast. And, when something goes wrong, well... let's just say no one dies quite as fast as an Enchanter.

New Enchanter Spells (since Kunark)

See p. 160 for Enchanter spell descriptions.

Level	Spell	Skill
8	Enchant Clay	Alteration
12	Intellectual Advancement	Alteration
20	Intellectual Superiority	Alteration
29	Haunting Visage	Conjuration
34	Gift of Magic	Alteration
39	Calming Visage	Conjuration
39	Wandering Mind	Conjuration
44	Summon Companion	Conjuration
44	Boon of the Garou	Divination
44	Enchant Velium	Alteration
49	Enchant Adamantite	Alteration
49	Enchant Brellium	Alteration
49	Enchant Mithril	Alteration
49	Enchant Steel	Alteration
49	Illusion: Imp	Divination
50	Improved Invisibility	Divination
52	Tricksters Augmentation	Divination
54	Beguiling Visage	Conjuration
55	Gift of Insight	Alteration
56	Horrifying Visage	Conjuration
58	Glamorous Visage	Conjuration
58	Spellshield	Abjuration
60	Gift of Brilliance	Alteration
60	Koadic's Endless Intellect	Alteration

Magician

by James Lewis (Ronaldor Vladimir)

Magicians are one of the more interesting and self-sufficient classes in the game. The main feature of the Magician class is the ability to summon a wide variety of pets to aid in battles throughout Norrath and Luclin. Not only can Magicians summon powerful Elementals (Earth, Air, Fire and Water), but they also have the ability to summon monsters to their aid as well.

As you progress through your career as a Magician, you can buy spells that enable you to buff your pet and increase its effectiveness. The trick to being a good Magician is to learn when to use the correct pet and how to keep it under control.

Magicians are also extremely adept at casting offensive spells, both area-effect and direct-damage. They are particularly well equipped for harming and even destroying (at higher levels) Elemental beings. The ability to cause damage by magical means is second only to that of a Wizard. Included in the Magician's ability to cause magical damage are damage shields. If used correctly and cast on whoever is being attacked the most, they can be a great source of irresistible damage to an enemy.

If that were not enough, Magicians also have the added ability to summon any number of magical items to sustain them in the field. These items include food, water, bandages, arrows, weight-reducing bags, rings of levitation, water-breathing stones and various items to aid night vision. Special note should be taken when using these items – they disappear 30 minutes after you log out. Be especially careful of leaving items in your weight reducing bags, as they will disappear, too. One more summoned item that requires caution in its use is the Modulation Rod. This magical item converts Hit Points to Mana (225 Hit Point to 150 Mana); however, if your Hit Points are below 225, you will be killed using it.

As far as defensive abilities go, Magicians receive three main defensive spell lines. These are Shielding (raises Hit Points and Magic Spell Resistance), Elemental Shielding (raises Fire and Cold spell resistance), and the Phantom Armor line (raises Armor Class and regenerates Hit Points at a faster rate). As pure spell casters, Magicians can also purchase the spell *Gate*, which enables them to magically transport to wherever *Bind Affinity* was last cast on or by them.

One of the last spells that makes Magicians extremely useful are the Malaise line of spells. When cast on a opponent, these spells reduces the target's resistance to nearly all types of magic.

To sum up, Magicians are one of the most powerful classes you can play in *EverQuest*, but don't let this fool you into thinking they are an easy class to play. Even with all this power, it takes months to master all the tricks and skill required to become an Arch mage. While Magicians are an excellent class to play solo (mainly due to the huge power of pets in combat), they can also bring much to a group. This is especially true later in life, when the *Call of The Hero* and other powerful spells are available.

New Magician Spells (since Kunark)

See p. 162 for Magician spell descriptions.

Level	Spell	Skill
12	Summon Elemental Defender	Conjuration
20	Summon Phantom Leather	Conjuration
29	Expedience	Alteration
29	Summon Phantom Chain	Conjuration
34	Monster Summoning I	Conjuration
34	Summon Shard of the Core	Conjuration
39	Summon Companion	Conjuration
39	Summon Phantom Plate	Conjuration
44	Elemental Maelstrom	Evocation
49	Summon Elemental Blanket	Conjuration
50	Monster Summoning II	Conjuration
52	Transons Elemental Infusion	Conjuration
54	Veil of Elements	Divination
55	Burnout IV	Alteration
55	Wrath of the Elements	Evocation
56	Rod of Mystical Transvergance	Conjuration
58	Transons Phantasmal Protection	Abjuration
59	Valiant Companion	Alteration
60	Anti Summoning Shield	Conjuration
60	Monster Summoning III	Conjuration
60	Shock of Fiery Blades	Conjuration

Starting Out as a Magician

by James Lewis (Ronaldor Vladimir)

As a young Magician, or Mage, you start out without the ability to summon elementals. (These spells are not available until level 4.) The first thing to do is look in your inventory. You should have two spells, a note, book, dagger, candle, and food and water. Memorize both spells into your spell book, then read the book and the note. (You can destroy the book unless you wish to be a PK.) Put the dagger and the candle into your hands, and you are ready to start your first quest. As you probably guessed, the note you just read starts the quest. Follow the instructions, and by the end, you should receive experience and a nice (albeit not-so-new) robe to wear. During this quest, look for merchants who sell spells you'll need in the future. Before rushing off to kill nasty monsters, practice casting your new spells so they don't fail you in combat.

You're now ready to gain experience and levels. Head away from your starting town and seek out rats, snakes and beetles. Start killing them using a combination of melee and spells, but don't venture so far that the guards can't protect you from the stronger creatures that wander in from time to time. Collect anything these creatures drop so you can sell them to merchants in the town to earn money to buy spells. Buy *Summon Food* and *Summon Water* first – these two save money and time.

By level 4, you can buy your first pet (you only really need one pet type at this level). Spend some time getting used to the commands and making sure your pet is by you at all times. Creating hotkeys for the "/pet" commands is much easier than typing them in each time – pets do tend to wander off at inappropriate moments.

Next, you're ready to wander a little further away from the city. The Magician is one of the only two classes capable of surviving long periods of time away from a city. Remember, though, to stock up on Malachite (the spell component that allows pet summoning) before you leave town.

Monk

by Airik Wolfe (Vonairik of Bristlebane)

So you want to become a Monk, do you? First, you must learn about the path. As a young Monk, you will have your work cut out for you, and you will not see the strengths of this class until later in life. Once trained in the Sneak (Level 8) and Feign Death (Level 17) skills, you will see the world open up, but until then, you must fight long and hard to make it.

Having the ability to sneak and then feign death when you are attacked will often save your life and allow you to travel where others cannot. This helps you become one of the better classes in Norrath in that you can pull for your hunting parties. When trained properly, this ability will allow you to split groups of monsters and bring only one back to the party, as well as enable you to retrieve corpses after a lost battle.

As a Monk, you are an amazing damage dealer in battle, but lack the Hit Points to stand toe-to-toe with monsters like the Warrior class can. Similarly, you cannot top the upper Rogues' Backstabbing abilities. While this may make a Monk seem weaker at the start, in the long run, this class can out-damage all but the Rogue melee class and take less damage while doing it.

So, tell me, my young friend, have you given thought to what race you will choose for your Monk? You must choose between the Human and the scaled Iksar as a starting race. The Human Monk is one who most other races love, and the one that can gain entrance into all but the most evil of cities. The Iksar Monk, on the other hand, must first prove that he is a friend, not a foe, before entering any but a few cities in Norrath. Proving yourself is a long and tedious task. At the same time, questing for faction is no different than any other quest, and well worth the effort.

Now, what about Luclin and the Monk? For those of us called Monk, Luclin is a ripe new territory to explore and experience. Venture out and abroad and make yourself known to the new race called the Vah Shir. (You can find them in the grand city of Shar Vahl on Luclin.)

The Vah Shir Beastlord has much in common with the Monk, and supplies will be on hand for most of your needs. The Iksar have not yet sent a representative for the Monk Class to Luclin; therefore, you need to return to Kunark for any training you require. However, Humans have traveled far (as always) and are spreading out in Luclin. Currently, there is a trainer located deep in the new Luclin territories for the Human Monk.

Necromancer

by Dave Harrod (Sslithiss Elghinn`Faer)

While openly accepted in evil societies, the art of Necromancy only exists in the shadows of other civilizations. A Necromancer is the most feared and hated of all classes. Not only does he call forth a supernatural spirit to follow his sadistic commands; he also plays upon the fear of our own mortality.

While most classes concentrate on outward forces, the Necromancer manipulates magic to control the body or spirit of themselves or others. They've even learned to control the very shadows in which they hide. Necromancers can tap into the life essence of others to heal themselves, or sacrifice their own to heal friends. They can poison others, inflict diseases, cause blood to burn from within, burst internal organs, and control the heart rate of others. Their mastery of the undead allows them to summon servants to their sides and to damage the undead with spells. Necromancers can speed the attacks of their servants or slow undead foes. Necromancers also have some group effect spells that can be used to steal stats, mana or even Hit Points from an enemy and award them to the entire group.

The Necromancer's strongest solo attack is Fear Kite. Casting *Darkness* reduces the speed of your target. At this point, send in your pet and cast *Fear*. Try to keep track of how long these two spells last to ensure that they affect your target at all times. Generally, *Darkness* lasts twice as long as *Fear*. The order in which you perform these basic steps varies depending upon your target. You may, for instance, send your pet first against a caster so that its attention will be focused upon your pet, not you. A harmful volley of spells cast against you could prove disastrous.

In a group, the Necromancer's role changes slightly. Your biggest weapon is your pet, but it can also be your bane. If anything hits your pet (or you) by either melee or spell, it is added to your pet's hate list — even if it's friendly fire. A pet that prematurely hits an NPC that was mesmerized could cause disaster. When fighting multiple critters, back your pet off early in order to clear its hate list before the target dies.

During raids, the Necromancer's role changes yet again. Many useful spells are now being used by someone else or don't stack with other spells. Situations change frequently during raids; coordinate with other raid members to see which spells are most useful at any given time. A majority of your time and mana will be spent on gaining points for others in your group. Almost always, you'll use your *Allure/Lich* (Hit Point-to-Mana) spells up to gain mana quickly. Your subversion spells transfer your mana to another player, usually a healer, and your life tap series helps restore low Hit Points. Remember even if a spell is resisted, you still rank pretty high on the target's hate list. Use caution when in these situations, and if you feign, stay down for some time to keep those NPCs off of you!

New Necromancer Spells (since Kun.)

See p. 163 for Necromancer spell descriptions.

Level	Spell	Skill
12	Focus Death	Alteration
20	Shackle of Bone	Alteration
29	Eternities Torment	Alteration
34	Torbas Acid Blast	Conjuration
39	Chilling Embrace	Alteration
39	Shackle of Spirit	Alteration
44	Summon Companion	Conjuration
44	Corpal Empathy	Alteration
44	Dead Man Floating	Abjuration
44	Incinerate Bones	Evocation
49	Insidious Retrogression	Conjuration
50	Improved Invisibility to Undead	Divination
52	Degeneration	Alteration
54	Succussion of Shadows	Alteration
55	Augmentation of Death	Alteration
55	Conglaciation of Bone	Evocation
56	Crippling Claudication	Alteration
58	Mind Wrack	Alteration
60	Arch Lich	Alteration
60	Zevfeer's Theft of Vitae	Alteration

Paladin

by Dador Caduceus, Realm of Valor (Mithaniel Marr)

The noblest of all the classes in Norrath, a Paladin exemplifies truth, honor and devotion. He is part Warrior and part Cleric. However, most consider the Paladin to be mostly Warrior and only partly Cleric. Though he gets healing and buffing spells, the Paladin never meets the proficiency of his Cleric brothers. The Paladin does retain a gift from his god in that he can Lay on Hands once per day to nearly completely heal himself or another in critical danger. This ability is available at birth, and will remain a valuable asset throughout his life.

The newly discovered moon of Luclin beckons to the adventurous Paladin. The Paladin will find a new world filled with wondrous and strange creatures. Like Norrath, many of these creatures will be hostile. The cat-like Vah Shir, inhabitants of Luclin, will accept the Paladin with some distrust. With his pious and noble ways, the Paladin can gain favor with these inhabitants and trade freely in their city.

A young Paladin traveling to Luclin would do well to seek out the city of Shar Vahl and make this his new home until he returns to Norrath. From there he can venture into Shadeweaver's Thicket or Hollowshade Moor. Like all other places, the moon of Luclin is not void of the undead. The Paladin can use his various undead spells to his advantage to help him destroy or sneak by the numerous skeletons and other undead creatures that roam these areas.

The Dwarf is probably the best-suited overall to engaging the role of Paladin. Dwarves have high Strength, Stamina, and Dexterity. They also have relatively high Wisdom. Remember to get and keep Agility above 75, or suffer the consequences to armor protection.

An Erudite does not have suitable starting stats to take the profession of Paladin. However, a judicious use of his bonus points can make a playable character. The Erudite Paladin is extremely rare, so this might be a good choice for a dedicated player.

Finally, the Half Elf has low Strength, Stamina, and Wisdom but relatively good Dexterity and Agility. Again, smart points allocation at creation can make a viable Half Elf Paladin.

New Paladin Spells (since Kunark)

Paladin spell descriptions begin on p. 165.

Level	Spell	Skill
9	Cease	Evocation
15	Desist	Evocation
30	Instrument of Nife	Abjuration
39	Divine Purpose	Alteration
39	Divine Vigor	Alteration
49	Thunder of Karana	Evocation
49	Valor of Marr	Alteration
50	Flame of Light	Evocation
53	Divine Glory	Alteration
54	Quellious' Words of Tranquility	Evocation
55	Wave of Healing	Alteration
56	Breath of Tunare	Alteration
59	Celestial Cleansing	Alteration
60	Brell's Mountainous Barrier	Alteration
60	Divine Strength	Alteration

Ranger

by Andrea Silva (Cryth Thistledown, Bristlebane)

Rangers are one of the hybrid classes, a mix between a Warrior and a Druid. They excel in melee with their Dual Wield and Double Attack abilities. Rangers can also take a few more hits than their Druid brethren. However, Rangers are limited to chain armor and do not have the Hit Points or armor class to rival that of a pure Warrior. To compensate for this lack of strength, Rangers can cast some of the less-powerful spells from the Druid spell book.

Many adventuring parties invite a Ranger to join the group because of the Ranger's ability to cast *Snare* and *Spirit of Wolf.* Just as in Norrath, a Ranger makes an invaluable addition for an expedition to Luclin.

The one skill a Ranger has in which he or she easily excels above all other classes is the ability to track. Creatures that are within a Ranger's tracking radius appear on a special tracking screen. The creature names are displayed in their "/con" color (blue, for example), making it easy for a Ranger to pick out creatures that yield the most party experience.

As a Ranger, you should familiarize yourself with several commands in order to get the most out of your tracking ability.

/trackfilter [red/yellow/white/blue/green]

(Ranger-specific) Specifies what NPC /con colors you do not want to see in your tracking display. For example, "/trackfilter Red" will remove all red (dangerous) NPCs from your tracking display. Repeating this command toggles the filter on/off.

/trackplayers [on/off/group]

Allows anyone with the tracking skill to indicate whether or not they want player characters to show up in their tracking list.

/tracksort [normal/distance/consider/rdistance/rconsider]

(Ranger-specific) Controls how your tracking display sorts targets. *Normal* sorts them by how long they have been in the zone, listing the "oldest" NPCs first. *Distance* puts the closest NPC on top of the tracking list. *Consider* places the highest level NPCs on top. *Rdistance* lists the closest NPC last, and *Rconsider* sorts the tracking list by difficulty, with the lowest level NPCs on top and the highest level NPCs on the bottom.

New Ranger Spells (since Kunark)

Ranger spell descriptions begin on p. 166.

Level	Spell	Skill
9	Tangling Weeds	Alteration
15	Hawk Eye	Alteration
30	Riftwind's Protection	Abjuration
39	Call of Sky	Alteration
39	Natures Precision	Evocation
49	Force of Nature	Alteration
50	Call of Earth	Abjuration
51	Strength of Nature	Abjuration
52	Falcon Eye	Alteration
54	Call of the Falcon	Conjuration
54	Jolting Blades	Conjuration
55	Call of Fire	Alteration
55	Cinder Jolt	Alteration
56	Mark of the Predator	Abjuration
58	Eagle Eye	Alteration
60	Call of the Predator	Abjuration
60	Warder's Protection	Abjuration

Rogue

by Luneshadow

Often misunderstood and mistrusted, Rogues fall into the damage-dealing group of classes. Their job is to put out as much damage as they possibly can, but without ever attracting the attention of the mob they're fighting. Because of their sneakiness, Rogues perform those tasks very well. The Evade skill helps, and a variety of other skills just make a Rogue's life in Norrath easier.

Their presence is preceded by their reputation, and Rogues are generally considered to be thieves. Still, many Rogues resent that comparison and in actuality, are very loyal and supply a number of valuable services to their group. Rogues find and disarm traps, hide and sneak through places others can't follow, create and use poisons to make weapons more deadly, and open doors that have no keys. And, when a Rogue is behind a mob flailing away, there's always Backstab to help out a friend.

Which brings us to the real downside of being a Rogue ... the view! You spend most of your time staying behind the mob you're fighting. Wood Elf Rogues are a bit taller, but Dwarves will find little to watch besides the backs of their enemies. Many Rogues find that scouting and pulling mobs for the group is much more satisfying than engaging in blow-for-blow group melee.

Rogues aren't as strong as some of the other classes, but they're fast and quiet. So what if your Rogue lacks the stature of a well-built Warrior? One good swipe of your blade can do enough damage to get the job done.

Rogues come from nine different races, including the new Vah Shir. Your choice of heritage will probably stem from what abilities you want. Want to be a nighttime scout or underground adventurer? If so, you'll likely want your character to be of Dwarven or Elven descent. If you desire more Strength, perhaps a Barbarian is a better choice.

With so many Rogues in so many cities, it's not too hard to find a friend or group with which to mingle. When visiting the new city of Vah Shir, however, you'll have to prove your worthiness to the locals to really be accepted — even among your colleagues.

Shadow Knight

by Kevin Freet (Skoriksis)

Fear, pain, cruelty ... these are the things a Shadow Knight feeds on every day of his or her life. What could have been the proud Warrior or the noble Paladin has instead been tainted by the darker arts.

Shadow Knights are formidable fighters in combat, even without dark abilities. They specialize in the use of a single weapon and a shield, or perhaps take up the overwhelming power of a two-handeded weapon. Their ability to wear heavy plate armor gives them little fear of walking into the middle of combat and they always expect to emerge from a battle alive.

Although not as powerful in the ways of the dark rites as a Necromancer, a Shadow Knight has enough power to be deadly. Shadow Knights excel in the theft of an opponent's abilities. Whether they tap into the raw strength of their foe or drain their victim's lifeforce and add it to their own, it's clear that a Shadow Knight is a force to be reckoned with. These dark casters can even summon the spirits of the fallen creatures of the land and command them as undead skeletal pets.

With the price of power, there are always consequences. Don't expect the citizens of the world to understand why you have chosen the path of a Shadow Knight in your life. You can fully expect to be hated almost everywhere you go. But, once you find a place where the practitioners of the dark arts reside safely, you will have all the tools you need to continue your unholy crusade.

New Shadow Knight Spells (since Kunark)

See p. 168 for Shadow Knight spell descriptions.

Level	Spell	Skill
9	Despair	Alteration
15	Scream of Hate	Alteration
29	Strengthen Death	Alteration
30	Scream of Pain	Alteration
39	Scream of Death	Alteration
39	Shroud of Hate	Alteration
50	Shroud of Pain	Alteration
51	Summon Corpse	Conjuration
52	Summon Companion	Conjuration
52	Abduction of Strength	Alteration
52	Mental Corruption	Alteration
54	Torrent of Hate	Alteration
55	Shroud of Death	Alteration
56	Torrent of Pain	Alteration
58	Torrent of Fatigue	Alteration
60	Cloak of the Akheva	Conjuration
60	Death Peace	Abjuration

Shaman

by Stephen Reinsborough (Tarthug)

Shaman are the spiritual leaders of the more primal races. They are among the most diverse classes available in *EverQuest*. Able to heal, cast pre-combative spells, and invoke devastating spells that can kill or seriously degrade an opponent's ability to fight, Shaman have abilities to fit nearly every situation. Shaman can dabble in alchemy, a trade skill unique to this class that allows them to brew many functional potions. This class has the best of all worlds — besides being one of the more capable soloing classes, Shaman are also in high demand by people who hunt in groups.

When playing a Shaman, you can select from five races: Barbarians, Ogres, Trolls, Iksar or Vah Shir. Each race brings its own advantages and challenges to playing a Shaman. Training locations, however, tend to be very limited, as are locations where your faction allows you to buy alchemy components.

Of all the priest-like classes, Shaman are the most physical. They are able to cast spells and, in a pinch, even engage in melee combat. For many of the less cultured races, a Shaman is the only real choice for those who want to play a caster class.

New Shaman Spells (since Kunark)

Shaman spell descriptions begin on p. 169.

Level	Spell	Skill
9	Talisman of the Beast	Alteration
19	Grow	Alteration
29	Imbue Amber	Alteration
29	Imbue Sapphire	Alteration
29	Form of the Bear	Alteration
29	Imbue Ivory	Alteration
29	Imbue Jade	Alteration
34	Shock of the Tainted	Conjuration
39	Spirit of Bih`Li	Alteration
39	Tumultuous Strength	Alteration
44	Summon Companion	Conjuration
44	Blast of Poison	Conjuration
49	Harnessing of Spirit	Alteration
50	Spirit Quickening	Alteration
52	Disinfecting Aura	Alteration
54	Plague of Insects	Conjuration
55	Chloroblast	Alteration
55	Form of the Great Bear	Alteration
56	Regrowth of Dar Khura	Alteration
58	Cannibalize IV	Alteration
58	Talisman of Epuration	Abjuration
60	Focus of Spirit	Alteration
60	Khura's Focusing	Alteration

Warrior

by Falaanla Marr, Human Magician of Fennin Ro

Being a Warrior means one thing — you are tough. You can take the most punishment of any class, and can also dish out a respectable amount of damage. Being a Warrior isn't about being pretty or acquiring matching pieces of armor. Your goal is to be an effective tank, plain and simple.

Various races can be Warriors — Barbarians, Ogres and Trolls are the largest. By virtue of their size, these races can take more punishment before dying, and also deal more damage due to their strength. Warriors also gain the ability to Bash, which, if successful, interrupts an opponent's spell casting. (Larger Warriors can Slam, even without a shield!)

Throughout their career, Warriors have access to various skills to assist in dealing damage and protective combat skills. Dual Wield allows the Warrior to wield two weapons at once, while the Riposte skill allows a Warrior to turn an enemy's attack against him.

If you're playing a Warrior and want to take an early trip to the moon, you first need to head to the Nexus. You will then likely want to head to the city of Shar Vahl, where the cat people known as the Vah Shir reside. Shade Weaver and Hollowshade have portals to Shar Vahl. They are friendly to travelers, so there's no need to watch your back.

After arriving, try to find a caster to bind your soul to the city of Shar Vahl, so you can easily return there if you die. After being bound, climb down into the moat-like area around the city and fight there until level 4 or 5. After you get level 5, you will want to head out to Shadeweaver's Thicket.

After gaining a few more levels, you may want to start searching for a group. Remember, as a Warrior, your goal is to take damage and protect the rest of the group. Knowing this, rely on your Taunt ability if a mob decides to attack your group's healer or caster, and use it in order to get the enemies to attack you instead.

While the life of a Warrior may at first seem boring, remember one thing. YOU are the person that stands between the mob and the caster, and you are the one that gets to chop the enemy into little pieces (or bludgeon him to death, if you so prefer). If you're tough, enjoy getting up in the enemy's face, and don't mind mismatched armor, being a Warrior may be the right career for you!

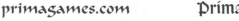

Wizard

by Moonshadow Litherial

If you haven't played a Wizard before, you'll find that it's a pretty straightforward career choice. Wizards only buff themselves, and they'd rather sit back and cast spells than engage in melee fights. After level 20 or so, most Wizards lounge around casting damage spells at the enemy and regaining mana.

What that viewpoint misses, however, is the amazing breadth of the Wizard's magical damage. At almost every level, a Wizards gets fire-based, cold-based, and magic-based damage spells. Rain type spells deliver damage in waves, and point-blank area-effect spells hit anything that gets too close. Targetable area-effect spells allow Wizards to "multikite" (take on multiple) creatures at a time. Last, but not least, Wizards get the most mana-efficient direct damage spells in the game.

If you had to give this class a title to proclaim its presence, it would have to be "Master of versatile damage." Add to that the Wizard's unique ability of planar travel and compatibility with traveling Druids, and it's easy to see why many players choose the life of a Wizard.

New Wizard Spells (since Kunark)

Wizard spell descriptions begin on p. 171.

Level	Spell	Skill
12	O'Keils Embers	Abjuration
20	Garrisons Mighty Mana Shock	Evocation
24	Combine Gate	Alteration
29	Imbue Fire Opal	Alteration
29	Minor Familiar	Conjuration
34	Great Divide Gate	Alteration
34	Iceclad Gate	Alteration
34	Iceclad Portal	Alteration
34	O'Keils Flickering Flame	Abjuration
39	Cobalt Scar Gate	Alteration
39	Elnerick Entombment of Ice	Evocation
39	Great Divide Portal	Alteration
39	Invisibility to Undead	Divination
39	Translocate: Combine	Alteration
39	Translocate: Fay	Alteration
39	Translocate: North	Alteration
39	Translocate: Tox	Alteration
39	Wakening Lands Gate	Alteration
44	Cobalt Scar Portal	Alteration
44	Enticement of Flame	Evocation
44	Translocate: Cazic	Alteration
44	Translocate: Common	Alteration
44	Translocate: Nek	Alteration
44	Translocate: Ro	Alteration
44	Translocate: West	Alteration
44	Wakening Lands Portal	Alteration
49	Lesser Familiar	Conjuration
49	Translocate: Cobalt Scar	Alteration
49	Translocate: Great Divide	Alteration
49	Translocate: Iceclad	Alteration
49	Translocate: Wakening Lands	Alteration
50	Translocate	Alteration
52	Firetrees Familiar Augment	Alteration
52	Translocate: Group	Alteration
54	Familiar	Conjuration
55	Improved Invisibility	Divination
56	Decession	Alteration
58	Garrisons Roaming Vision	Conjuration
60	Greater Familiar	Conjuration
60	Hsagra's Wrath	Evocation
60	Ice Spear of Solist	Evocation
60	Porlos' Fury	Evocation

Rites of Passage for a Young Vah Shir

by Moonshadow Litherial for Lunemew Gernawl

The life of a young Vah Shir is an interesting progression. When you determine which path you wish to follow – Warrior, Rogue, Bard, Shaman or the new Beastlord – your guildmaster will first send you off to become an official citizen. (See the story at the start of this chapter on p. 8.)

After citizenship is granted, guildmasters provide new and increasingly challenging tasks for their young trainees. You'll be sent first around the city, and then later around adjoining zones to learn more about your surroundings, all the while improving your armor and weapons. As you progress in level, the guildmasters entrust you with more challenging tasks. Between tasks, there's plenty of time for you to adventure on your own terms, tussle in the arena with your friends or littermates, and even time to meet up with one of the king's dancers in the Merchant's Quarter Celebration House.

In an interesting parallel to Vah Shir society, later tasks require you to work closely with other classes to complete your tasks. Items you need to complete your work are only available from Vah Shir who study other professions. These quests illustrate the deep-rooted sense of cooperation and information sharing that has fostered the Vah Shir society over the years and preserved their strong presence on the harsh surface of Luclin.

The path you have chosen will lead you through many lands and help forge many long-lasting friendships. When your journey is finished, the strength in your heart will serve as a light for generations to come. May you serve our society as it serves you, young one ...

Races

Vah Shir

The Vah Shir are a noble, cat-like people, not quite as vicious and hated as the Iksar, but not nearly as socially adept as the Elven races. Their arrival on Luclin is largely undocumented, though oral history concurs that it happened many years ago as a result of the Erudites' experimentation with magical weapons, culminating in one

colossal event called "The Shifting." Whether it was through accident or intention, the entire city and most of its inhabitants were flung into space through "The Hole." The remaining Vah Shir were herded together and isolated on Kerra Isle, while the transported cats found themselves settling in a cold, inhospitable climate of immeasurable solitude. Today, upon the far-reaching moon of Luclin, the prosperous city of Shar Vahl houses their proud descendants.

The Vah Shir bear many appearances, ranging from a handsome grey coat with wispy strokes of silver to the classic black-and-orange hide of their Kerran forefathers. Proud and rugged, this feline race are friendly to their own kind and tolerant of most outside visitors. Tempers can quickly become inflamed if the situation merits it, but most often, conversations are accompanied by a salutatory purr or low growl of agreement. They welcome most races, though their fur may stand on end if someone causes a disturbance in their home city.

The Vah Shir take great pride in their past and require all adolescents to complete a ritual of citizenship before apprenticing in any of the town's trades. Although many may exclaim that the rites of passage make citizenship difficult to obtain, the respect that comes with adulthood brings both privilege and opportunity. Few question the loyalty or trustworthiness of fully registered sisters and brethren.

The Vah Shir are great fighters, possessing both stealth and prowess on the battlefield. Blessed with lightness of paw and some inherent protection from falling, the Vah Shir know little fear. While many choose to follow the path of a Warrior, others use their innate skills for more roguish activities. Still, the call of nature resounds deeply in the soul of all Vah Shir. They communicate well with all manner of beasts, and many young Vah Shir pursue Beastlord status, developing a deep kinship with tigers and training them as "warders." Those few that exhibit an aptitude for alchemy or enchantment adopt the life of a shaman, while the musically inclined tend to apprentice with local Bards and release their abilities through a finely crafted instrument.

Vah Shir Starting Statistics

Starting City Shar Vahl
Racial Tensions None
Special Abilities Sneak, Safe Fall

	STR	STA	AGI	DEX	WIS	INT	CHA	Bonus AP
Beastlord	90	85	95	70	80	65	70	+20
Bard	95	75	90	80	70	65	75	+25
Rogue	90	75	100	80	70	65	65	+30
Shaman	90	80	90	70	80	65	70	+30
Warrior	100	85	95	70	70	65	65	+25

Tips on Playing a Vah Shir

Newbie Hunting. As a young cat, you can hunt from levels 1-5 in the crater surrounding the Vah Shir home city of Shar Vahl. To get down there, you will need to find a bridge (north or south), go across the bridge and climb the wall down on that side. (It's great having Safe Fall – you take less falling damage.) In the crater, you'll find Grimling Runts, Scorpions, Xakra Worms and Hoppers. This should get you to level 4 or so. Once you outgrow the crater, head to Shadeweaver's Thicket (south bridge) and hunt more of the same.

What quests should I do first? Unlike many other societies, the Vah Shir put gaining citizenship right up at the top of their list of "things you should do after being born." First things first – find Animist Sahdi and get a note. Then, find Registrar Bindarah in the courtyard near the south gate and give him the note. He'll send you off to get a slate and to persuade the Tax Collector to stamp your paperwork. Another NPC by the name of Mignah gives you a slate ... if you ask nicely. Try "I am in need of a personal acrylia slate." Take these items to the Registrar, and then make the requisite visit to Raja Kerrath in the Royal Palace. Once you return back to the Registrar, you're properly registered and can begin taking on class-specific quests handed down by the appropriate guildmaster.

Aspiring **Beastlords** should visit the Royal Palace and find Elder Animist Sadhi to get a cloak, and then Animist Poren to get started with the handwrap adventures.
New Vah Shir **Bards** should locate the Elder Hymnist Hortitosh in the Bards' guild (on top of the Royal Palace). Bring him back proof of your citizenship to get the claw quest.
Shaman Vah Shir should seek Fehril, near Animist Sadhi in the Royal Palace. She sends you on a cloak quest.
Rogue Vah Shir must find Rakutah to get their first real quest. A Rogue Trainer is also "hidden" on an upper floor near the city gates.
Warrior Vah Shir must seek out High Armsman Trukhanah for guidance.

Finally, if you're looking for more Shar Vahl quests, see Dronqam Runghi (alchemy quest), Master Barkhem (shield quest), Taruun Rolom (wage quest), or Arms Historian Qua (Wolf Bane weapon quest).

Cooperation: The name of the game. One important fact you'll learn early on is that the Vah Shir rely heavily on each other's skills. You'll need to master the skills of your own profession, and in turn, rely on others' career skills. Each class has items that can only be crafted or gained through mastery, and it won't take long to figure out that you need to work cooperatively with other Vah Shir to complete many of the game's quests.

Innate abilities. The Vah Shir are naturally skilled in Sneak and Safe Fall. The city of Shar Vahl isn't particularly peaked or dangerous, but these skills will prove useful when you venture away from your home den. While these skills cater to effective Warrior abilities, they also help those Vah Shir with, well, less stringent morals. Watch your pockets!

Who the heck is the "Raja"? Heirarchy is another integral part of the Vah Shir society, which is built upon honor, loyalty and respect for one's elders. The Raja is the Vah Shir's ruler, and quite a regal spectacle. You can find him in the Royal Palace, in the northern part of the city, flanked by two bodyguards.

What do I do with a warder? The warder is the Beastlord's equivalent of a pet, only this pet is good for life past level 9 and isn't afraid to move into new zones with you. Basically, your pet is about evenly matched with you and progresses as you gain experience. That said, pay special attention to all of the "Spirit of" spells you get at certain levels.

These pet-buffing spells have several different purposes. They can temporarily raise the level of your warder and can even make it self-sufficient in battle against things that normally con blue against you. Other spirit spells give your warder additional damage potential, and still other spells heal your pet. Finally, at higher levels, warders employ additional attack types — for instance, Bash and Kick.

Barbarian

by Gnish, Mage of Death

Barbarians are generally regarded as the gentle giants of the North. Due to their size, they make great fighters and good Shaman or Rogues.

Luckily for Barbarians, the path to Luclin lies through a portal and not a Gnome-powered rocket ship. The Vah Shir regard them indifferently, so your first stop should be to visit Shar Vahl, which is easily accessible from the Nexus. It would be wise for Barbarians to tread softly in the other cities, as they don't take too kindly to outsiders. However, there are ways to earn the trust of those cities and it would be wise to do so through quests that increase faction standing.

Many adventures await Barbarians on Luclin, and it's a challenge they will openly welcome, for most of the gentle giants love a good time (and a good ale, which they shall discover in Luclin as well). Luclin will provide many ample opportunities for Barbarians to prove their worth.

Dark Elf

by Airik Wolfe (Vonairik of Bristlebane)

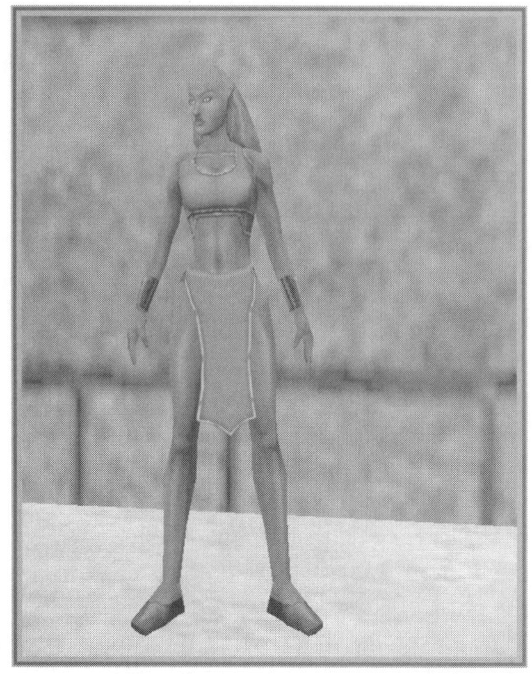

Playing a Dark Elf Necromancer on Luclin offers a distinct challenge to the average player. Katta Castellum and Sanctus Seru are off-limits to darker class and race combinations, such as Dark Elf Necromancers. Most Dark Elves will be marked as kill-on-sight (KOS).

From the Nexus arrival point, head into the Bazaar to bank your funds, and look around Shadow Haven while you're at it. Shadow Haven offers Dark Elves the challenge of overcoming bad faction, as you'll find yourself dubious to the residents at first. Fear not, for within you will find a faction quest that could help you become a happy citizen.

Head out of Shadow Haven and through the Paludal Caverns and beyond to get to Shar Vahl and other great adventures. Shar Vahl is home to the Vah Shir, who are currently indifferent to Dark Elves. It has been said that the Vah Shir hold lengthy councils about this and might be changing their views, so treat them well while you visit. Currently, Shar Vahl is the only city on Luclin that caters to the Dark Elves' needs.

If you've progressed to higher levels and are up for more adrenaline-inducing adventures, head to Fungus Grove and seek the outpost within this amazing territory.

Dwarf

by Brandon de la Cruz

The discovery of Velious strengthened the Dwarven race immeasurably, as the old world Dwarves sought to establish good relations with their newfound brethren, the Coldain. But this does not mean they are complacent to sit by after portals to Luclin have been discovered — the moon is obviously rich in precious gems and minerals. Rumors tell of even more exotic delicacies and brews than were found in the jungles of Kunark or the harsh, icy lands of Velious.

Dwarves are a hardy race, and a good addition to any expedition. They tend to excel in the less subtle arts of exploring — bashing, hacking, and quite a bit of kicking. Occasionally, you can also find a Dwarf who has mastered the healing arts as a Cleric or Paladin, which, along with a strong kicker, supplies some recovery magic as well. Any way you look at it, you can't go wrong with a good Dwarf at the head (or waist) of your party.

Erudite

by Dave Harrod (Sslithiss Elghinn`Faer)

Once merely a faction of the Human race, Erudites fled Antonica to escape persecution. The children of this new society were surrounded by scholars and had no choice but to becomes scholars themselves. Erudites eventually became a race dependent upon their mental capabilities. No longer did they choose to rely solely upon steel, and even those that did decide to pick up a sword only did so while knighted. Erudites consider themselves far too superior to practice Shamanistic magic, or to live off the land and "become one with nature." And, to even consider that an Erudite would engage in the seedy practice of Rogues would meet with open disdain.

When the dark arts were re-discovered, the Erudites were separated into two factions. For the first time in history, Erudites were at war with themselves. In an effort to end the conflict, a mighty spell was cast by the high council that carved a great hole in the ground and even sent pieces of Norrath deep into space. The heretics built a city there and called it Paineel. Here, they broke through to the Plane of the Underfoot, releasing its denizens. In a tentative alliance, both societies worked together to seal the plane with a wall of living rock before Odus could be overrun. The heretics rebuilt Paineel on the rim of the hole after sealing the entrance to their former home.

As a modern Erudite, you won't be killed on sight in Shar Vahl, but don't expect any red carpets – especially if you're a dark class. Some merchants might also refuse to trade with you. You can try your hand in the other cities of Luclin, but Katta Castellum and Sanctus Seru may resent your presence.

Gnome

by Gnish, Mage of Death

Gnomes are generally regarded as a neutral race and as such, they are allowed in the most cities of any race. The main exception is that all Trolls and Ogres hate Gnomes, but that figures — Gnomes are a delicacy dish for them. Gnomes also boast the only race capable of tinkering, the skill to create new and unusual devices. In fact, tinkerers have created ways to breathe underwater and the most famous tinkerer (although outlawed) has created a clockwork dragon.

Everyone loves, or at least tolerates, the Gnome race on the mainland. So, it figures that Luclin is no different. The Vah Shir are rather unconcerned by your presence, so your first stop should be to visit the Vah Shir city of Shar Vahl, easily accessible from the Nexus. Even a Gnome Necromancer is tolerated in the cats' home city. Other interesting stops are the Bazaar and Shadow Haven, where Gnomes are tolerated, but not loved. Some merchants — even Gnome vendors — won't sell to darker classes, such as Necromancers. Unfortunately, the other cities on the moon wish to hang evilish Gnomes by the toes.

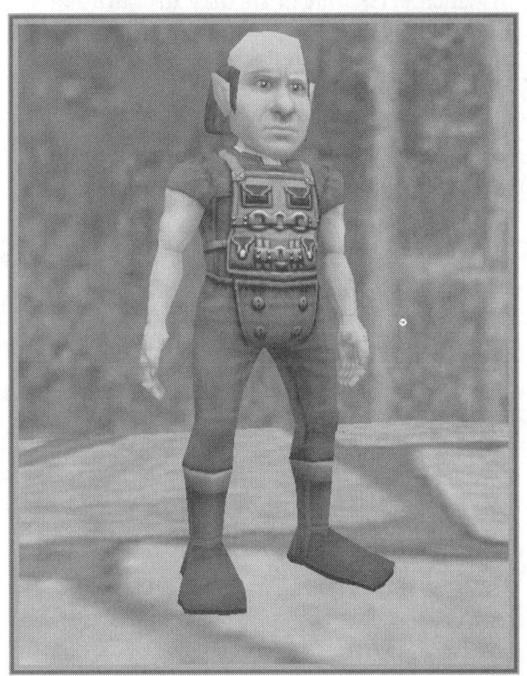

It seems that Gnomes may have been one of the first races to reach the moon, as they have several establishments there. In fact, some tinkers live in Luclin's cities; it is encouraging to see that they have not forgotten their roots. Hopefully, Luclin's Gnomes can offer some some new recipes, since gravity boots will be sorely needed on certain parts of the moon ...

Half Elf

by Jason Reisz (Reijas)

Part Elven and part Human, Half Elves share the characteristics of both, while not completely fitting in with either. Half Elves are taller and stronger than their Elven descendants, but over the years, have maintained their ability to see in the dark.

On the Human side, Half Elves are more balanced as far as statistics are concerned, but can only wear medium armor due to strength considerations.

Half Elves can start in both Human cities, Qeynos and Freeport, and in the Elven city of Kelethin. Because of their heritage, Half Elves are neither liked nor disliked in the "good" and "neutral" cities but, depending on which class and faith they are, are not typically welcome in the darker cities of Norrath.

Half Elves can choose from several different professions. When the opportunity presents itself, Half Elves can be Bards, Paladins, Rangers, Warriors and Druids.

Halfling

by James Lewis (Ronaldor Vladimir)

Halflings are often regarded as the most fun-loving of all the races. They are light-hearted souls, relaxed and brimming with curiosity. Their quest for fun often leads them to pranks, so anyone near a Halfling should be aware of this. Despite their mischievousness, they are also known for their hospitality, and should anyone find themselves in the town of Rivervale (where Halflings reside), they will be greeted with a warm welcome.

Halfling characters are easily distinguishable, as they are not of normal stature. They are shorter than Humans and not nearly as broad as Dwarves, but do not be fooled — this does not hinder their strength, and they are surprisingly strong. However this is not the only quality they possess; Halflings are dexterous and agile, and they have acquired a good base of wisdom due to their curious nature. Navigation is also aided by their infrared vision.

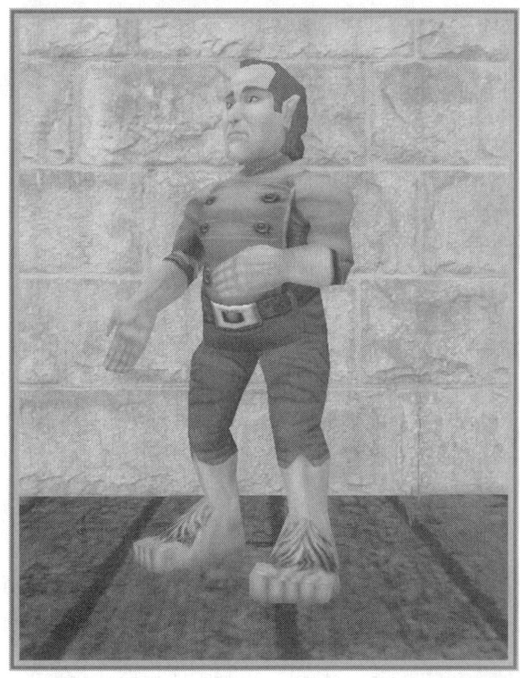

The Halflings' easygoing attitude and natural ability to travel has held them in good stead with other races. There are few which they do not get along with, and this has granted them access to the aligned cities without much difficulty. Yet despite their traveling feet, they will always find themselves coming home, to Rivervale.

Halflings can make excellent Rogues, Clerics and Warriors, but their main calling seems to be to nature and the Druid class.

High Elf

by Dador Caduceus, Realm of Valor (Mithaniel Marr)

Among the Elven people, the High Elves stand as the nobility. The High Elves consider themselves more dignified and eloquent than their lesser cousins. These cousins, the Wood, Dark and Half Elves, all share the same mother of Tunare with the High Elves.

The High Elves make their home in the beautiful city of Felwithe on the continent of Faydwer. It is a majestic castle-like fortress of marbled walkways and grand ballrooms. Vendors can be found in the outskirts of the yards in various wooden shacks.

The continent of Faydwer is mostly wilderness. Many beasts roam the forests, but the High Elves' arch enemy remains the Orcs of Crushbone. The castle of the Crushbone Orcs is located near Felwithe, and the High Elves are constantly battling to keep the Orcs at bay.

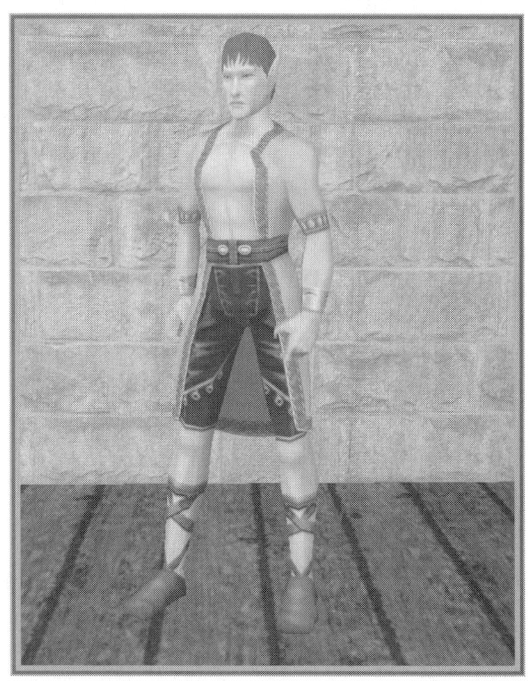

High Elves have heard of the recent discovery of life on the moon of Luclin. Early reports indicate that the High Elf people will not encounter any unusual racial hostility. However, early travelers relay that the moon contains many strange and hostile creatures. Rumors about a new, cat-like race have also surfaced. Fortunately, the Vah Shir cat people seem to accept High Elves into their home city of Shar Vahl with only minor distrust.

Young High Elves starting out on a life of adventure should be able to find a new world for discovery if they choose to make their way to Luclin. As good practice, though, a young High Elf should have passed five or six seasons before setting out to the new world.

Human

by Alex Harkness
(Zandar, Arch Mage, Bristlebane)

The Human race is well known for its resilience, both to the surrounding environment and to the hostile creatures that inhabit Norrath. Humans are young compared to some of the more ancient races in Norrath, but their amazing adaptability assures they can make the most of every situation, be it good or bad.

When playing a Human character, you can rest assured you will be in good company. Due to their natural ability to propagate the species quickly, you will no doubt find them in every nook and cranny of Norrath. Some of the very first explorers to the moon of Luclin were in fact Humans.

History may lead you to believe otherwise; however, if you ask a commoner in any part of Norrath, they will surely give high praise to the kindness and compassion so often shown by the Human race.

Humans do have a more or less serious issue of night blindness. Still, it does not take too long to obtain items that alleviate that problem. Humans have the ability to play nearly every class in the game, with the exception of Beastlord and Shaman, and can start from either Freeport or Qeynos.

Iksar

by Kevin Freet (Skoriksis)

Since the beginning of their existence, the reptilian race of the Iksar have been brutalized and enslaved. Noble, cunning, and cruel, the Iksar trust no one but their own kind. Their lizard-like bodies provide them with a natural armor and protection from the heat; however, they avoid the cold whenever possible. They also are imbued with a natural regeneration and are excellent swimmers from birth. The Iksar have been forced to live off the land through the ages and have the ability to forage from their surroundings.

The Iksar were once enslaved by a powerful and evil race of intelligent snake men known as the Shissar – that is, until a mysterious plague destroyed the Shissar and left the Iksar free to study the dark arts of Necromancy. This would lead to the foundation of the Iksar knowledge and philosophy.

From their harsh beginnings as slaves to the Shissar to the war with the dragons of the Ring of Scale, it's clear to see why the Iksar don't trust anyone. Although they thrive in their hometown of Cabilis, a rumor has surfaced that an ancient enemy long since thought dead has been reported on the moon of Luclin and the call to arms can be heard once more.

It seems that the hatred Iksar have felt for generations on Norrath isn't felt as hard on Luclin. Perhaps it is because lizard scales aren't the strangest thing that the citizens of Luclin have seen wandering around their cities. But, this doesn't mean that you won't have trouble finding friends.

The cat-like Vah Shir tolerate you, despite that fact that you are not covered head to toe in fur. So, if you wish to head to Luclin while you are still a young hatchling, you can find a home within the walls of Shar Vahl. However, they do not train in many skills known by the Iksar, so you will not find a Necromancer, Shadow Knight or Monk trainer.

Another place to call a home away from home is Shadow Haven. In this underground city, many races coexist peacefully. You can even find an elusive vendor of Necromancer and Shadow Knight spells. However, not everyone will avoid staring at your scaly hide. Expect many of the residents to look upon you with disdain, as though you had just stepped in at a horse stable. Some of the merchants may go so far as to refuse to sell to Iksar. It may take time and patience, but you will eventually find yourself a home.

During your stay on Luclin, just make sure that you "con" everyone from a distance before you run up to shake their hand. There are indeed places where you will certainly be unwelcome, such as the city of Katta. It would be best to avoid that town in particular.

Of course, young lizard, the biggest challenge is getting to one of the Nexus teleporter pads to transport you to Luclin. The closest one to your home of Cabilis is in the Dreadlands. For a young hatchling, this means a deadly journey, and possibly one you can't be expected to complete without a few deaths. If you can stand the sight of them, you might be forced to call upon a soft-skinned race for a teleport to a safer moon portal.

Ogre

by Jason Reisz (Reijas)

In the earliest days of Norrath, and long before the world was home to many races, the ethereal plane became populated by the gods. One such god, the Rallos Zek Fiery Warlord, was eager to place his mark on Norrath. Thus, he created a race full of ambition and driven toward power.

In this manner, Ogres entered Norrath and began to build a mighty empire, taking over most of Norrath. Unsatisfied, they set their eyes upon the planes of the gods to assist Rallos Zek in his coup efforts. When these attacks failed, the Ogres were punished by the other gods for taking part in Rallos Zek's attempt to rule the planes. As part of their punishment, Ogres, once powerful and brilliant, were reduced to the least intelligent race on Norrath.

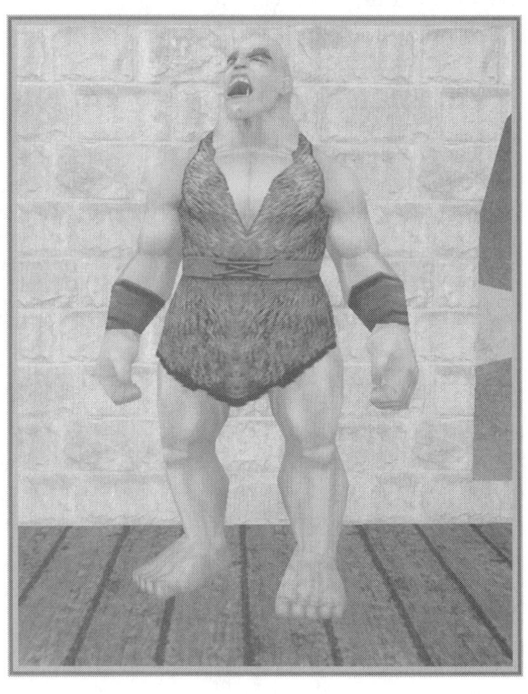

Today, the descendants of these Ogres are gargantuan creatures who boast great strength. Even Trolls, who possess nearly equal stamina, cannot match their brawn. Ogres are unstunnable from the front, making them an excellent race for Warriors and Shadow Knights. More intelligent Ogres even take up the priest-like ways of a Shaman.

Historically, Ogres have had difficulty gaining entry into many of Norrath's cities. Many Ogres expect that their reputation will invoke distrust among the newly discovered Vah Shir. However, the cat race is generally unconcerned with tensions on Norrath and treats every race neutrally – though always with a slight mistrust. Like all newcomers to Luclin, Ogres must prove themselves through good deeds. The best place to get started is in the Vah Shir's home city of Shar Vahl.

Troll

by Falaanla Marr, Human Magician of Fennin Ro

You is Troll! You not smartest, prettiest, or wisest being out there, but you strong and tough. You also quick to heal!

As a Troll, you can be a Warrior, Shadow Knight or Shaman. If you plan to head to Luclin and want to train at Shar Vahl, choose either the Warrior or Shaman class. (The Vah Shir do not know much about the dark arts practiced by Shadow Knights.)

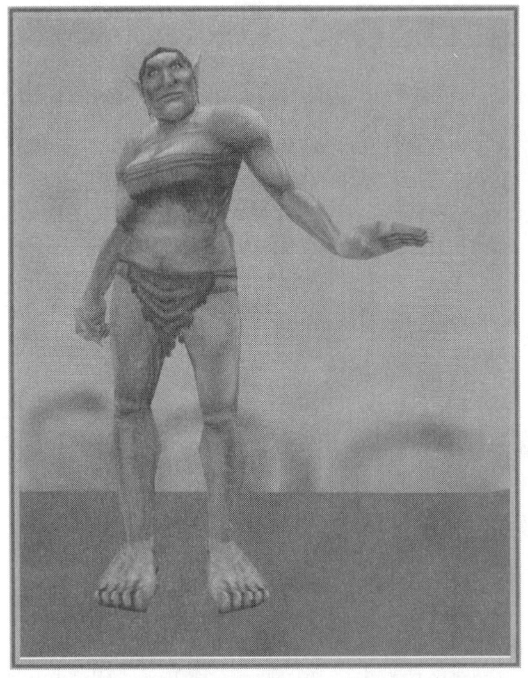

Heading to the moon can be a perilous journey when you are less experienced, but it can be done. Simply head to the closest Nexus portal and then head to Shar Vahl. There, be sure to find a caster to bind your soul to the city — you don't want to die and have to run back here again! After you have done this, you have a couple of choices as to where to hunt. If you want to remain in the city, simply climb down the rocks near the zone exit, into the moat-like area around the city. Down here are various beasts that allow you to practice your skills until you are level 4 or 5. You can also head out to Shadeweaver's Thicket, though you may be better off waiting until level 5 — there's not much there to hunt at level 1.

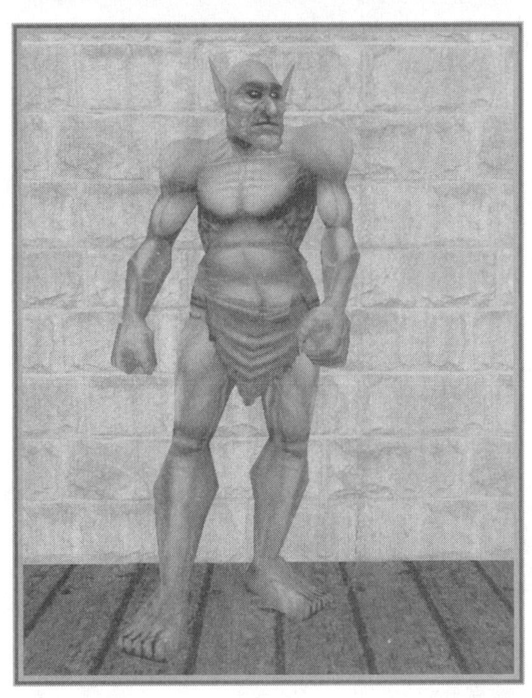

The hardest part about playing as a Troll on Luclin will be getting there. The Vah Shir are a friendly bunch, and will tolerate your presence, though you may need to endear yourself to some by completing quests. Their trainers will even take the time to train you in the ways of the Warrior and Shaman, provided you have proven yourself.

Enjoy the trip to the moon, young Troll!

Wood Elf

by Andrea Silva (Cryth Thistledown, Bristlebane)

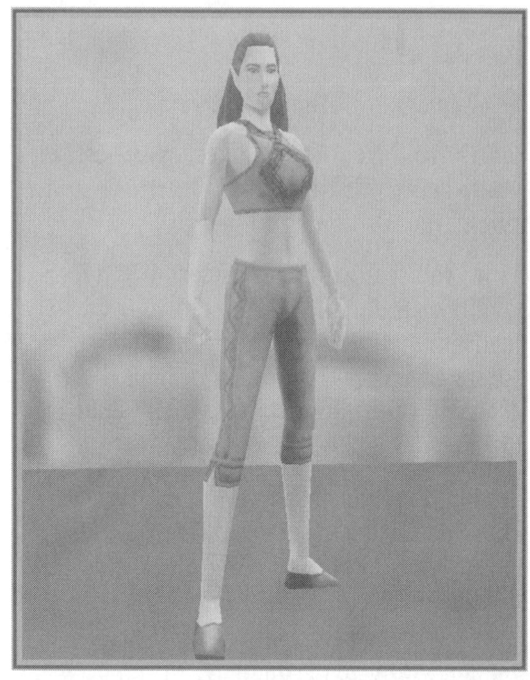

Wood Elves, also known as the Fier'Dal, are commonly regarded as a good-aligned race. The Wood Elves boast many explorers and adventurers among their kind, so a trip to the moon of Luclin is just one more direction in which the Wood Elves can expand their horizons.

Upon reaching Luclin, a Wood Elf will generally be regarded with either apprehension or indifference by the existing inhabitants. This is not to say that Wood Elves can walk around with impunity, for Luclin has its own variety of hostile creatures that all intelligent creatures treat with caution. They will, however, be allowed to enter the cities of Shar Vahl and Shadow Haven, as well as trade wares in the great Bazaar located near the Nexus.

The Vah Shir city of Shar Vahl and the varied residents of Shadow Haven are apprehensive toward most foreign races, but if an adventurer comes with honest intentions, they will be welcomed. The Wood Elves are no exception to this rule and can sell and buy from merchants, deposit and withdraw items from their bank vaults, as well as perform tasks to improve their faction standings.

Skills

Each character starts out with some skills. Everyone, for instance, has the basic ability to trade, tolerate alcohol, beg, fish, sense direction and swim. Also, varying hand and weapon combat skills are available to each of your characters from the start.

You can also get other skills based on your class and race. Rangers, for instance, get the Tracking skill, and Warriors receive Kick at level 1. Over time you gain the ability to develop other skills, as shown in the tables on the next two pages.

As you play the game and earn experience, you progress in level and earn skill points. To raise your ability in a skill, you spend skill points on that ability.

It's a good idea to plan out your character before you get too far into the game. Figure out what you want to be able to do at higher levels, and save your points accordingly.

Finally, keep in mind that you can only advance an ability so many times. Once you're stellar at doing something, there's no room for improvement.

Skill Tables

Level Limits. For most skills, the highest a skill can go is no higher than 5 times your current level, plus 5. For example, if you're currently at level 20, your highest skill could be no higher than 105 [(20 x 5) + 5 = 105]. There are no level limits on most trade skills.

Skill Caps. There are absolute caps on each skill (but the cap will often depend on your class). You can't exceed this cap no matter how much experience your character has. For about half the skills, the maximum you can achieve in a skill – its skill cap – is level 200.

First Training Point. In general, the first point you put into a skill gives you that skill at your current experience level. (For example, if you are a Bard and put your first point into Stringed Instruments at level 36, you immediately have Stringed Instruments at level 36.) Waiting so that you can increase this initial boost isn't usually a good idea – if it's useful, you want to be practicing and improving it as soon as possible.

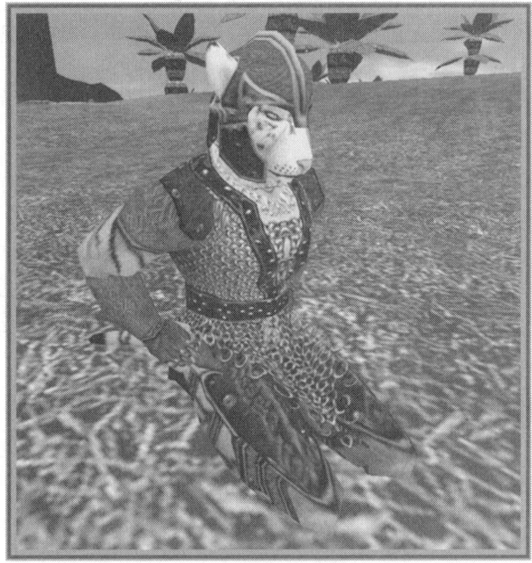

Most trade skills are the exception to this first-point rule. You never start a general trade skill higher than level 20, regardless of your experience level when you begin learning it.

Skills

Common Skills

Skills	Bs	Bd	Mk	Ro	Wr	Pl	Rn	Dr	Cl	Sm	SK	En	Mg	Wz	Nc
Trade[1]	1	1	1	1	1	1	1	1	1	1	1	1	1	1	1
General[2]	1	1	1	1	1	1	1	1	1	1	1	1	1	1	1
Basic Combat[3]	1	1[3]	1	1	1	1	1	1	1	1	1	1	1	1	1

Additional Combat Skills

Skills	Bs	Bd	Mk	Ro	Wr	Pl	Rn	Dr	Cl	Sm	SK	En	Mg	Wz	Nc
Piercing	1	1		1	1		1			1	1	1	1	1	1
Throwing	1	1	1	1	1		1					1	1	1	1
1H Slashing		1		1	1	1	1	1			1				
2H Slashing		1			1	1	1				1				
Archery				1	1	1	1				1				
Taunt					1	1	1				1				
(Berserking)					(1)										
Dodge	10	10	1	4	6	10	8	15	15	15	10	22	22	22	22
Parry		53		12	10	17	18				17				
Riposte	40	58	35	30	25	30	35				30				
Disarm			27	27	35	40	35				40				
Double Attack			15	16	15	20	20				20				
Dual Wield	17	17	1	13	13		17								
Bash					6	6					6				
Kick	5		1		1		5								
Instill Doubt			18				22								

Monk

Skills	Bs	Bd	Mk	Ro	Wr	Pl	Rn	Dr	Cl	Sm	SK	En	Mg	Wz	Nc
Mend			1												
Safe Fall		24	3	12											
Round Kick			5												
Tiger Claw			10												
Block			12												
Feign Death			17												
Eagle Strike			20												
Dragon Punch/ Tail Rake			25												
Flying Kick			30												

[1] Baking, Blacksmithing, Brewing, Fletching, Jewelry Making, Pottery, Tailoring; Tinkering is only available to Gnomes, Lvl 16.

[2] Alcohol Tolerance, Begging, Fishing, Sense Direction, Swimming

[3] Offense, Defense, Hand to Hand, Bind Wound, 1H Blunt, 2H Blunt; but not 2H Blunt for Bards

Rogue

Skills	Bs	Bd	Mk	Ro	Wr	Pl	Rn	Dr	Cl	Sm	SK	En	Mg	Wz	Nc
Sneak		17	8	1			10								
Hide		25		3			25				35				
Pick Lock		40		6											
Pick Pockets				7											
(Sense Traps)				(8)											
Backstab				10											
Apply Poison				18											
Make Poison				20											
(Disarm Traps)		(30)		(21)											

Ranger

Skills	Bs	Bd	Mk	Ro	Wr	Pl	Rn	Dr	Cl	Sm	SK	En	Mg	Wz	Nc
Track		35					1	20							
Forage		12					3	5							

Bard

Skills	Bs	Bd	Mk	Ro	Wr	Pl	Rn	Dr	Cl	Sm	SK	En	Mg	Wz	Nc
Singing		1													
Percussion Inst.		5													
Stringed Inst.		8													
Brass Inst.		11													
Wind Inst.		14													

Caster

Skills	Bs	Bd	Mk	Ro	Wr	Pl	Rn	Dr	Cl	Sm	SK	En	Mg	Wz	Nc
Channeling						9	9	4	4	4	9	1	1	1	1
Meditate		(10)				12	12	8	8	8	12	4	4	4	4
Research												16	16	16	16
Alchemy										25					
Casting Skills (Abjuration, Alteration, Conjuration, Divination, Evocation)	9					9	9	1	1	1	9	1	1	1	1
Specialize Skills (Specialize: Abjure, Alteration, Conjuration, Divination, Evocation)								30	30	30		20	20	20	20

Alternate Advancement

by Alan VanCouvering (edited by Moonshadow Litherial)

What is Alternate Advancement?

The alternative advancement system allows anyone who has purchased and installed *EverQuest: Shadows of Luclin* to further customize their high-level (level 51+) characters. Customized features include things such as minor permanent statistic and resistance boosts, unique skills based on your class (Warrior, Magician, etc.) or archetype (fighter, magic user, and priest), plus general skills available to everyone. These skills include anything from enhanced metabolism to improvements in skills already available to your class. You can also gain a title for your character based on the choices you make when enhancing your character. These titles will be visible to other players.

Gaining these alternate skills and powers requires you to spend experience points you've earned. You can funnel incoming experience into either your alternative advancement pool *or* into your standard experience pool. You can even choose to have a percentage of your incoming experience go into each pool.

Once enough experience has entered the alternative advancement pool, you receive training points that can be used to acquire enhancements. When you collect the proper amount of training points, you have the option of choosing which enhancement you wish to gain. Some enhancements may have prerequisites. A prerequisite is a skill (or multiple skills) you will need to obtain before you can get the enhancement.

Experience loss due to death suffered by the character will be subtracted from the "leveling" experience pool; it does not impact your alternative advancement pool.

Note

All characters will be able to open the interface screen for Alternate Advancement. But only players who purchase the Shadows of Luclin expansion will be able to earn any of these abilities.

Earning and Spending Skill Points

When you divert experience towards alternate advancement, a second experience bar appears on your character screen. When you "ding" in this bar, you will have gained one skill point. It is these skill points that allow you to purchase alternate advancement abilities. Each ability costs a different number of skill point's. These costs are detailed in the complete list of alternate advancement abilities (p. 65). You can – and for later skills, must – gain several skill points before spending them on an ability. This allows you to gain the experience you need while you're deciding what skills you really want.

Raising Ability Skill Levels

Every ability in the alternate advancement system has an associated skill level. For many abilities, only one skill level exists – once you purchase the ability, you attain all the skill available for that ability. Other abilities have more than one skill level. Gaining a second or third (or more) skill level in an ability will improve it. However, it is important to note that a second skill level is usually more costly than the first, and the third even more costly. That expense is rewarded, however, by a greater increase in the power of that ability.

Let's look at two examples:

Improved Natural Strength has five skill levels. Each skill level for this ability costs one skill point. Each time you raise your skill level with this ability you gain two points of strength.

Healing Adept (from the Priest Archetype) has three skill levels. Each skill level costs progressively more skill points. The first skill level costs two skill points for a 2% improvement in healing spells. The second skill level costs four points, but improves that percentage to 5%. The third skill level costs six skill points, but raises the percentage to 10%.

Passive vs. Active Abilities

Abilities can be passive or active. Passive abilities are always on and always have effect. Most abilities are passive. In fact, all General and all Archetype Abilities are passive.

You must trigger (activate) active abilities. Every active ability has a refresh timer, meaning that once you use it, you can't use it again for some period of time.

Why Use Alternate Advancement?

Unique to *EverQuest: Shadows of Luclin*, alternate advancement provides additional challenges for higher-level players. It also allows you to individualize your characters. A number of skills exist in the game. Therefore, for each character, you must decide which ones will most positively affect your playing style. For instance, you might give your Warrior tank Combat Fury in order to do more damage, while another player might choose Combat Stability to allow his Warrior to survive more attacks. Similarly, one caster might concentrate on Subtlety to avoid aggroing, and another might concentrate on Fury for damage.

When the Temple of Solusek Ro was added to the game and caster specialization enabled, many Druids divided into "alteration" and "evocation" specialties in order to differentiate themselves from other Druids. Alternate Advancement does the same thing, only on a larger scale. There are so many skills that few characters will ever get all of them. The ones you choose should reflect your character's personality and approach to life in Norrath.

It's worth a little research to decide what you want. You can click on alternate advancement abilities in the Alternate Advancement screen to view their descriptions. Skill points are expensive, so make sure you're careful when spending them. Unlike specialization, a few hundred platinum pieces cannot undo this decision.

Alternate Advancement Ability Types

There are three types of alternate abilities – general, archetype and class abilities. Each is a stepping stone for the next. Attaining a certain number of general abilities is required before you can learn any abilities from your archetype. Similarly, you will have to attain a prerequisite number of abilities from your Archetype to start gaining abilities from your class group. There are also level requirements for each of these levels. Also, remember that you can't gain any of these abilities unless you own *Shadows of Luclin*.

You can raise general, archetype and class abilities anywhere from 1 to 5 levels, depending on the skill. The first skill level of each archetype ability costs two skill points. The second skill level of each archetype ability costs four skill points. The third skill level of each archetype ability costs six skill points. All Archetype abilities are passive.

The following requirements are in addition to any prerequisites needed for some abilities:

General abilities. A character must be level 51 or higher to open up the general abilities. Each general ability costs 1 skill point per level; all general abilities have either three or five levels. All general abilities are passive.

Archetype abilities. A character must have spent 6 skill points on General abilities and be level 55 or higher to open up the Archetype abilities. The first skill level of each archetype ability costs two skill points. The second skill level of each archetype ability costs four skill points. The third skill level of each archetype ability costs six skill points. All archetype abilities are passive.

Class abilities. A character must have spent 12 skill points on Archetype abilities and be level 59 or higher to open up the class abilities. There are two types of class abilities. The first type is similar to the archetype abilities, with three skill levels.

The cost for those types of skills are always the same – the first level costs three skill points, the second skill level costs six skill points, and the third skill level costs nine skill points.

The second type of class ability only has one skill level. However, that one skill level costs a varying number of skill points, depending on the ability. Most, but not all, class abilities are passive.

General Abilities

General abilities are available to all classes.

First Aid

Increases the max that you can bind wound by 10 percent for each ability level.

Cost 1, for each of 3 levels

Improved Natural Agility

Raises your base Agility by 2 points for each ability level.

Cost 1, for each of 5 levels

Improved Natural Charisma

Raises your base Charisma by 2 points for each ability level.

Cost 1, for each of 5 levels

Improved Natural Cold Protection

Raises your base Save vs Cold by 2 points for each ability level.

Cost 1, for each of 5 levels

Improved Natural Dexterity

Raises your base Dexterity by 2 points for each ability level.

Cost 1, for each of 5 levels

Improved Natural Disease Protection

Raises your base Save vs Disease by 2 points for each ability level.

Cost 1, for each of 5 levels

Improved Natural Fire Protection

Raises your base Save vs Fire by 2 points for each ability level.

Cost 1, for each of 5 levels

Improved Natural Intelligence

Raises your base Intelligence by 2 points for each ability level.

Cost 1, for each of 5 levels

Improved Natural Lung Capacity

Increases the amount of air you have by 10, 25, and 50 percent.

Cost 1, for each of 3 levels

Improved Natural Magic Protection

Raises your base Save vs Magic by 2 points for each ability level.

Cost 1, for each of 5 levels

Improved Natural Metabolism

Decreases your food consumption by 10, 25 and 50 percent.

Cost 1, for each of 3 levels

Improved Natural Poison Protection

Raises your base Save vs Poison by 2 points for each ability level.

Cost 1, for each of 5 levels

Improved Natural Regeneration

Raises your regeneration ability by 1 point per ability level.

Cost 1, for each of 3 levels

Improved Natural Run Speed

Slightly modifies your base run speed. This modification does NOT stack with movement rate spell effects.

Cost 1, for each of 3 levels

Improved Natural Stamina

Raises your base Stamina by 2 points for each ability level.

Cost 1, for each of 5 levels

Improved Natural Strength

Raises your base Strength by 2 points for each ability level.

Cost 1, for each of 5 levels

Improved Natural Wisdom

Raises your base Wisdom by 2 points for each ability level.

Cost 1, for each of 5 levels

Archetype Abilities

Archetype Abilities by Class

	Caster	Melee	Priest
Bard	√	√	
Beastlord		√	√
Cleric			√
Druid			√
Enchanter	√		
Magician	√		
Monk		√	
Necromancer	√		
Paladin		√	√
Ranger		√	√
Rogue		√	
Shadow Knight	√	√	
Shaman			√
Warrior		√	
Wizard	√		

Along with general abilities, you also get different archetype abilities based on your class. The following chart shows which classes get which archetypes.

Caster

Channeling Focus

Increases max channeling to reduce the chance of interruption. Percentages are approx. 5, 10 and 15 percent reduction.

Cost 2 (level 1), 4 (level 2), 6 (level 3)

Mental Clarity

Increases natural mana regeneration by 1 point per ability level.

Cost 2 (level 1), 4 (level 2), 6 (level 3)

Spell Casting Deftness

Reduces casting time of beneficial spells with a cast time greater than 4 seconds. Percentages are approx. 5, 15, and 25 percent.

Cost 2 (level 1), 4 (level 2), 6 (level 3)

Spell Casting Expertise

Removes possibility of spell fizzling. First level removes fizzle on spell below 20, second below 35, and third below 52.

Cost 2 (level 1), 4 (level 2), 6 (level 3)

Spell Casting Fury

Gives you a chance to land a critical hit with direct damage spells. Percentages are 2, 4, and 7 percent increase chance to critical.

Cost 2 (level 1), 4 (level 2), 6 (level 3)

Spell Casting Mastery

Gives an increased chance of making your specialization check for that spell casting skill. It also reduces the chance to fizzle and increases the chance to reduce the mana cost for the spell at a percentage of 5, 15, and 30 percent.

Cost 2 (level 1), 4 (level 2), 6 (level 3)

Spell Casting Reinforcement

Increases the duration of beneficial spells by 5, 15, and 30 percent.

Cost 2 (level 1), 4 (level 2), 6 (level 3)

Spell Casting Subtlety

Reduces the amount of hate generated by the spell 5, 10 and 20 percent.

Cost 2 (level 1), 4 (level 2), 6 (level 3)

Melee

Combat Agility

Increases your avoidance ability to melee damage by 2, 5 and 10 percent.

Cost 2 (level 1), 4 (level 2), 6 (level 3)

Combat Fury

Increases the chance to land a critical hit. Non-Warriors nearly approach the original critical percentages of Warriors, while Warriors remain significantly ahead of other classes in the percentage chance to critical.

Cost 2 (level 1), 4 (level 2), 6 (level 3)

Combat Stability

Increases your mitigation ability to melee damage by 2, 5 and 10 percent.

Cost 2 (level 1), 4 (level 2), 6 (level 3)

Fear Resistance

Gives a bonus resistance to fear type spells of 5, 10 and 25 percent. It also increases the chance of breaking fear.

Cost 2 (level 1), 4 (level 2), 6 (level 3)

Finishing Blow

Gives you a chance to finish a fleeing mob off. The NPC must be below 10 percent health and fleeing. Non-Warriors must first place 1 ability point into Combat Fury to get this ability to work.

Cost 2 (level 1), 4 (level 2), 6 (level 3)

Improved Natural Durability

Increases max Hit Points by 2, 5 and 10 percent. The percentages are based on base Hit Points including stamina and stamina effects.

Cost 2 (level 1), 4 (level 2), 6 (level 3)

Improved Natural Healing

Raises your regeneration ability by 1 point per ability level.

Cost 2 (level 1), 4 (level 2), 6 (level 3)

Priest

Channeling Focus

Increases max channeling to reduce the chance of being interrupted. Percentages are approx. 5, 10 and 15 percent reduction in being interrupted.

Cost 2 (level 1), 4 (level 2), 6 (level 3)

Healing Adept

Increases the max value of healing spells by 2, 5 and 10 percent.

Cost 2 (level 1), 4 (level 2), 6 (level 3)

Healing Gift

Gives the priest a chance to cast a critical heal by 3, 6 and 9 percent. This will double the healing value of the spell

Cost 2 (level 1), 4 (level 2), 6 (level 3)

Mental Clarity

Increases natural mana regeneration by 1 point per ability level.

Cost 2 (level 1), 4 (level 2), 6 (level 3)

Spell Casting Fury

Gives you a chance to land a critical hit with direct damage spells. Percentages are 2, 4 and 7 percent increase chance to critical.

Cost 2 (level 1), 4 (level 2), 6 (level 3)

Spell Casting Mastery

Gives an increased chance of making your specialization check for that spell casting skill. It also reduces the chance to fizzle and increases the chance to reduce the mana cost for the spell at a percentage of 5, 15, and 30 percent.

Cost 2 (level 1), 4 (level 2), 6 (level 3)

Spell Casting Reinforcement

Increases the duration of beneficial spells by 5, 15 and 30 percent.

Cost 2 (level 1), 4 (level 2), 6 (level 3)

Class Skills

Finally, on top of general and archetype abilities, you can get class-specific abilities.

Bard

Archetype

Channeling Focus
Combat Agility/Fury/Stability
Fear Resistance
Finishing Blow
Improved Natural Durability/Healing
Mental Clarity
Spell Casting Deftness/Expertise/Fury/Mastery/Subtlety/Reinforcement

Class

Ambidexterity

Increases your chance to use Dual Wield successfully.

Cost 9

Acrobatics

Reduces the damage taken from falling.

Cost 3 (level 1), 6 (level 2), 9 (level 3)

Advanced Trap Negotiation

Reduces reuse time on sense and disarm traps.

Cost 3 (level 1), 6 (level 2), 9 (level 3)

Body and Mind Rejuvenation

Gives you 1 additional point of mana and Hit Point regeneration.

Cost 5

Extended Notes

Gives the song increased ranged of 10, 15, and 25 percent.

Cost 3 (level 1), 6 (level 2), 9 (level 3)

Instrument Mastery

Allows for specialization and improved use of all instrument types.

Cost 3 (level 1), 6 (level 2), 9 (level 3)

Jam Fest

Allows you to sing songs at a higher casting level. Note: This does not allow them to sing songs that are higher than your level.

Cost 3 (level 1), 6 (level 2), 9 (level 3)

Physical Enhancement

Gives you additional improvement in Natural Durability, Avoidance Boost, and Mitigation Boost abilities.

Cost 5

Scribble Notes

Reduces the amount of time it takes to memorize a song.

Cost 3

Singing Mastery

Allows for specialization and improved use of the specific instrument type.

Cost 3 (level 1), 6 (level 2), 9 (level 3)

Beastlord

Archetype

Channeling Focus
Combat Agility/Fury/Stability
Fear Resistance
Finishing Blow
Healing Adept
Healing Gift
Improved Natural Durability/Healing
Mental Clarity
Spell Casting Fury/Mastery/Reinforcement

Class

Ambidexterity

Increases your chance to use Dual Wield successfully.

Cost 9

Body and Mind Rejuvenation

Gives you 1 additional point of mana and Hit Point regeneration.

Cost 5

Double Riposte

Gives you an increased chance to execute a double riposte 15, 35 and 50 percent of the time.

Cost 3 (level 1), 6 (level 2), 9 (level 3)

Pet Discipline

Allows you to give your pet a "hold all aggression" command. The pet will not attack anything that attacks it or its master until told to attack. Usage: /pet hold.

Cost 6

Physical Enhancement

Gives you additional improvement in Natural Durability, Avoidance Boost, and Mitigation Boost abilities.

Cost 5

Cleric

Archetype

Channeling Focus
Healing Adept
Healing Gift
Mental Clarity
Spell Casting Fury/Mastery/Reinforcement

Class

Bestow Divine Aura

Gives you the ability to cast a Divine Aura spell on a PC target.

Cost 6

Celestial Regeneration

Gives you the ability to cast a large heal over time spell at no mana cost.

Cost 5

Divine Resurrection

Allows you to provide a resurrection that provides 100 percent experience return.

Cost 5

Innate Invisibility to Undead

Allows you to become invisible versus undead without the need to memorize a spell.

Cost 3

Mass Group Buff

Turns your next group buff into a beneficial area effect spell, hitting everyone within its radius. It also doubles the mana cost of the spell used.

Cost 9

Purify Soul

Allows you to cast a spell that cures all ailments except for charm, fear, and resurrection effects.

Cost 5

Spell Casting Reinforcement Mastery

Increases the duration of beneficial buffs by an additional 20 percent.

Cost 8

Turn Undead

Gives you an area-effect fear DoT spell against undead that with each ability level amplifies the damage.

Cost 3 (level 1), 6 (level 2), 9 (level 3)

Druid

Archetype

Channeling Focus
Healing Adept
Healing Gift
Mental Clarity
Spell Casting Fury/Mastery/Reinforcement

Class

Dire Charm

Gives you the chance to permanently charm an NPC.

Cost 9

Enhanced Root

Reduces the chance that an NPC will break root against direct damage spells cast by you with this ability by 50 percent.

Cost 5

Exodus

Gives you the ability to cast an instant casting no mana cost evacuation or succor spell.

Cost 6

Innate Camouflage

Allows you to become invisible without the need to memorize a spell.

Cost 5

Mass Group Buff

Turns your next group buff into a beneficial area effect spell, hitting everyone within its radius. It also doubles the mana cost of the spell used.

Cost 9

Quick Direct Damage

Reduces the casting time on direct damage spells by 2, 5 and 10 percent.

Cost 3 (level 1), 6 (level 2), 9 (level 3)

Quick Evacuation

Reduces the casting time on evacuation and succor spells by 10, 25, and 50 percent.

Cost 3 (level 1), 6 (level 2), 9 (level 3)

Spell Casting Reinforcement Mastery

Increases the duration of beneficial buffs by an additional 20 percent.

Cost 8

Enchanter

Archetype

Channeling Focus
Mental Clarity
Spell Casting Deftness/Expertise/Fury
Spell Casting Mastery/Reinforcement
Spell Casting Subtlety

Class

Dire Charm

Gives you the chance to permanently charm an NPC.

Cost 9

Gather Mana

Allows you to recover all your mana.

Cost 5

Jewel Craft Mastery

Reduces the chance of failing on a jewel craft combination by 10, 25, and 50 percent.

Cost 3 (level 1), 6 (level 2), 9 (level 3)

Mass Group Buff

Turns your next group buff into a beneficial area effect spell, hitting everyone within its radius. It also doubles the mana cost of the spell used.

Cost 9

Permanent Illusion

Allows you to zone without losing your illusion.

Cost 3

Quick Buff

Reduces the casting time of beneficial spells with a duration by 10, 25 and 50 percent. Some spells may be excluded.

Cost 3 (level 1), 6 (level 2), 9 (level 3)

Spell Casting Reinforcement Mastery

Increases the duration of beneficial buffs by an additional 20 percent.

Cost 8

Magician

Archetype

Channeling Focus

Mental Clarity

Spell Casting Deftness/Expertise/Fury/Mastery/Reinforcement/Subtlety

Class

Elemental Form Air

Allows you to turn into a Air elemental, gaining many of the benefits innate to the NPC and some of the negative.

Cost 3 (level 1), 6 (level 2), 9 (level 3)

Elemental Form Earth

Allows you to turn into a Earth elemental gaining many of the benefits innate to the NPC and some of the negative.

Cost 3 (level 1), 6 (level 2), 9 (level 3)

Elemental Form Fire

Allows you to turn into a Fire elemental gaining many of the benefits innate to the NPC and some of the negative.

Cost 3 (level 1), 6 (level 2), 9 (level 3)

Elemental Form Water

Allows you to turn into a Water elemental gaining many of the benefits innate to the NPC and some of the negative.

Cost 3 (level 1), 6 (level 2), 9 (level 3)

Elemental Pact

Removes component cost of summoning pets.

Cost 5

Frenzied Burnout

Allows you to cast a buff on your pet that will cause it to go berserk doing increased damage. When the effect wears off the pet will explode damaging everything around it.

Cost 6

Improved Reclaim Energy

Increases the amount of mana returned to you when reclaiming your pet.

Cost 3

Mass Group Buff

Turns your next group buff into a beneficial area effect spell, hitting everyone within its radius. It also doubles the mana cost of the spell used.

Cost 9

Mend Companion

Allows you to cast a Lay of Hands type spell on your pet.

Cost 5

Pet Discipline

Allows you to give your pet a hold all aggression command. The pet will not attack anything that attacks it or its master until told to attack. Usage: /pet hold.

Cost 6

Quick Summoning

Reduces the casting time of summoning spells by 10, 25, and 50 percent.

Cost 3 (level 1), 6 (level 2), 9 (level 3)

Turn Summoned

Gives you an area-effect fear DoT spell against summoned that with each ability level amplifies the damage.

Cost 5

Monk

Archetype

Combat Agility/Fury/Stability
Fear Resistance
Finishing Blow
Improved Natural Durability/Healing

Class

Ambidexterity

Increases chance to Dual Wield successfully.

Cost 9

Acrobatics

Reduces the damage taken from falling.

Cost 3 (level 1), 6 (level 2), 9 (level 3)

Critical Mend

Gives you a chance to do a superior mend 5, 10 and 25 percent of the time.

Cost 3 (level 1), 6 (level 2), 9 (level 3)

Double Riposte

Gives an increased chance to execute a double riposte 15, 35 and 50 percent of the time.

Cost 3 (level 1), 6 (level 2), 9 (level 3)

Dragon Punch

Gives you the ability to proc a knockback spell off of Dragon Punch.

Cost 5

Purify Body

Removes all negative effects from body except for fear, charm and resurrection effects.

Cost 9

Rapid Feign

Reduces your reuse time on feign death by 10, 25 and 50 percent.

Cost 3 (level 1), 6 (level 2), 9 (level 3)

Return Kick

Gives you the chance to do a flying kick attack on ripostes in addition to the normal riposte attack 25, 35 and 50 percent of the time.

Cost 3

Necromancer

Archetype

Channeling Focus
Mental Clarity
Spell Casting Deftness/Expertise/Fury
Mastery/Reinforcement/Subtlety

Class

Call to Corpse

Allows you to cast a no component summon corpse spell.

Cost 6

Dead Mesmerization

Allows you to cast an area-effect, low-resist, undead mesmerization spell.

Cost 3

Dire Charm

Gives the chance to permanently charm NPC.

Cost 9

Fearstorm

Allows you to cast an area-effect, low-resist fear spell.

Cost 5

Flesh to Bone

Turn any meat or body part item into bone chips. Hold the item on your cursor. *Warning* This ability will use magical and no drop items if held on the cursor.

Cost 3

Innate Invisibility to Undead

Allows you to become invisible versus undead without the need to memorize a spell.

Cost 3

Life Burn

Allows you to cast a no-resist, direct-damage spell equal to that of your current Hit Points. The effect drains your life and gives you a life bond effect that does 250 pts of damage for 6 ticks.

Cost 9

Mass Group Buff

Turns your next group buff into a beneficial area effect spell for everyone in its radius. It also doubles the mana cost of the spell used.

Cost 9

Mend Companion

Allows you to cast a Lay Hands type spell on your pet.

Cost 5

Pet Discipline

Allows you to give pet a "hold all aggression" command. The pet will not attack anything that attacks it or you until told to attack. Usage: /pet hold.

Cost 6

Paladin

Archetype

Channeling Focus
Combat Agility/Fury/Stability
Fear Resistance
Finishing Blow
Healing Adept
Healing Gift
Improved Natural Durability/Healing
Mental Clarity
Spell Casting Fury/Mastery/Reinforcement

Class

Act of Valor

Allows you to transfer all of your Hit Points to a target PC, killing yourself.

Cost 3

Body and Mind Rejuvenation

Gives you 1 additional point of mana and Hit Point regeneration.

Cost 5

Divine Stun

Allows you to have the chance to stun NPCs with spells up to level 60. Normal resist rules apply.

Cost 9

Double Riposte

Gives you an increased chance to execute a double riposte 15, 35 and 50 percent of the time.

Cost 3 (level 1), 6 (level 2), 9 (level 3)

Fearless

This ability makes you permanently immune to fear spells.

Cost 6

Holy Steed

Gives you the ultimate holy steed.

Cost 5

Improved Lay of Hands

Turns your Lay of Hands into a complete heal.

Cost 1

Mass Group Buff

Turns your next group buff into a beneficial area effect spell, hitting everyone within its radius. It also doubles the mana cost of the spell used.

Cost 9

Physical Enhancement

Gives you additional improvement in Natural Durability, Avoidance Boost and Mitigation Boost abilities.

Cost 5

Slay Undead

Turns your criticals into massive damage when fighting undead monsters.

Cost 3 (level 1), 6 (level 2), 9 (level 3)

2 Hand Bash

Allows you to bash with any two-handed weapon.

Cost 6

Ranger

Archetype

Channeling Focus
Combat Agility/Fury/Stability
Fear Resistance
Finishing Blow
Healing Adept
Healing Gift
Improved Natural Durability/Healing
Mental Clarity
Spell Casting
Fury/Mastery/Reinforcement

Class

Ambidexterity

Increases your chance to use dual wield successfully.

Cost 9

Archery Mastery

Gives increased archery damage based on ability level up to 30, 60 and 100 percent.

Cost 3 (level 1), 6 (level 2), 9 (level 3)

Body and Mind Rejuvenation

Gives you 1 additional point of mana and Hit Point regeneration.

Cost 5

Double Riposte

Gives you an increased chance to execute a double riposte 15, 35 and 50 percent of the time.

Cost 3 (level 1), 6 (level 2), 9 (level 3)

Endless Quiver

Prevents you from ever running out of arrows.

Cost 9

Innate Camouflage

Allows you to become invisible without the need to memorize a spell.

Cost 5

Mass Group Buff

Turns your next group buff into a beneficial area effect spell, hitting everyone within its radius. It also doubles the mana cost of the spell used.

Cost 9

Physical Enhancement

Gives you additional improvement in Natural Durability, Avoidance Boost and Mitigation Boost abilities.

Cost 5

Rogue

Archetype

Combat Agility/Fury/Stability
Fear Resistance
Finishing Blow
Improved Natural Durability/Healing

Class

Acrobatics

Reduces the damage taken from falling.
Cost 3 (level 1), 6 (level 2), 9 (level 3)

Advanced Trap Negotiation

Reduces reuse time on sense and disarm traps.
Cost 3 (level 1), 6 (level 2), 9 (level 3)

Ambidexterity

Increases chance to Dual Wield successfully.
Cost 9

Chaotic Stab

Allows you to do minimal backstab damage on your attempt, even if not behind a monster.
Cost 6

Double Riposte

Gives you increased chance to execute a double riposte 15, 35 and 50 percent of the time.
Cost 3 (level 1), 6 (level 2), 9 (level 3)

Escape

Removes you from all hate lists. If you are out of immediate combat, this ability will also make you invisible (similar to hide ability).
Cost 9**Poison Mastery**

Reduces chance of failing on a poison combination by 10, 25 and 50 percent. It also reduces the time to apply poison by 2.5 secs for each ability level. Once one point is applied, you no longer fail in poison application.
Cost 3 (level 1), 6 (level 2), 9 (level 3)

Purge Poison

Removes all poison affects from you.
Cost 5

Shadow Knight

Archetype

Channeling Focus
Combat Agility/Fury/Stability
Fear Resistance
Finishing Blow
Improved Natural Durability/Natural Healing
Mental Clarity
Spell Casting Deftness/Expertise/Fury/Mastery/Reinforcement/Subtlety

Class

Body and Mind Rejuvenation

Gives you 1 additional point of mana and Hit Point regeneration.
Cost 5

Double Riposte

Gives you an increased chance to execute a double riposte 15, 35 and 50 percent of the time.
Cost 3 (level 1), 6 (level 2), 9 (level 3)

Fearless

Makes you permanently immune to fear spells.
Cost 6

Leech Touch

Gives you a life tap harm touch. This ability uses the existing Harm Touch timer.
Cost 6

Pet Discipline

Allows you to give your pet a “hold all aggression” command. The pet will not attack anything that attacks it or its master until told to attack. Usage: /pet hold.
Cost 6

Physical Enhancement

Gives you additional improvement in your Natural Durability, Avoidance Boost and Mitigation Boost abilities.
Cost 5

Soul Abrasion

Gives you increased damage off of your self buff lifetap procs.

Cost 3 (level 1), 6 (level 2), 9 (level 3)

Super Harm Touch

Gives you a low resist Harm Touch. This ability uses the existing Harm Touch timer.

Cost 6

2 Hand Bash

Allows you to bash with any two-handed weapon.

Cost 6

Unholy Steed

Gives you the ultimate unholy steed.

Cost 5

Shaman

Archetype

Channeling Focus
Healing Adept
Healing Gift
Mental Clarity
Spell Casting Fury/Mastery/Reinforcement

Class

Alchemy Mastery

Reduces the chance of failing on an alchemy combination by 10, 25, and 50 percent.

Cost 3 (level 1), 6 (level 2), 9 (level 3)

Cannibalization

Gives you a new cannibalize spell.

Cost 5

Mass Group Buff

Turns your next group buff into a beneficial area effect spell, hitting everyone within its radius. It also doubles the mana cost of the spell used.

Cost 9

Pet Discipline

Allows you to give your pet a "hold all aggression" command. The pet will not attack anything that attacks it or its master until told to attack. Usage: /pet hold.

Cost 6

Quick Buff

Reduces the casting time of beneficial spells with a duration by 10, 25 and 50 percent. Some spells may be excluded.

Cost 3 (level 1), 6 (level 2), 9 (level 3)

Rabid Bear

Turns you into a rabid bear, boosting all your offense capabilities.

Cost 5

Spell Casting Reinforcement Mastery

Increases the duration of beneficial buffs by an additional 20 percent.

Cost 8

Warrior

Archetype

Combat Agility/Fury/Stability
Fear Resistance
Finishing Blow
Improved Natural Durability/Healing

Class

Ambidexterity

Increases your chance to use Dual Wield successfully.

Cost 9

Area Taunt

Allows for you to taunt everything in a small radius.

Cost 5

Bandage Wound

Gives you increased healing capabilities through bandage by 10, 25 and 50 percent.

Cost 3 (level 1), 6 (level 2), 9 (level 3)

Double Riposte

Gives you an increased chance to execute a double riposte 15, 35 and 50 percent of the time.

Cost 3 (level 1), 6 (level 2), 9 (level 3)

Flurry

Allows for you to have up to 2 additional attacks off of your primary hand.

Cost 3 (level 1), 6 (level 2), 9 (level 3)

Rampage

Allows for you to attack everything in a small radius.

Cost 5

Warcry

Allows you to give your entire group immunity to fear for a period of time based on ability level.

Cost 3 (level 1), 6 (level 2), 9 (level 3)

Wizard

Archetype

Channeling Focus
Mental Clarity
Spell Casting Deftness/Expertise/Fury
Mastery/Reinforcement/Subtlety

Class

Exodus

Gives you the ability to cast an instant casting no mana cost evacuation or succor spell.

Cost 6

Improved Familiar

Makes your familiar immune to spells and resistant to melee damage.

Cost 9

Mana Burn

Allows you to do irresistible damage based on your current mana.

Cost 5

Nexus Gate

Gives you an instant cast self gate spell to the Nexus.

Cost 6

Quick Direct Damage

Reduces the casting time on direct damage spells by 2, 5 and 10 percent.

Cost 3 (level 1), 6 (level 2), 9 (level 3)

Quick Evacuation

Reduces the casting time on evacuation and succor spells by 10, 25 and 50 percent.

Cost 3 (level 1), 6 (level 2), 9 (level 3)

Spell Casting Fury Mastery

Gives you an increased percent chance to critical with direct damage spells.

Cost 3 (level 1), 6 (level 2), 9 (level 3)

Strong Root

Gives you a nearly irresistible root spell.

Cost 5

Alternative Servers

primagames.com

Every new player to EverQuest comes with different expectations and a unique style of play. Therefore, the designers have established several variant servers, where the rules of play have been modified to accommodate different tastes in roleplaying. These alternative servers include several where player versus player (PvP) combat is not only allowed but encouraged (under varying strictures and guidelines) as well as the new Firiona Vie server, which is devoted to encouraging in-character roleplaying.

As a general rule, it is more of a challenge to establish a character in these alternative servers than it is in servers that use the normal rule set. Therefore, it is recommended that new players establish their first characters on one of the regular rules servers, and move on to an alternative server when they feel they have mastered the game and are ready for a new challenge.

Firiona Vie

The Firiona Vie server is set up with a very different ruleset than the other servers. The intention is to encourage roleplaying on the server. Here is a list of the rules that vary from those of the standard servers:

Firiona Vie Server Feature List

- † The designers consider Firiona Vie a "PvE" (Player vs. Environment) server, *not* a PvP (Player vs. Player) server. This means it's a standard "blue" server with the same rules and features regarding PvP as the vast majority of EQs servers. It is not one of the "Zeks."
- † Auction is restricted to city zones: Qeynos, Surefall Glade, Highkeep, Freeport, Rivervale, Erudin, Halas, Neriak, Grobb, Oggok, Greater Faydark, Ak'Anon, Kaladim, Felwithe, Paineel, Cabilis, Kael and Thurgadin.
- † Beneficial buff spells do not work on characters 20 or more levels lower than the caster.
- † Each character is assigned an "alignment" upon creation. This alignment will be described in brief on the character creation screen (in the same location as their deity).
- † Each character is allowed to change their alignment *once*, any time after they reach 10th level, if they choose to. A character is not required to change alignments. You can choose from a list of alignments based on your race, class and deity.
- † Your alignment sometimes determines whether or not you can group with other characters. Good characters cannot group with Evil characters.
- † A character's alignment determines an experience bonus or penalty when grouping with other characters. Grouping with similarly aligned characters provides a bonus; grouping with characters of disparate alignments gets you a penalty. It is important to

note that the penalties for all group members combined can never exceed the bonus normally given for grouping.

- Your alignment determines if you can cast beneficial spells on other characters (including resurrections). If you can't group with someone, then you can't aid them (or receive aid from them) with spells.
- Language skills improve only through group chat in the same zone, and from **/say**.
- Languages can only improve 1 point each hour, and are capped at (level x 5)+5 skill points.
- The Common tongue does not exist. A Human language does, and is easily available only to certain races.
- Only one character per account on Firiona Vie.
- The Trivial Loot Code (see below) is in effect in all zones.
- Very few items are No-Drop. Exceptions will include things such as newbie notes and epic weapons.
- Bind Affinity is restricted for all characters to locations where melee characters can bind on other servers.
- **/emote** is language specific.
- All characters are **/roleplay**.
- **/alignment** displays the alignment of your character and a more detailed description of that alignment.

Trivial Loot Code

If you kill an NPC and that NPC does not yield experience (because there is a significant power discrepancy between the NPC and you or someone in your party), then the Trivial Loot Code takes effect. If *any* member of a group does not get experience for a kill, the Trivial Loot Code takes effect. The Trivial Loot Code prevents magical, lore and no-drop items from appearing on the corpse. Normal items and coins appear on the corpse in all cases as usual.

Choosing an Alignment

This server introduces the idea of alignment into the world of Norrath. This is an idea used in many roleplaying games to help the players and the game master further describe their characters, to express their social and emotional personality in much the same way as they describe a character's physical appearance.

Written descriptions of each of the nine possible alignments are provided on pages 81-83. Each description is an outline of the ideals of that alignment type. Alignments are usually chosen to match the personality of your character. If you are neutral, but refuse to aid a dark elf or troll because you believe them to be evil, perhaps you would be better defined as neutral good.

Characters change and develop as they are played. When you started out with a new character you may have had a certain

Life on Firiona Vie

By Gilles "Barawin" Andre

The seasoned player creating a new character on Firiona Vie will be surprised, at first, by the disappearance of spam in the chat box. The `/ooc` channel is disabled, `/shout` has a limited range, and `/auction` is only available in towns. As a result, the usual (and sometimes annoying) spam encountered on other servers completely disappears on Firiona Vie. The new chat rules are much more realistic and, except for `/tell` and `/group` which are still available, you actually have to meet and face the persons you want to talk to.

A second rule directly influencing chat is the removal of the "common language" concept. Every race speaks its own language, and you need to learn the other races' tongues in order to communicate with them. Language skill development is limited to 1 point per hour, which makes learning new languages rather time consuming and difficult. The direct result of this rule is that players tend to team among their own race (for better communication), which reinforces the "role-play" side of the game. New tactics have to be designed, specific to this or that race's assets. A typical Ogre tactical unit, for instance, might include 2 Shaman, 2 Warriors and 2 Shadow Knights. The lack of a Cleric offers the Shaman a prime healer role, as they were originally designed, giving them a more satisfying task than the buffing role they have on other servers. Also, the limited healing power forces the players to design new tactics among tanks to trade aggro against difficult opponents.

Another new feature on the server is alignment: good/neutral/evil and order/

concept in mind. You might have seen her as tolerant of both good and evil, willing to help anyone that needed it. But as she travels and meets people, she might realize that helping evil people has never been a pleasant experience, and that she feels more comfortable, and more honorable, obeying the rules. Perhaps she learns to despise rogues. A character that you thought would be orderly when you created her may end up being orderly good after she experiences Norrath a bit.

This is why you have to wait to choose the permanent alignment of your character until you reach level 10. Your character is given an alignment when you choose his class, race and deity. That alignment matches the ideals of that character's teachers. If your character starts as an agnostic human warrior, he will have left his training with all the impressions that his teachers gave him about the world. Because the character spent so long under the tutelage of people who insisted that a warrior must follow the middle road and be willing to fight when and where he was needed, he will enter his career as a neutral. But adventuring changes people, and after ten levels of such adventure you will be able to decide your character's alignment, within restrictions determined by that character's race, class and deity. For example, High Elves must be good, and are restricted to good alignment options when they reach level 10, or at any time thereafter.

You can only make this change once, so choose wisely. Get to know your character before choosing.

Alignment Descriptions

Neutral (N)

A person of neutral alignment can be very different from another person of the same alignment. For example, a Druid might actively defend the center, holding a strong desire that neither good nor evil, order nor discord gain control in the world, for each of them is inherently unbalanced and unnatural. But a Warrior of neutral alignment might be unconcerned about such things and simply wish that all those with such strong opinions keep them to themselves. In either case, the neutral character is not strongly allied with the idea of order or discord, good or evil.

Discordant Neutral (DN)

This is a character of unruly nature. Whether one is in opposition to the tenets of order or just desires to be unconstrained is immaterial. These folk tend to be unmindful of the rules of society, preferring to do what seems correct to them at the moment. This isn't a destructive kind of chaos such as would make a person evil, nor is it a gentle chiding of the rules intended to show where constraints hinder the ability for one to do what is good. Folks of this alignment are most often just unable to understand why others have the right to blanket their lives with rules when those rules can't be accurate for any of the specific situations they find themselves in.

neutral/discord. Your race, deity and class all restrict your choice, but you will be allowed one change in alignment once you reach level 10. It directly influences who you can group with (players with same or close alignment) and who you can buff and get buffs from.

The combination of alignment and language rules results in players not wasting their time learning each and every language in the game, but giving preference to those from races they will actually team with. The same applies to guilds. Many are race-specific, and those accepting multiple races will actually be either good or evil oriented. The result is a much more realistic world, with no Dark Elf Necro/High Elf Cleric/Troll Warrior/Wood Elf Druid teams!

Last, for those who hate twinking and think it unbalances the game, Firiona Vie is the server of choice. The trivial loot code is in effect in *all* zones (no farming allowed!) and players are only allowed one character per account on this server. Players do not fight over a particular piece of loot that is much needed for one team member, but would also be sooo cool on another player's twink!

The server rules can be very disorienting for veteran players. They also make the world much more realistic and challenging, predominantly because of the lack of key classes in most groups. Each race has to design its own fighting tactics and adapt to the new environment. I wouldn't advise this server to brand new players, for life is much harder than on other servers, but veterans getting tired of the play style on their server can try Firiona Vie and discover a world designed in a very different way … almost a brand new game!

Orderly Neutral (ON)

Characters of this alignment believe foremost that sentient races must have rules to abide by, or they will become lost in uncivilized discord. This does not necessarily make them proselytizers of order. It is just as likely that one of this alignment would hold only themselves to such restrictions. Even so, their belief in the ordering of things is strong and they will often find it challenging to allow discord to work around them. One of this alignment will follow the rules of any society he finds himself in, and will tend to avoid the company of those that hold no rules or laws important.

Neutral Good (NG)

Characters of this alignment believe that being good is more important than being orderly or chaotic. If rules make certain people happy, then they should have such rules. If rules cause others to be troubled, then they should be able to go where such rules do not apply. But neither rules nor a hatred of such rules should be an excuse for a person to be evil. Above all else, being good is what matters. This may only be a personal goal, or it might be something that the character desires for others. In any case, such a person will be unable to abide evil in any form. How they respond to such evil will vary from person to person, but they will never encourage evil and will never aid one that does evil.

Neutral Evil (NE)

Characters of this alignment are uninterested in order or discord. Such disinterest might stem from a lack of concern, or it might spring from disdain. For the most part, a person of this alignment strives primarily to achieve evil ends. Their goals might be personal, or they may wish to impress evil upon others. But evil is in them, and they cannot tolerate goodness. They will never aid a person of goodly demeanor, and depending on their personal desires will either hinder them or shun them.

Orderly Evil (OE)

Characters of this alignment form the heart of many evil societies. Their rules may be cruel, perhaps even frightening, but they are the devices that keep society in line. Evil to the core, these characters understand the power of organization and order, and they know that the way of discord is the way of self-destruction. If you want your dreams to come true, either as a person or as a society, then you must have the strength of order to build on. Structure is what makes evil terrible and mighty. Ambitious orderly evils desire the destruction of all that is good, and often have a plan for making that happen.

Discordant Evil (DE)

Characters of this alignment eschew rules as restrictive to the purpose of evil. They believe that confusion and mayhem are the most effective tools available. They find those of order to be far too constrained by their own rules to be effective. Only those willing to throw off the shackles of order can ever truly be great. Seething chaos is the soil that nourishes true evil. Honor is for fools and Paladins, both of which make fine mulch for the garden.

Alternative Servers: Alignment Descriptions

Orderly Good (OG)

Characters of this alignment believe that good is enhanced by order. True peace can only be achieved through the foundation of just rules and true goodness. Discord breeds evil, for those who are unwilling to follow rules most often do so because those rules enforce what is good. Certainly some rules are unjust and should be defied. But such rules are only created by those who are evil at heart. Societies, families, and individuals alike should be willing to do what is right, and to set what is right down as law. Some might be asked to make sacrifices for the good of others. Those unwilling to do so, those who say that rules are too constraining and are unwilling to abide by them because it discomforts them to do so, are selfish. Selfishness often leads to evil. Evil is intolerable.

Discordant Good (DG)

Characters of this alignment believe that being good is an internal measure, not a societal one. Many of the rules that societies create have nothing to do with being good, but are designed to restrict people so that they can't be evil. A fine distinction, to be sure, but how can a rule, written onto a piece of paper or carved into stone by someone days, months or even years prior have any pertinence to an action taking place right now? Stealing is against the rules in many places, but it is not by its very nature evil. It is only the intent of the person doing the stealing that determines the goodness of the act. Stealing money from an evil man and using that money to feed those who have little is a good act, not an evil one. Rules hinder many acts that are indeed good.

Racial Alignments

Each of the races of Norrath has a society, where they learn how to behave themselves (or, for some, how to misbehave). Below are very brief descriptions of the alignment tendencies of each race. The alignments available to characters of each race are listed in parentheses after the description. The most common alignments appear first, with those after each successive dash being less common than those previous.

Barbarians

These isolationists tend toward neutrality and slightly toward goodness. They also tend to be orderly, primarily because the most commonly worshiped deity in Halas is the Tribunal. However, they are a wild people in a wild land, and not a few of them feel constrained by rules and follow the ways of discord. For the most part their society honors bravery and skill over trickery and greed, and desires of power or other evil thoughts are channeled and controlled by the overwhelming need to prove themselves to their people. (N/NG/ON - OG/DG/DN)

Dark Elves

Driven primarily by the hatred that created them, Dark Elves are strongly evil. Their society is orderly (as order is the only thing that keeps their society stable), but in some the urge for evil is unrestrained by the rules of their society. There are discordant elements among the Dark Elves, primarily among those of the necromantic arts. Upward movement in the society of Neriak requires great cunning and self-control, however, and it is rare that those who do not possess orderly minds gain power in those circles. But Dark Elves are driven by all kinds of hatred — wild, flaring, dangerous hatred as well as cold, seething, dangerous hatred. (OE/NE - DE)

Dwarves

As sturdy of mind as they are of body, Dwarves tend strongly toward order. Moved more by the smooth strength of steel and the beauty of precious stones, they are rarely motivated by the temptations of good or evil. However, through a long and occasionally strained relationship with the High and Wood Elves, and from continuous battle with the evil of the goblins, they will stray toward goodness rather than evil, if indeed they stray at all. The Dwarven society prides itself on its honor, steadfastness in times of trouble, and its loyalty to its kin. (ON - N/NG)

Erudites

Erudites are a people of two societies. The first was founded by Erud himself and still hold his strong beliefs at its core. Meticulous might be a good way to describe these folk. Their lives are ever bent toward discoveries of the mind. Their society reflects this. They are generally peaceful and orderly, and have become even more dedicated to the ideals of peace and order since their civil war gave a face to those among them who were dedicated to evil.

The heretics of Paineel are just as orderly and meticulous as their estranged cousins in Erudin. Where the Erudites see order as a device that allows people the freedom to be good, the heretics see it as a tool that gives strength to their evil. Their daily lives are no less organized than the people's of Erudin, but their social goals involve powers of dark necromancy and evil, rather than the enlightenment of good and kindness.

It isn't unreasonable to envision these two societies as distillations of the two faces of order. Both have a tendency to be harsh in their adherence to order, as they have very real evidence of what can happen when one strays from the path of good/evil. Erudites (ON/OG/NG), Heretics (OE - NE)

Gnomes

Gnomes run the gamut, being as likely to follow one path as any other. They are, however, unlikely to follow the strict life of order. They tend to be an unstructured people, and their amazing skill and detailed work seems to come from an inherent understanding of things, rather than any strict organizational skills. The rising influence of Bertoxxulous in Ak'Anon is considered by some among other races as evidence of the disorganization of the Gnomes. There exists an odd truce between the worshippers of the gods of the Gnomes, almost as if they are too busy or absentminded to take notice of the potential conflict that exists within the cavern walls of their clockwork city. (N/DN/NG/NE/DG/DE)

Half Elves

Being born of Humans and Wood Elves, and having a tendency to be independent of either society in any case, Half Elves can be of any alignment. They tend to fall into professions and forms of worship that suit their dispositions rather than conform to the needs of any society. It is possible to find Half Elves as members of almost any religion. In this fashion they take after their Human parents. (ANY)

Halflings

These little folk tend to be kindly and warm, outgoing and inquisitive. While some are less friendly and some are more orderly than is most common, on the whole they are a pleasant people. While some will take up duties and keep at them tenaciously, this is stubbornness rather than orderliness. Unfettered and gregarious, these folk tend to chafe at rules they don't understand. Sure, it's wrong to hurt people, but everyone knows that, so why do you have to make a rule that says you can't? Despite what is often seen as rashness by some of the more stoic races of Norrath, Halflings are never swayed to evil. (DG/NG/DN/N)

High Elf

These children of Tunare embody her sense of order and goodness. They are a people of high values and great light. While some might be slightly less lawful or marginally less good than others, High Elves are incapable of evil and chaos. This does not make them immune to errors in judgment, and it is not uncommon for them to appear haughty and even rude due to their strong sense of self-worth. As a society, they value actions over words, though they do not take words lightly. They value the good hearts of their cousins, the Wood Elves, but find their flightiness disconcerting. (OG - ON/NG)

Humans

Diversity is both their strength and their weakness. Humans can be of any alignment, and much like their Half Elven kin, they tend to take up professions that suit their desires. Those who feel a need for structure in their lives will often settle in the cities they have built on Antonica. But it is just as likely that you will meet a lawless Human brigand on the road as a pleasant Human Cleric. With a Human you can never know what to expect until you get to know the individual. (ANY)

Iksar

Even though their empire has fallen, the Iksar are still an orderly society. Evil to the core, there is very little variance from the path of order and evil among the Iksar of Cabilis. Those who are too disorderly are exiled into the wilderness of Kunark, where most find only death. Those who are too weak are often killed trying to prove their strength. Their single-minded acceptance of Fear has given their society its strength, and has given them the reputation as a terrible and dangerous people. (OE - NE)

Ogres

Perhaps at the height of their society (if you believe such rumors), Ogres were the epitome of order and the strength of evil. But these days they are just too stupid to have much need for laws. Somewhat mellower than their green-skinned neighbors, Ogres tend to be just evil, as chaos and law require more work. Their society decays as their attentiveness to their old ways slowly fades. They can't be anything other than evil, but they can be motivated to be orderly or discordant, depending on how frequently they were dropped as children and on what part of their body they landed. (NE - DE/OE)

Trolls

Trolls are a people bent on destruction and tend to be both discordant and evil. There is no reason to believe that Trolls as a people ever had a society to speak of. They are ruled by the strongest and their society shifts with the latest battle, rarely fixing on a long-term goal. Their ferocity is their strength, serving them well enough in the place of rules. They are never other than evil, though some are less disorderly than the rest. (DE - NE)

Vah Shir

This noble race is never evil, and tends toward order or goodness, though they are unlikely to be so strongly aligned as to follow both. Seen as 'agnostic' by most others, the Vah Shir worship spirits and ancestors rather than specific gods. This is why they seem less 'cultured' in the ways of their religion, while still maintaining an organized and up-to-date society. It is their dedication to each other that makes their society strong and has allowed them to flourish on Luclin. As a rule these folk are calm and orderly, though there are always a few that tend to be less of one or the other. (N/NG/ON - OG/DG/DN)

Wood Elves

As the High Elves are an orderly folk, the Wood Elves are wild. They tend to be chaotic and willful. They represent all that is untamed in the forest and in their beloved Mother of All. They are at heart a loving people, though they do stray, some becoming more wild than good. They are never evil, however, no matter the consternation they cause their High Elven cousins. Their society is built on respect more than on a sense of order. It is only reasonable to take the advice of one's betters, but that does not mean that one is constrained to obey that advice as if it were the only path. (DG/DN - N/NG)

Class Alignments

Bard

Travelers, arbiters, tale-spinners, lore masters and often heroes, Bards have many personalities. While it is not uncommon for any given Bard to have several personalities all his own, as a group they are as diverse as the gods they follow. (ANY)

Beastlord

Similar in style and manner to a Ranger, these beast tamers are different in one key respect. Their dedication is rarely to a society as much as it is to their lives as masters of beasts and the beasts themselves. Also unlike a Ranger, the Beastlord is only respectful of nature in the way that he was trained. Vah Shir Beastlords worship the spirits of nature and the animals, as do Barbarians. But the evil races have grown to understand this worship differently, and often believe it to be a form of mastery over those spirits. (ANY)

Cleric

A Cleric is often the pinnacle of his society – a spiritual leader, and often lore master for the tales of a society or of the god that they worship. Only those whose souls are most closely bound to their deity will become Clerics, and so they have alignments restricted by that of their deity and of their race. (ANY)

Druid

A Druid fights for the balance. Not content to be a bystander in the battles that often occur between factions both religious and racial, a Druid might actively defend a forest from the ravages of good or evil alike. (N)

Enchanter

Enchanters are often known for their ability to disguise themselves and to cloud the minds of others. There is a tendency, therefore, for such a person to understand other races and to at least study them somewhat. (ANY)

Magician

Elemental mastery and the power over the servants of the elements are not preclusive to any attitude. The only true requirement for this profession is a strong will and perhaps an equally strong ego. (ANY)

Monk

In order to be able to control one's body to the degree that a Monk is capable, one must first control the mind. Monks must be orderly to follow the path that leads only along the razor's edge. (ON/OG/OE)

Necromancer

The desire to raise and manipulate the corpses of the dead is an unpleasant one at best. Most societies make rules against such activities, as disturbing the dead can have accursed consequences. Necromancers, therefore, are always evil and they rarely concern themselves with order. (DE - NE/OE)

Paladin

Paladins are the heroic knights of legend. They are the epitome of their people and their gods. This means that they must be goodly, and are most often orderly, but can be neutral good. (OG - NG)

Ranger

Rangers are the warriors of nature. They shy away from no duty that calls them to the service of their god. They share many of the beliefs of the Druids, though their methods may vary. A Ranger cannot be evil and tends indeed to be neutral, as do Druids. But they are closer to Paladins in this regard; they are more closely tied to the desires of their deity than to the balance of things. (N/DN - DG/NG - OG/ON)

Rogue

Rogues are just that, rogues. They find rules amusing things, obstacles at worst, toys at best. A rogue may not be orderly. They, in fact, tend to be discordant. (DN/N - DG/DE/NG/NE)

Shadow Knight

Often seen as the counterpoint to the Paladin, and justifiably so, Shadow Knights are knights of legend, too, though of the dark sort. A Shadow Knight must be evil, and tends to be orderly or discordant in resonance with their deity and society. (OE/DE)

Shaman

Much like Clerics, Shaman are the spiritual leaders of their people. Those who are most like unto their deity will be called to be Shaman. (ANY)

Warrior

The Warrior is as varied in personality as the battles he fights. They tend to be less extreme, for those of highly religious nature tend to become Paladins and Shadow Knights, but this does not mean that a Warrior can't be just as righteous as any Paladin. (ANY)

Wizard

Theirs is only the desire for knowledge and power. Their intent for that knowledge and power is dependent only on their character. (ANY)

Deity Alignments

Agnostic

Followers of no specific god, these characters are not restricted to any particular alignment, though they do tend to be neutral. (ANY)

Bertoxxulous - God of Disease/Decay

An unpleasant creeping comes to mind when thoughts turn to Bertoxxulous. It is often thought that without this god things might never fall into chaos and age. His followers are never good, nor are they orderly. (DE - NE)

Brell Serilis - Duke of Below

A complicated god to define, Brell Serilis's most prominent worshippers are, of course, the dwarves of Kaladim. However, if the rumors are indeed true, he is the creator of many races, good and evil, orderly and discordant. Regardless of the truth, many evil races do indeed worship Brell. However, the belief that he created such creatures is not held among most races of Norrath. In fact, the fundaments of his worship among most societies posit that he is not evil, but a lover of creation in its purest form. He is worshiped as a non-evil deity, and is most often considered an orderly being. Modern worship of him follows that course. (N/ON - NG/OG - DN/DG)

Cazic-Thule - God of Fear

Mindless terror is his goal; order and discord are irrelevant to this god, and he cares only to spread paralyzing fear. As long as the result is terror, the cause or method is of little consequence. How his followers choose to inspire fear is up to them. His followers must be evil. (NE - DE/OE)

Fizzlethorpe Bristlebane - God of Thieves

His followers accept only one tenet: Laws are something to be ridiculed. As his following among the Dark Elves might indicate, he is not necessarily only a god of fun and tricks. While each society will have a slightly different understanding of his nature, none of his followers can be orderly. (DN - DG/N/DE/NE/NG)

Innoruuk - God of Hate

His primary place of worship lies deep within Neriak, but his power is universal and touches everyone at some point in their lives. He has followers among many people of Norrath. His followers must be evil. (OE - NE/DE)

Karana - God of Storms

His essence is the torrential rain and fury of the storm, the discord of the storm and the goodness of the nourishing rain. His followers can't be evil or orderly. (N/DN/NG - DG)

Erollisi Marr - Goddess of Love

Her designs are in direct opposition to those of the god of Hate. It might indeed be true that her influence is as far reaching as Innoruuk's, and that even the darkest heart can be touched by Love. Her followers must be good. (NG/DG/OG)

Mithaniel Marr - God of Righteousness and Truth

Mithaniel Marr is a more dedicated force for goodness than his sister, Erollisi. Order and goodness are within his realm, and his sword arm defends both. His followers must be good and cannot be discordant. (OG - NG)

Prexus - God of the Oceans

Prexus is most often worshiped by those who sail the seas. For many, such worship is not just a desire to avoid his wrath while at sea. Prexus despises Bertoxxulous and calls Rodcet Nife ally. His followers cannot be evil, but you will find as many who love the seas for their wild waves as for their calm on a clear night. (N/NG/OG/DG/DN/ON)

Quellious - Goddess of Peace and Harmony

As seekers of inner peace, followers of Quellious can never be discordant or evil, and are most commonly both orderly and good. (OG - N/NG/ON)

Rallos Zek - God of War and Battle Lust

While there are indeed good and just reasons to do battle, those are not the only reasons. Rallos worshippers are those who love battle for any cause, and reason. They can never be good, though some are not as evil as others. (DE/NE/OE - N/DN/ON)

Rodcet Nife - Prime Healer

Only those of good heart can follow the god of healing. Whether they choose the path of order or discord is not important, as long as they heal the hurts and destroy the disease of the world as they travel that path. (NG/OG/DG)

Solusek Ro - God of Fire

Fire is, by its very nature, a discordant element. Often the followers of Solusek Ro worship him as a destructive force, a power of chaos and ruin. But not all of those who follow the Burning Prince see him that way, and some even see fire as a cleansing thing. His followers can't be orderly and tend not to be good. (DN/DE - N/NE - DG/NG)

Tribunal - God(s) of Justice

Justice is by no means the same thing as the truth and valor of Mithaniel Marr. For followers of the Tribunal, order is the primary concern. Some followers of the Tribunal believe that justice cannot exist without a measure of concern for those it affects, but it is argued (often and at great length) by most followers that this is a tainting of justice, not a tempering of it. Followers are almost always orderly, and some are good. (ON- OG - N)

Tunare - Mother of All

It is said that Tunare created the elves, who in time became the orderly high elves and the more discordant wood elves. Her power is that of growth and life, encompassing both order and discord as forces of nature. Her followers can be of any non-evil alignment. (N/NG/OG/DG/ON/DN)

Veeshan

Virtually unknown in Norrath, only bards know much of Veeshan's mythology and are still willing to worship her. She is believed to be the mother of all dragons and dragon kin. Otherwise, the lore about the nature of her worship is all but lost. Her followers interpreted what little they know about her and, perhaps as much through ignorance as through truth, have created a path of worship to her that eschews order, discord, good and evil equally. (N)

Sullon Zek

The Sullon Zek server is a relatively new server with a new rule set. The rules for this server are very different than those on any other *EverQuest* server. In general the server is based on the concept of a PvP teams server, like Tallon and Vallon Zek, but with the teams chosen based on which god the character worships rather than the race of the character.

- † You are unable to fight other players until you have gained enough strength to survive the struggle. Characters below 6th level cannot participate in PvP combat. As soon as you reach 6th level you are PvP enabled.
- † Combat can occur between any characters above level 6 that are not in the same alliance (or "Deity Team"). A level 50 character can attack and kill a level 6 character if that character is not a member of his alliance (see p. 93 for more on **The Alliances**).
- † You lose experience when killed in PvP combat, if the character that killed you is within 5 levels of you. The amount of experience lost is the same amount that is lost if you are killed by an NPC. Corpses can be resurrected by a Cleric to partially restore lost experience.
- † You can only loot coins from other characters, and then only if the victim is within 5 levels of the killer. Only the character who administered the killing blow will be able to loot the corpse.
- † You may only have one character at a time on this server. This means that you have to delete an existing character in order to create a new one.
- † Characters cannot group with anyone that is not of their alliance.
- † Characters cannot invite someone to join their guild that is not of their alliance.
- † All combat skills have their effective value capped at 2 levels above a player's current level. Losing two levels does not cause you to lose any combat skill effectiveness. Losing more than that will cause those skill caps to be lowered so that they remain only two levels above your current level. (This prevents players from leveling up a character and then "de-leveling" it so they can keep their high level skills and kill low level characters easily.)
- † Resistance debuff spells have a 50% increased effectiveness against player characters.
- † `/consider` returns only three kinds of results when used against player characters. Green means that the character is below your range. White or black mean that the character is within 5 levels of you. Red means that she is above your range.

- `/consider` also displays a message indicating what alliance the target belongs to. Members of your own alliance are displayed as allies. Evil and Good alliance members who `/consider` Neutral alliance members see them as apprehensive. Neutral alliance members see Evil and Good folks as apprehensive also. Good and Evil alliance members see each other as threatening.
- Faction hits for PvP are taken for killing characters within their racial home towns. Killing a Human in any Human starting city will cause a faction loss with the locals. Freeport, Qeynos and Surefall Glade are considered starting cities for Humans. All of Greater Faydark and Felwithe are considered starting cities for High Elves and Wood Elves. Half Elves have no starting city. Erudites have home towns that match their starting cities. Other cities are not considered home towns, despite being run and controlled by a certain race. For example, Highpass Hold is not a Human home town. Thurgadin is not a Dwarven home town.
- Rules such as the Play Nice Policy do not apply to this server. Characters have the ability on this server to deal with their conflicts through combat. Causing experience loss by "training" NPCs on other characters is not an offense that would warrant a warning on this server. However, all rules regarding general decency still apply. Cursing, threats and other such things are dealt with sternly, and are still unacceptable behavior on this or any other server.
- Beneficial effects cannot be used on members of another alliance.
- No one is able to bind in dungeon zones.
- "Buff" spells do not affect characters more than 20 levels lower than the spell level. Existing spell restrictions on spells over 50th level supercede this rule.
- Characters over level 20 that are killed in PvP combat drop an insignia. For more on **Insignias**, see the next page.
- Naked corpses *will* disappear when looted by a player character. If you are naked and killed by a player character, your corpse disappears when it is looted.
- Rogues can pick the pockets of player characters that are no more than five levels higher or lower than they are. They can only steal coins - but it is more difficult than stealing from an NPC. A Rogue can only pick the pockets on any given player character once every 30 minutes. Be aware that stealing is not regarded kindly by the governing authorities of Norrath ...
- Hiding or concealing yourself with an ability or spell will cause other PCs to lose their target on you - but beware the *See Invisibility* spell!
- Due to its intensive competitive nature, all players on Sullon Zek receive more experience for kills and quests than on other servers, and also lose less experience upon death (in both PvP and non-PvP situations).

The Alliances

The Good Alliance consists of the worshippers of Erollisi Marr, Mithaniel Marr, Rodcet Nife, Quellious and Tunare.

The Evil Alliance consists of the worshippers of Bertoxxulous, Cazic Thule, Innoruuk and Rallos Zek.

The Neutral Alliance consists of the worshippers of Brell Serilis, Bristlebane, Karana, Prexus, Solusek Ro, The Tribunal, and Veeshan.

There are no Agnostics on Sullon Zek. With the gods and their followers actively at war with one another, those that do not choose to follow a deity are regarded as enemies of all factions. Everyone now worships a deity, if not out of respect, love or fear of the god, then out of fear for their lives at the hands of the more militant faithful.

Barbarian Shaman and Warriors can choose to worship Mithaniel Marr. He was unwilling to abandon all of the noble Barbarians that served the good, and many declared themselves in favor of an alliance with his cause.

Monks will be able to worship Veeshan. The Temple in Qeynos has discovered some ancient writings that opened up new avenues of belief.

Necromancers are exclusively part of the evil alliance; however it is possible for good and neutral parties to summon corpses of fallen comrades from a distant point without the evil implications traditionally associated with that act. To do so, a Magician may trade greater insignias (see **Insignias**, below) for a *Summon Corpse* potion.

This world, more than others, is subject to change as the alliances grow in power and numbers. Please refer to the *EverQuest* web page at http://eqlive.station.sony.com for the most up-to-date information, as well as player rankings (see **Insignias**, below) and statistics.

Insignias

An insignia is obtained when a character of one alliance kills a character of a rival alliance. To produce an insignia the slain character must be above level 20, and within five levels of the slayer. Only the character who administers the death blow can take the insignia.

Insignias are specific to a given deity. An insignia from Karana is different from an insignia for Prexus. There are four levels of insignia: minor, normal, greater and superior. Minor, normal or greater insignias are obtained when a character dies as described above (depending on the level of the slain character). Ten minor insignias can be combined at a forge to create one normal insignia, ten normals create one greater insignia, and 10 greaters create one superior insignia. However, insignias can *only* be combined with other insignias of *the same deity.* Only minor, normal and greater insignias can be obtained by slaying another character; superior insignias can only be made by combining greater insignias.

Insignias have a double purpose — points are assigned for every insignia a player has in his possession, either in the bank or on his person, and rankings are done regularly based upon those points. Also a player can exchange the insignias as part of an alliance quest - losing the points associated with them but gaining valuable items in return.

Advice: How to Get Started on a PvP Server

By Brandon de la Cruz

If the idea of fighting against something a little smarter than a computer-controlled monster appeals to you, then you should give the PvP servers a try. Here's some advice to help get you started.

† *Choose a server.* Now that you've decided to go PvP, you still have to figure out which server to play on. Rallos Zek is a free-for-all for players who enjoy ultimate freedom in combat. The other three servers are team-based, so you can know who to rely on. Vallon and Tallon Zek have race-based teams, while Sullon Zek operates on a deity-team principle that makes for some interesting allies. Feel free to try them all out, if you like! (Note: you may only have one active PC on Sullon Zek. In order to create another you must delete the first one. You can have up to the standard 8 characters on the other PvP servers.)

† *Know the ruleset.* After you choose a server to play on, take the time to look over the ruleset for that server. What are the allowable PvP level ranges? What are you allowed to loot from other players? If you don't know these things you run the risk of being taken advantage of by more experienced players.

† *Be ready to die.* You have to start somewhere, after all – and on the PvP servers it's rock bottom. When you are first able to engage in PvP (level 1 on Rallos, Tallon, and Vallon Zek; level 6 on Sullon Zek) be aware that other players will know this, and see you as a potentially easy target. It can be frustrating to lose a battle, but if you take advantage of the resources you have – especially guards and teammates – you will be able to protect yourself long enough to learn the ropes.

† *Learn the customs.* Just like *EverQuest* in general, the PvP servers have their own vocabulary and customs. Try to figure out how players interact with each other on your server – what is acceptable, what is frowned upon, when and how to alert a zone to an enemy's presence – and you will soon find yourself with a host of new friends to help you, and enemies to battle against.

† *Have fun!* Don't forget that the PvP servers are supposed to be enjoyable … in their own way. If you aren't having fun, or are just starting out in *EverQuest*, you may want to consider a normal server instead. Even on the PvP servers, the actual game is still the same – you still need to level up by hunting and grouping with others. So, if you have learned these skills from the relative safety of a normal server, then it might be easier for you to make the transition over to PvP.

PvP Servers

The player vs. player (PvP) servers were set up at the request of players who wished to add a little more challenge to the standard *EverQuest* game. On these servers players can choose to engage in open combat with each other. The spoils of war vary from server to server, but on all PvP servers it is important to remember that the fundamental *EverQuest* game remains unchanged, and to be successful you will still need to hunt, group, and train your abilities just as you would on a normal server.

Rallos Zek is the oldest PvP server and the one with the simplest ruleset. Any character can attack any other as long as they are within 4 levels of each other. (A level 45 person may attack or be attacked by anyone from level 41 through 49.) In the event that you kill or are killed by another player on this server, the loot rules are "Coin + 1 item". You may loot (or have looted from you) all coin on the corpse, plus an item. Items in bags, in a melee slot (primary, secondary, ranged or ammo), or items marked NODROP may not be looted.

Vallon Zek and Tallon Zek are known as the PvP-Teams servers. Only races on opposing teams may attack, kill or loot each other. The four teams are:

Dark Races. Comprises Iksar, Dark Elves, Ogres and Trolls.

Short Races. Comprises Dwarves, Halflings and Gnomes.

Elven Races. Comprises Half Elves, Wood Elves and High Elves.

Human Races. Comprises Humans, Erudites and Barbarians.

Vah Shir will be assigned to one of these teams shortly.

Anyone on one team may engage in PvP combat with anyone on any of the other three teams, subject to an 8 level limit. That is, a level 42 person can attack or be attacked by anyone between levels 34 and 50, assuming that they are on opposing teams.

The loot rules on these servers differ from Rallos Zek. Only coin may be looted from a fallen opponent.

A recent revision of the PvP server rules has resulted in a removal of all "play nice" restrictions regarding PvP. Standard blue server rules still apply and sexual/racial harassment will not be tolerated. Everything else (training/bind point camping/exp killing, etc) is now completely legal. No PvP-related petitions will be handled by the CS staff. The standard blue server problems, such as lost corpses, bugs, lost items, etc., will still be handled.

Antonius Bayle (UK Server)

This server is the first EQ server located in the United Kingdom. It has the same rules as other standard servers. Those that play *EverQuest* from somewhere outside the United States (where the majority of servers are located) might want to try playing on Antonius Bayle, as it may provide a faster and more stable connection.

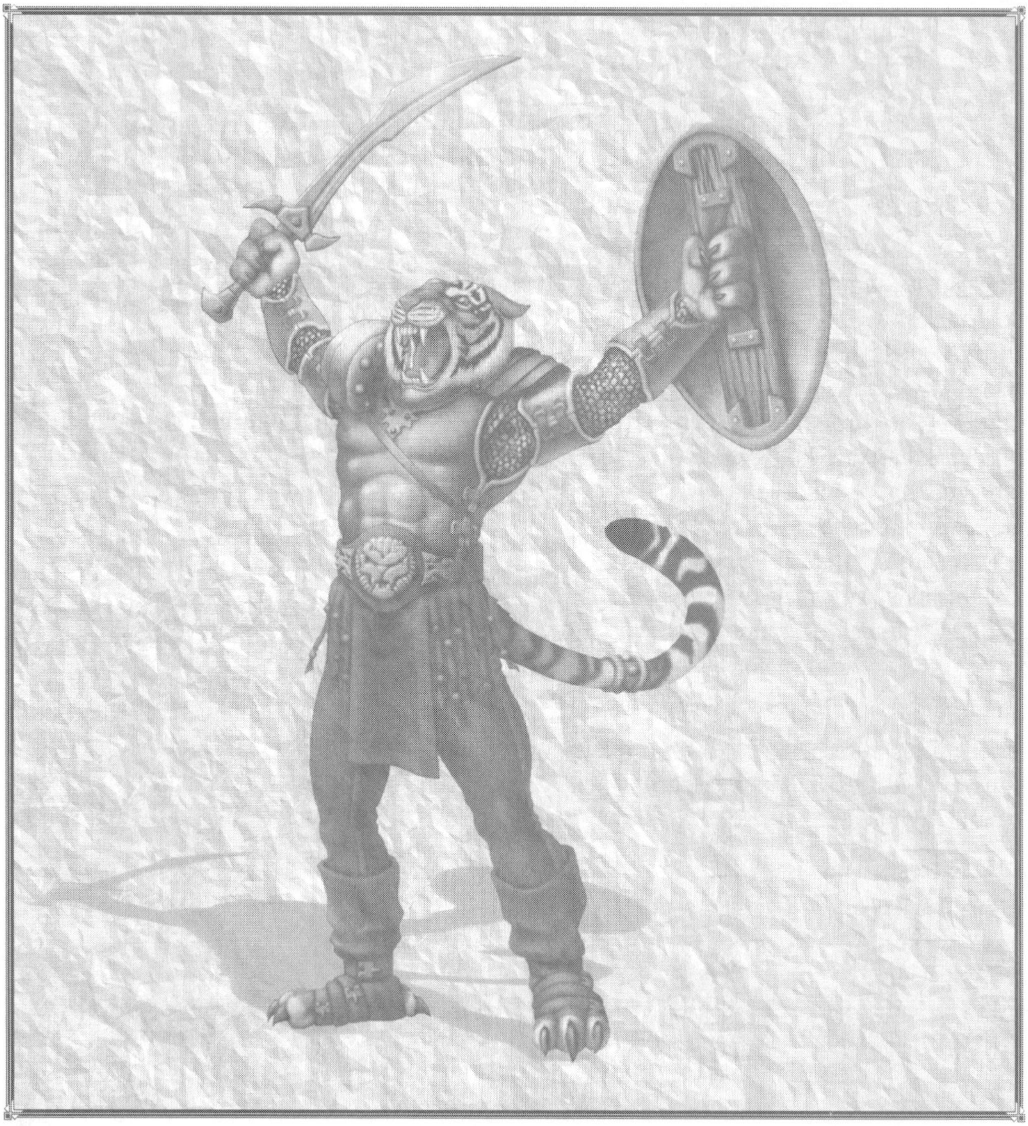

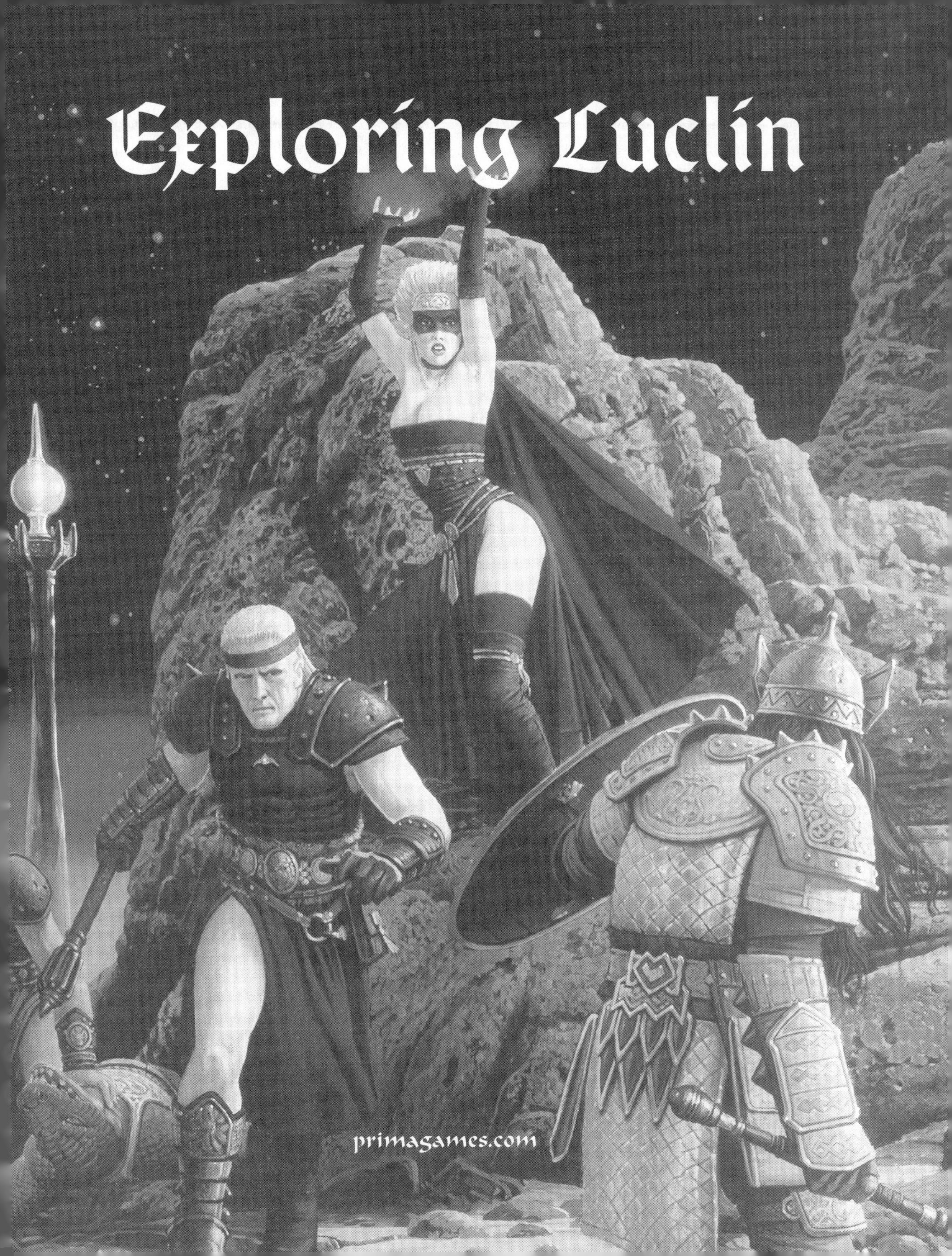

Exploring Luclin

primagames.com

Luclin is the moon of Norrath. Hidden for ages, disguised by the power of the god of the same name, this moon has only recently been discovered by those now living on Norrath.

But some of the children of Norrath have long known of Luclin, for it is their home. Whether they arrived by accident, purpose or war, these remnants of ancient Norrath have had to make their new homes among the creatures of Luclin's creation.

Luclin is a land of light and shadow. A place where it is understood that light creates shadows, and that in shadows darkness thrives ...

To get to Luclin from Norrath, travel to one of the four great spires, located in the Great Devide, Greater Faydark, South Korana, and Tox. You will find there a Wizard who, either by gift or by stealth, has obtained the spell needed to activate the spires for use as transmitters to Luclin. Wait patiently and soon the Wizard will offer to transport everyone in the immediate area to the Nexus on Luclin. Be there and say yes, and you'll soon be exploring this wondrous new world.

EQ Atlas

www.eqatlas.com

All maps are copyright EQ Atlas website, and used here with permission. EQ Atlas has an excellent array of high-quality maps, not just of the cities, but also of the areas in between.

Muse, the Half Elf Cartographer, has been wandering Norrath since the early days of the Beta, drawing maps and making them available to his fellow adventurers.

Shar Vahl

Shar Vahl is a grand walled City and home of the Vah Shir. It is composed of beautiful buildings constructed from acrylia, a native Luclin stone. The city was built by the Vah Shir after they were blasted onto the surface of Luclin during a war between the Erudites and the Heretics. Shar Vahl lies in the center of a large crater created by the impact of the hunk of Norrath that was blasted away from the planet and onto the moon. Protected by the canyon around the city, the Vah Shir had time to build and fortify against any intrusion.

Young Vah Shir, using their excellent agility to climb the dangerous walls of the crater, find their challenges within the crater canyon itself. Some of the native creatures bear their young in the canyon, where they are out of sight of many of the predators of Luclin. While those beasts are too young or weak to make their way out of the canyon, they make fair challenges for young Vah Shir trying to prove themselves.

Welcome to the City of Shar Vahl!

Welcome to the home of the Vah Shir, the city known as Shar Vahl!

Inside this city, you will find most anything that a traveling adventurer would need. Whether you enter through the North Gate (from Shadeweaver's Thicket) or the South Gate (from Hollowshade Moor), you will find that the city seems to be on top of a pillar, with two bridges leading to it. The city was built to take advantage of the crater that was made when the large hunk of Norrath that was blasted away from the planet impacted on the moon.

After crossing the bridge and making your way inside the actual city, you will find a residential area. Various Vah Shir live and work here. The city's Registrar is in the Northern Residential area – this is good to know since young Vah Shir must visit it to become citizens of the city. There are also pubs dotted around these areas.

After some more walking, you will come to the area that deals with the city's commerce. In this area is another pub – even the Vah Shir need a drink or two after a long day's work! – a bank, a general store that sells various supplies for adventurers, an alchemist's shop and other general merchants. There is also an Arena here, so that you and your friends can do battle with each other.

When you are done with your business here, you can then proceed to the center of the city. The King Raja resides here. You will find a few more merchants outside his palace who will sell you any goods you may not have been able to find in the rest of the city. You will also see the King's Temple, a towering structure that is a magnificent sight to behold. If you decide to walk in to pay the King a visit, don't be afraid of the large tigers. They are quite friendly … provided you don't try to hurt them!

It's interesting to note that there is a jail under the temple. That is definitely a place you do *not* want to be: no one really knows *how* the Vah Shir treat their prisoners. I am sure, though, that if you play nice in their city, you won't ever need to see this place ...

Whatever your reason for coming to the moon, be sure to stop by the fine city of Shar Vahl – you will surely enjoy the trip!

– Falaanla Marr (Human Magician of Fennin Ro)

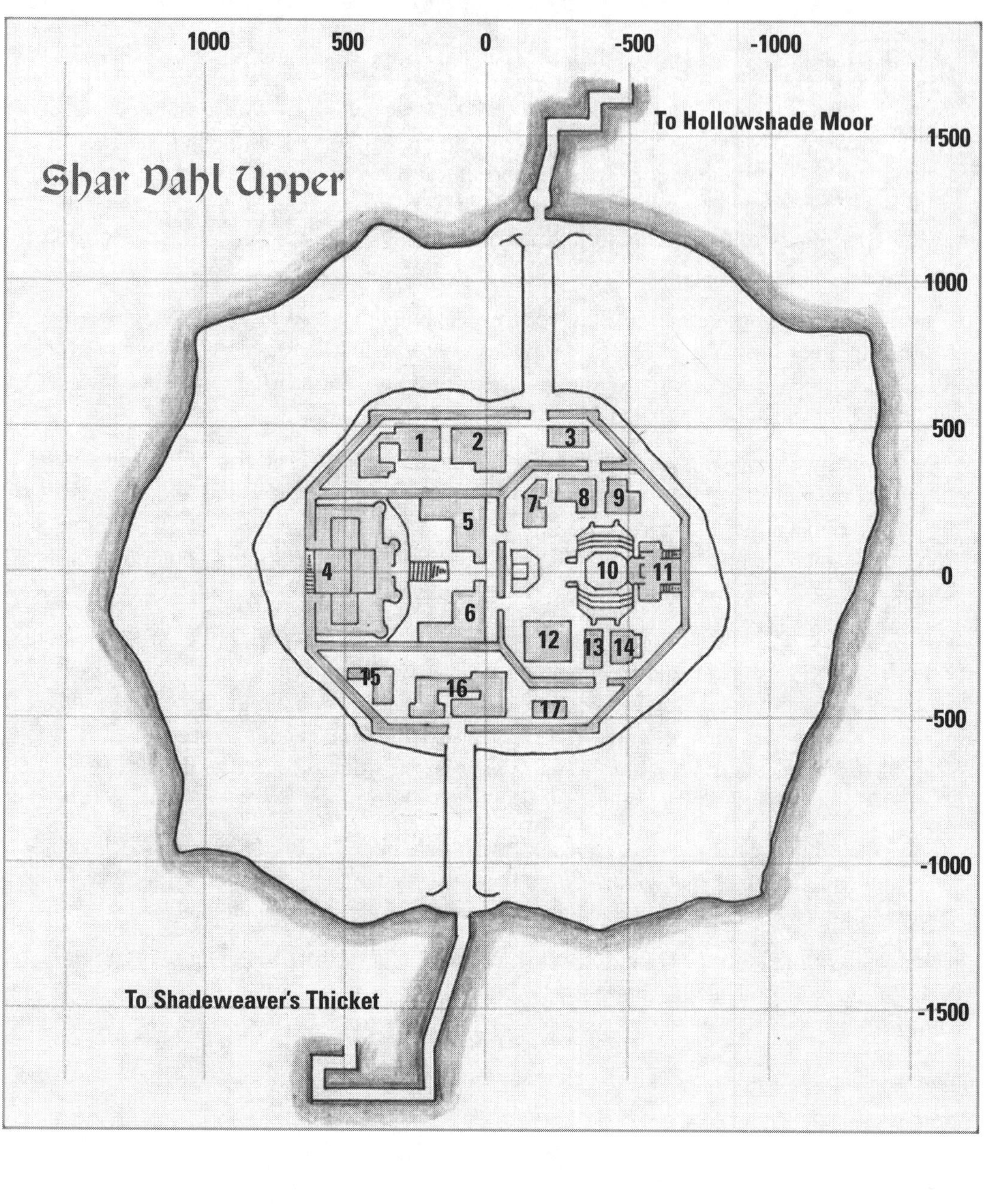

Shar Vahl Upper

1000 500 0 -500 -1000

1500
1000
500
0
-500
-1000
-1500

To Hollowshade Moor

To Shadeweaver's Thicket

1 2 3 4 5 6 7 8 9 10 11 12 13 14 15 16 17

1 Merchants selling ore/stone/smithing hammers, forges
2 Food and other goods, baking supplies, shoes, food and other goods, cooking books, shield/parrying dagger
3 Alcohol
4 Castle, Bard Trainer and Bard spells on roof
5 nothing
6 nothing
7 Blacksmithing molds
8 Brewing supplies, metals/gems,
2nd floor: sewing supplies, sewing kit
9 Pottery supplies, instruments, pottery sketches, clay/ore/smithing hammer, kilns, pottery wheels
10 Arena
11 Royal Stand
12 Alcohol and food, brewing supplies, brew barrel, oven
13 Alchemy supplies, potions/magic stones
14 Tax collector, bank
15 Merchants selling alcohol, fletching and bowmaking supplies, poison supplies
16 Registrar; Merchants selling food, bags, wooden practice weapons, alcohol, ovens, chainmail patterns
17 Merchants selling alcohol, pottery supplies, pottery wheel, fishing supplies

---

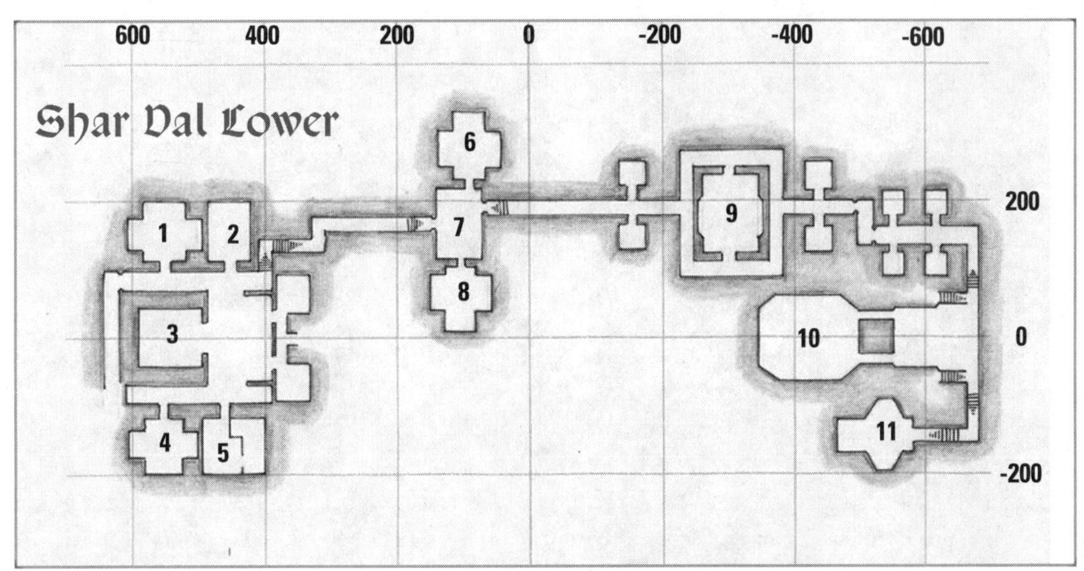

1 empty
2 empty
3 Throne Room
4 empty
5 Cooking books and supplies, oven
6 Beastlord Trainer
7 Shaman, Beastlord spells
8 Shaman Trainer, alchemy supplies
9 Rogue Trainer
10 Arena
11 Weapons, Warrior Trainer

Katta Castellum

Katta Castellum is the first of the Combine cities established on Luclin, when a group of the Combine loyal to Tsaph Katta left Norrath. The city is built on the cliffs and the cliffsides of the Tenebrous Mountains that overlook the Twilight Sea. It is considered by many to be the most majestic of the cities of Luclin. Access to the city is guarded on one side by a great wall and guard towers carved of the native mountain stone, and on the other by the cliffs and Twilight Sea.

The top level of government in Katta Castellum is the Concilium Universus, an elected council of nine officials that govern according to their interpretation of the wills of Tsaph Katta. Directly under the command of the Concilium Universus are eighteen governors who carry out the orders of the council within the city, and the Validus Custodus, the city militia. Every able-bodied young man spends time in service of the Validus Custodus, and many remain in the ranks of the militia for their whole lives.

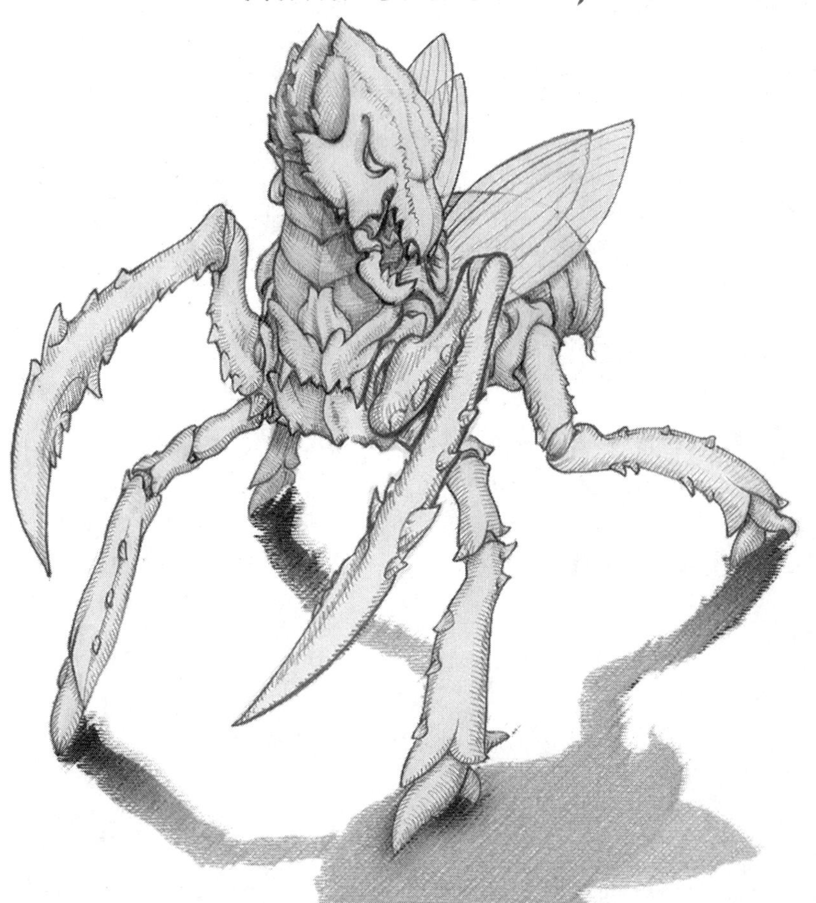

Sanctus Seru

Another stronghold of the Combine, Sanctus Seru was named in honor of their leader, Seru.

The people of Sanctus Seru are orderly to a fault. They spent long years building their city to exacting standards. Geometrically precise structures, arrow-straight streets, even rows of buildings and high walls were constructed. They are not afraid of hard work or dedication, and it shows in the nature of the city. Nothing is allowed to look worn — constant maintenance of the city insures this.

The government of the city is just as orderly as its streets, though its leader, Seru, has not been seen in public in living memory. The organization of the people of Sanctus Seru is so deeply rooted that every citizen falls under the structure of the government. Unfortunately for some, these folk find strangers to be somewhat untrustworthy and disorganized, and are reluctant to embrace visitors.

Shadow Haven

Built within a series of large caverns in the heart of Luclin, this city is indeed a haven for its residents. Citizens of Shadow Haven consider themselves free-thinking folk, willing to see beyond the petty conflicts that seem to embroil the others that have come to Luclin from Norrath. Primarily merchants and traders, these folk are not above profiting from the conflicts of others.

Shadow Haven is ruled by the trade families, who control the flow of goods throughout most of the city, and who claim responsibility for creating the Bazaar. It is the Bazaar that attracts the most money to Shadow Haven. People of all sorts come to see if they can buy or sell goods in the Bazaar, which is easily the busiest part of the city.

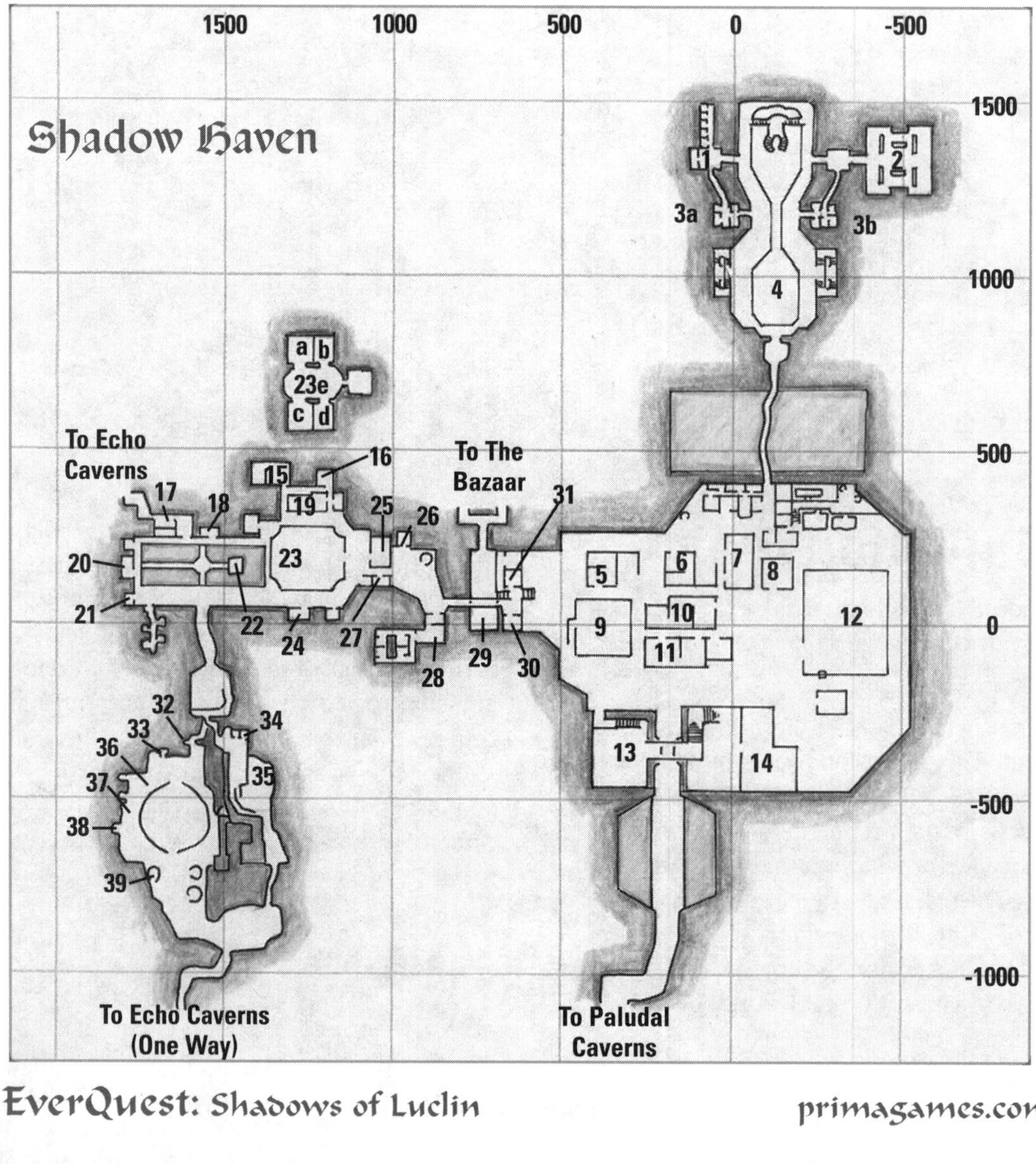

Shadow Haven

1 Upstairs — Inn and bank; downstairs — Magician supplies
2 Library with Enchanter, Wizard and Magician spells
3a Meats and stews, food, jewelry supplies
3b Izbat's Wondrous Robes — robes and cloaks, food and goods, alchemy supplies, robes, staves, talking scrolls — Generic spells
4 Necromancer, Shadow Knight spells
5 Large cloth armor, cloth armor, food and goods
6 Sewing kit, baking molds, basic smithing equipment, forge, large molds, armor molds, blacksmithing molds
7 empty
8 The fordel hold — bank
9 Grimthor's Distillery — food and goods, alcohol, brew barrels
10 empty
11 Instruments, food and goods, fordel scout armor, fordel weapons, rough hide armor, boots
12 Paladin and Cleric Trainers, Paladin and Cleric spells
13 Oven, alcohol
14 Warrior Trainer
15 Alcohol, brew barrel
16 The Black Kettle — alcohol
17 Rogue Trainer
18 Large rough hide armor, sewing kit
19 empty
20 Bank
21 Heavy and regular boxes and bags
22 Transporter to Shadow Haven
23 Teleporter to underground
23a Ranger Trainer and spells
23b Druid Trainer and spells
23c Beastlord Trainer and spells
23d Shaman Trainer and spells
23e Tree, click to go back to 23
24 Food and goods, basic blacksmithing supplies, forge, blade molds, shield molds
25 Bard Trainer, alcohol, oven
26 Merchants
27 Marchop's Micro Metals — tinkering supplies
28 Shandeling's Roost — inn
29 Alcohol
30 Jewelry supplies, metals and gems
31 Sewing patterns, rough hide armor
32 The Lost Turnip —oven, vegetables, bags outside
33 Deepcarver Plate and Pickbringers Chain armor
34 Basic blacksmithing and dyeing supplies, small armor molds, forge
35 Oven, pottery Wheel, small leather armor, alcohol, fishing supplies, pottery sketches, Basic pottery supplies, potions/crystals
36 Food
37 Boots
38 Bank
39 Food

The Bazaar

The Bazaar is a huge cavern filled with row upon row of open stalls. "Hectic" would only be sufficient to describe the place on a slow day. With the flow of travelers that the Nexus now brings in from Norrath, the Bazaar has become almost overwhelmingly busy. This, of course, pleases the citizens of Shadow Haven greatly. These visitors spend a lot of money, and they probably "lose" more than they spend.

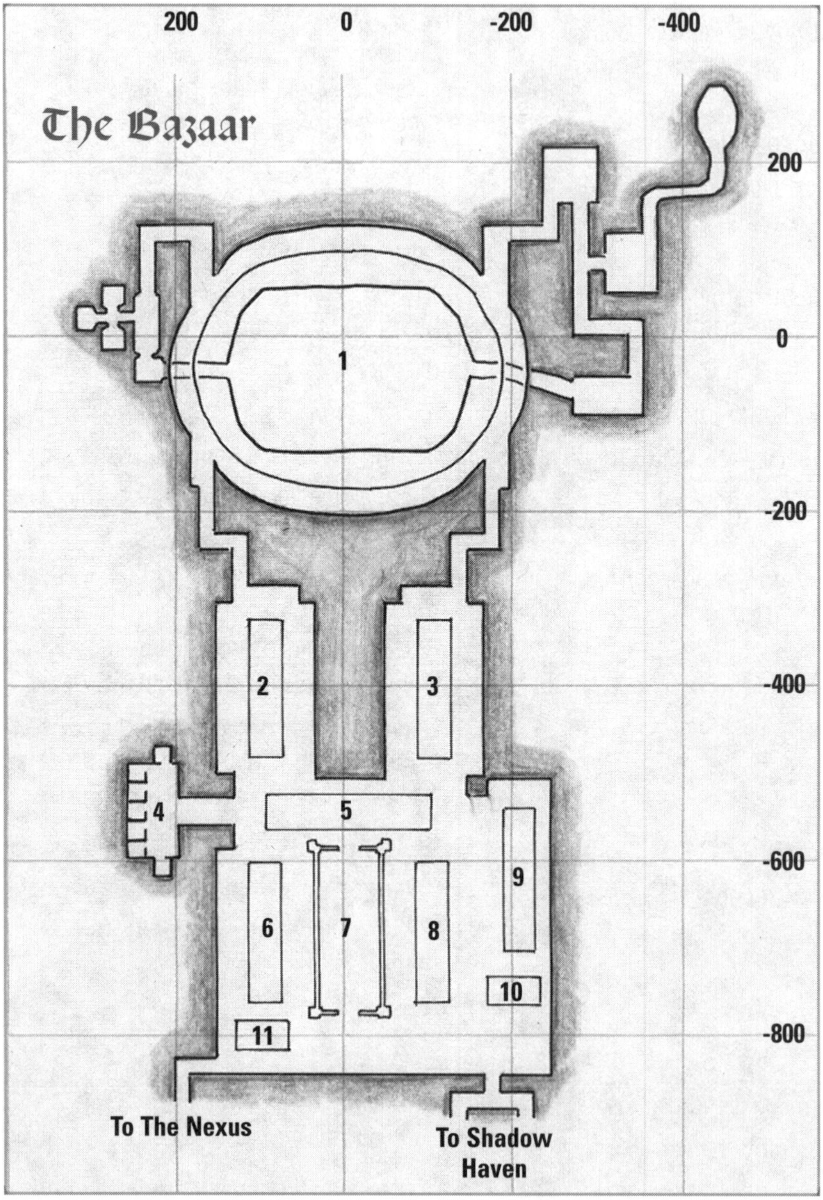

The Bazaar

To The Nexus

To Shadow Haven

1 The Palaestra, the Arena
2 empty
3 Sewing kit
4 Stable with forge
5 empty
6 Oven
7 Merchants selling tailoring patterns, books, and kit, Basic dying and smithing supplies, spell components, coffins (small, medium, and large), Plate molds, and alcohol
8 Pottery wheel, forge
9 Pottery wheel, kiln
10 Bank
11 Bank

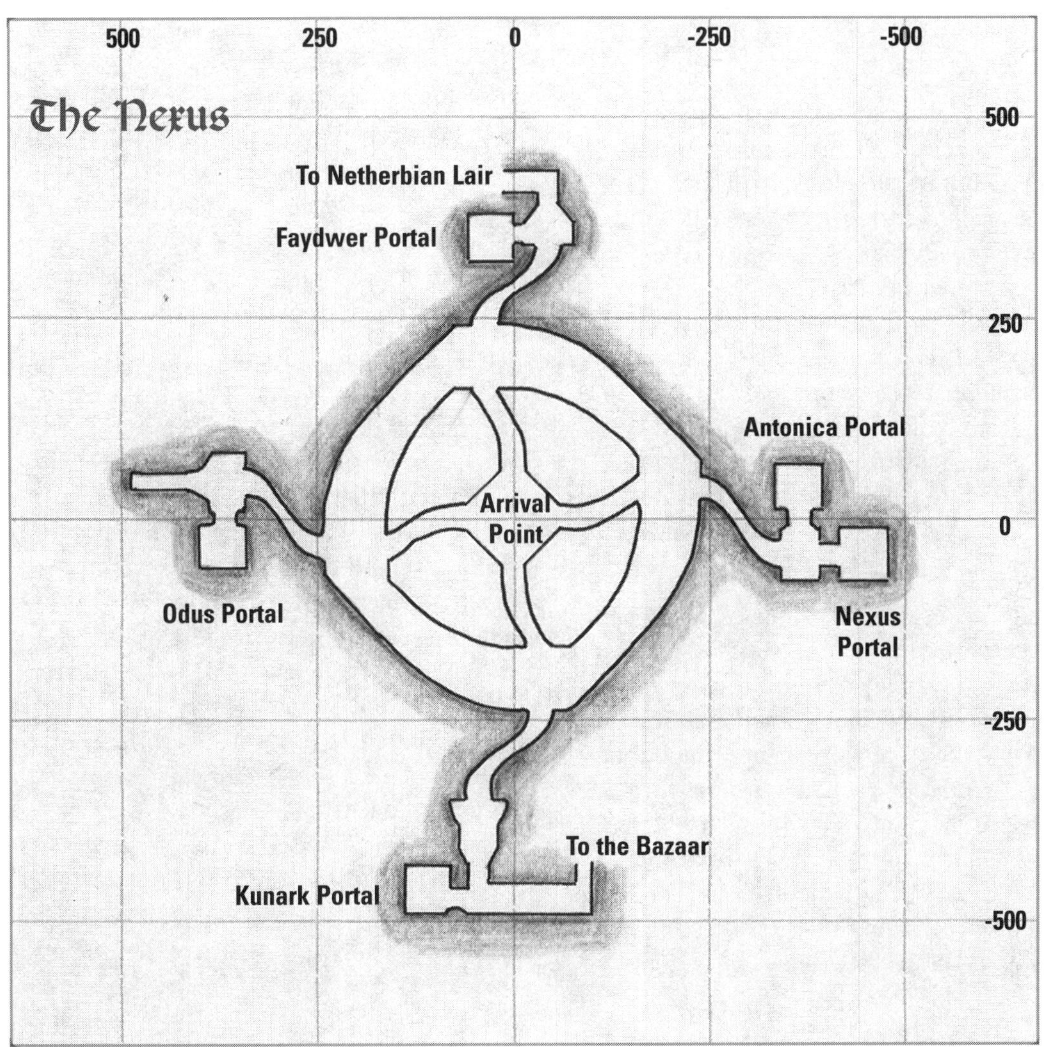

The Nexus

Now that Norrath and Luclin have moved closer together, the magic that once allowed travel between the two has been restored. The Nexus is the only location on Luclin with a strong enough magical transportation focus to allow this to happen.

The Nexus is of unknown origin, although it appears to be of Combine design. Its original function is uncertain, but it is evident from its design that it was meant to transport people between the moon of Luclin and the different continents of Norrath. The fact that it only teleports people to the continents that the Combine Empire had significant involvement in: Antonica, Odus, Faydwer, and Kunark, but not Velious, lends more strength to the theory that it was Combine-built.

Now that Luclin and Norrath are much closer, the magical energies that once infused it and allowed the transportation have again empowered the Nexus to take people to and from Norrath. Everyone coming to Luclin arrives on the central platform, where the magical energies are focused. In each wing, there is a separate transporter to take people to Norrath. To the north is the Faydwer portal, east is Antonica, south is Kunark, and west lies the portal to Odus. These are activated on a specific schedule to take travelers back to Norrath.

The Nexus is also important as a waypoint for Luclin itself. The trade families of Shadow Haven lay claim to the Nexus, which has direct connections to both Shadow Haven to the east and the Bazaar to the south. To the north lies the entrance to Netherbian Lair, which leads to Marus Seru and Dawnshroud Peaks, and from there to the city of Sanctus Seru. The Nexus is probably the single busiest place on all of Luclin at the present time.

Paludal Caverns

The Paludal Caverns are an ancient network of caverns beneath the surface of Luclin, one of the many that have been opened up and used by the current surface inhabitants to get around the moon. This set of caves runs between Shadeweaver's Thicket and Hollowshade Moor, and also connects to the more extensive caves that make up Shadow Haven deeper beneath the surface.

The Moor above feeds large amounts of water slowly into the caverns, leaking slowly through their ceilings, creating many small and some very large underground bodies of water. The damp air and loose rocky soil allow these caverns to be filled with fungi, mosses, and slimes, which thrive here. In fact, there is a rumor of a very large form of the sentient fungi that lives here.

There are other inhabitants of the caverns as well. A large race of insectoid creatures makes part of the caverns their home, and a whole race of fiends lives here also, feeding on fungi and adventurer alike. The least indigenous inhabitants are the bandits that can be found hidden here and there in the caverns. Since the Paludal Caverns is the quickest way to the surface from Shadow Haven, and lies on the trade route between Shar Vahl and Shadow Haven, it is a perfect place to raid caravans going between the two places. The bandits have set up their permanent homes near the ancient chasm that is adjacent to the Shadow Haven entrance.

Netherbian Lair

It is believed that these caverns were created by a family of large worms for use as their home. But it has since become inhabited by the Netherbians. Members of the Combine discovered these tunnels while searching for a better route to the topside of Luclin. Always interested in ore, they fortified the tunnel before knowing about the inhabitants that lay deeper in the maze of the cavern system. The entrance to Shadow Haven and most of the constructed areas, which serve as the road between Sanctus

Seru and Shadow Haven, are watched over by guards and functionaries from Shadow Haven and patrolled by the Hand of Seru. However, opening up onto this large tunnel is a network of winding ancient mines, now inhabited by more hostile occupants. Travel along the main corridors is safe, but travel through the mines does not come with that reassurance. The natural tunnels with their unusual population offer no such protection.

Echo Caverns

These caverns have several openings and lead travelers out of Shadow Haven to places much more dangerous. The caverns themselves are twisting and convoluted, and many unusual creatures make their lairs there. But it is also rumored that some disreputable folk have taken up residence in the caverns. Life in the caverns has taken its toll on these people, and some of them may not even be recognizable as members of a sentient race.

Shadow Haven extends its protection a short way into these caves, but once an adventurer passes through the door, that marks the end of that protection — anything can happen.

The Fungus Grove

Underneath the Twilight Sea, connecting the ocean to the great caverns under the surface of Luclin, is The Fungus Grove. For the most part this area is a single colossal cavern with all variety of fungi and subterranean mosses. Small tunnels and burrows exist that stray from the main cavern, but none of them seem to lead anywhere. Winding its way through the cavern is a small river known as the Glowater. A dim glowing species of algae runs thick in the slow moving river, giving it an eerie luminescent quality. The Glowater ends in a large pond located in the northern portion of The Fungus Grove, emptying via a crack in the bottom of the pond.

The Fungus Grove consists of a varied collection of gargantuan fungi. These "trees" grow together in clumps and copses scattered about, leaving large areas devoid of large plant life. Over the centuries the stone of the cavern and the organic remains of beasts have combined to create a rich soil able to sustain the ancient fungi of the region. Life and death follow each other at a furious pace in The Fungus Grove.

The Deep

The Deep is a section of the many caverns found in the depths of Luclin. This cave system, like many others, sprawls out in many directions. Most of the tunnels are dead ends, but at least one of them does manage to reach the surface. The Deep is a very dark and treacherous cavern that very few have explored and to which even fewer have returned. It is rumored that this cavern leads to a source of great evil.

The most notable feature of these caverns is the Abyss, a fissure of incredible depth. No exploration unit recorded has been able to cross the Abyss. Many of the convoluted tunnels in The Deep meet their endings in the Abyss. It is expected that many adventurers have done the same, but the Abyss could be considered much less frightening than some of the inhabitants of The Deep.

Acrylia Caverns

The Vah Shir have enjoyed great prosperity on Luclin. They built a beautiful, majestic city and encased their buildings and structures in acrylia. They acquired most of this acrylia from their mines, mines that are a series of tunnels and shafts that extend deep into the surface of Luclin. The upper mines are sparsely populated with unusual native fauna. Occasionally an adventurer will come upon a vein of acrylia and sometimes the ore can be found in the possession of some of the creatures of the mines, who are very protective of the resource.

But the delving of the Vah Shir uncovered an ancient Grimling stronghold. The Grimlings have since reclaimed the mines for their own, and their fierce and powerful determination to keep it has won out over all attempts by the Vah Shir to wrest the place from them. It is one of the goals of the Vah Shir to reclaim these mines, as there is always more use for the acrylia that it produces.

Shadeweaver's Thicket

Shadeweaver's Thicket is a sparsely forested area adjacent to the Vah Shir city of Shar Vahl. The thicket is dotted with low brushes and thick-boled trees. Many of the plants have luminescent or bright colored leaves. It is roughly divided into two areas. On the southeastern side of the thicket lies the city of Shar Vahl, guarded by the crater formed from the impact of the Norrathian shard. It is from here that the bold Vah Shir guards keep vigil over their young. The young Vah Shir use this area as a training ground to improve upon their skills in the wild. There is a large cluster of well-guarded tents and buildings right by the city's walls where this training occurs. By fighting the local fauna and performing tasks for the merchants who have set up shop here, a young Vah Shir can progress quite far in this area alone. This area is also where the old trade route between Shar Vahl and Shadow Haven runs, although the area has become more dangerous lately as the Loda Kai bandits have moved into the region and started threatening caravans moving between the two cities.

The western half of the thicket consists of rocky terrain with sparse vegetation, and is much more dangerous. This is the area that gives the thicket its name. The shades of fallen Vah Shir soldiers travel this area, tormented by the evil spirits that seem to be becoming more aggressive lately. The ground is also rougher and life has to struggle to grow in this area. These living dead have started to move into the safer regions east

Acrylia Caverns, Shadeweaver's Thicket

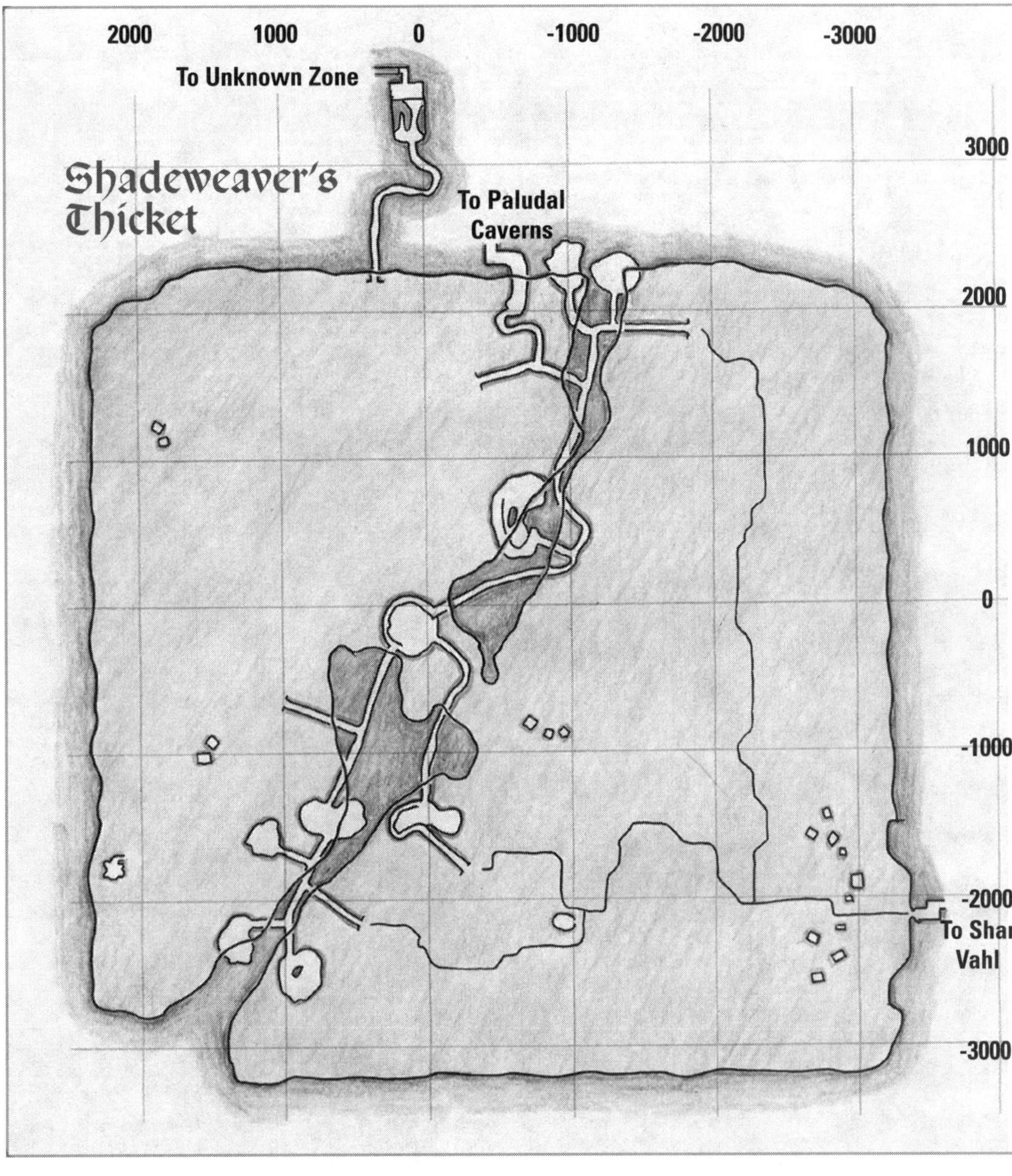
2000
1000
0
-1000
-2000
-3000
To Unknown Zone
Shadeweaver's Thicket
To Paludal Caverns
3000
2000
1000
0
-1000
-2000
-3000
To Shar Vahl

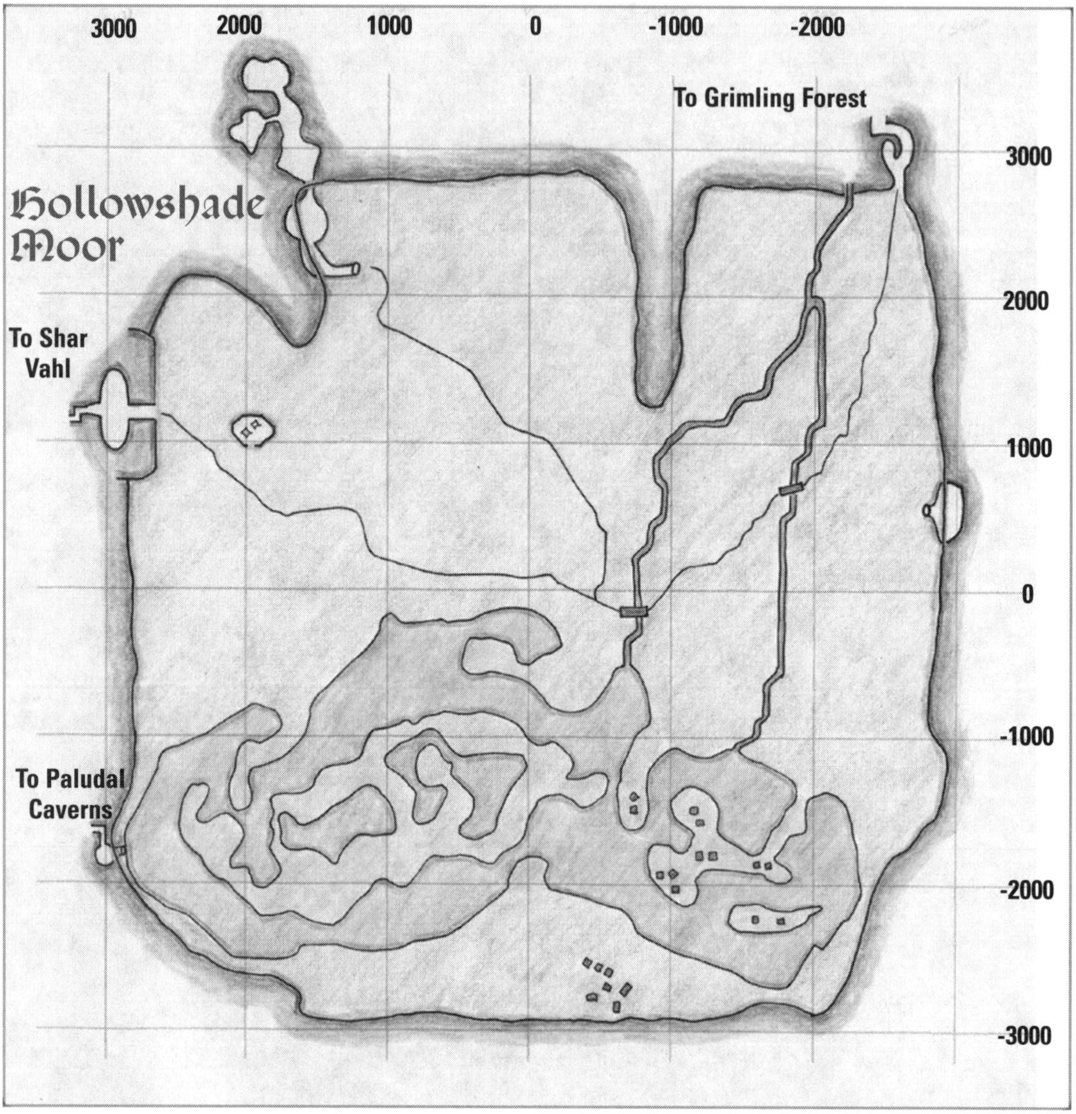

Hollowshade Moor

3000 2000 1000 0 -1000 -2000

To Grimling Forest

To Shar Vahl

To Paludal Caverns

3000
2000
1000
0
-1000
-2000
-3000

of the mountains, sometimes accompanied by the Loda Kai.

In between the two halves of the Thicket is a rough, impassable mountain range, riddled with underground caverns. In the north, a small section of these are used as part of the trade route between Shar Vahl and Shadow Haven, but most of the cavern complex remains unexplored by outsiders.

Hollowshade Moor

Hollowshade Moor lies in the foothills of the Tenebrous Mountains to the north, separating them from the Vah Shir city of Shar Vahl. Several small rivers wind their way down from the mountains to end in the watery moor that makes up the southern half of the area. The Hollowshade Moor is lightly forested with thick-barked, squat trees. The Vah Shir have built a road of acrylia that runs through Hollowshade Moor, from the gates of their city all the way to the acrylia mines in Grimling Forest, higher up in the foothills of the mountains to the north. Hidden near the moor lies the nearly submerged entrance to the Paludal Caverns.

Ownership of the Moor is hotly contested by the local inhabitants, and the Vah Shir tend to stay out of the conflict as much as possible, while defending their interests as best they can. The grimlings from the forest to the north also have set up fishing villages on the moor. To get here, they need to travel through the territory of the sonic wolves, who live in caverns not far from the passage to Grimling Forest. Both of these groups are in constant conflict with the thick-skinned and squat owlbears. These aggressive creatures prowl about the moor in large numbers, traveling from the cover of their caves in search of water and food. The owlbears claim most of the Moor as their own, and use their caves near Shar Vahl to raise their young. These three groups are in a very delicate balance, with small skirmishes happening all the time, but larger battles occurring only infrequently.

The Vah Shir have learned to avoid getting involved in these conflicts, and try to stay to their own. Attempts in the past to fight off one or more groups have only led to the other groups becoming more hostile in an attempt to take over more of the Moor. At present, the Vah Shir leave all the groups be, and move quickly on the road through the contested territory.

Grimling Forest

The Grimling Forest lies at the base of the Tenebrous Peaks. It is made of rolling foothills and occasional boulders. The forest is sparse when compared with some on Norrath, but it is a dense forest by comparison to others on Luclin. The combination of short, brightly colored trees and towering fungus make this an unusual forest by all accounts. A river flows from the mountains to the north. As it winds south through the forest it divides into several streams that feed the moor below the forest.

Many paths wind through the forest, but most have been overgrown. The Vah Shir

are too busy dealing with the Grimlings to keep these paths maintained. Rumor has it that one of these paths leads from Hollowshade Moor to the entrance of what was the acrylia mines. The entrance lies near the base of the Tenebrous Peaks. Old handcarts and rusted mining tools are strewn about near the mine entrance – signs of a hasty evacuation. The Grimlings have effectively driven the Vah Shir from the mines, which the Vah Shir are not pleased about. Many an innocent traveler has been caught up in the fierce skirmishes between the Vah Shir and the Grimlings.

The Tenebrous Mountains

The Tenebrous Mountains reach towards the starlit skies north of the Grimling Forest, on the dark side of Luclin. While the higher altitudes of the mountain range are illuminated by the perpetual starlit night sky, the lower altitudes are cloaked in the darksome shadows of the mountains. The eerie vegetation of the Grimling Forest extends into the Tenebrous Mountains at the lower altitudes, then thins out. On the highest of the mountains, the atmosphere is too thin to support the mysterious inky foliage. The western edge of the Tenebrous Mountains is composed of cliffs that fall away into the Twilight Sea. Perched on the cliff edge and extending down its face is the city of Katta Castellum.

The Dawnshroud Peaks

This mountain range is unique because of its strange coloration compared to the rest of the area. Dawnshroud is such a deep green that from a distance these mountains look like they are covered in moss. This might be the most fertile land on the surface of Luclin. Green grasses, wide-leafed trees and small clear pools of water cover the land. But where there is such lush plant life there will also be animals. The Legionnaires of Sanctus Seru guard the entrance to their city, and they try to keep the pathways of Dawnshroud safe. But the Lightcrawlers and other native creatures feel safe in their lush world, and they have little fear of the once-mighty Combine Empire, or any adventurers that might cross their paths.

Marus Seru

North of Sanctus Seru lies the Sea of Seru, Marus Seru. It is a place of extreme landscape, with smooth expanses of surface rock and sheer escarpments and fine sand, all under the harsh actinic glare of the sun. This landscape is believed to have been formed as the moon made close passage to the sun, when temperatures reached nearly a thousand degrees hotter than they are now.

The life found in this zone is varied, but all the native creatures have evolved in a region where light is ever present and extreme heat is a constant. Due to the abundance of solar energy, creatures here have evolved to make use of this, including the plant life.

Mons Letalis

Located between Marus Seru and The Grey, the Deadly Mountain is a contrast of towering peaks that seem to reach for the heavens and the deep valleys that surround them. Barren and scattered with tremendous stones, Mons Letalis is a harsh place, both in appearance and in actuality.

Thought to have been subjected to the same astrological and geological events that affected Marus Seru, Mons Letalis' surfaces are shaped by exposure to extreme heat, rounding and smoothing the terrain. Atmospheric effects have further served to give the land an organic shape rather than the jagged mountainous moonscape one would expect. Despite the bleakness of these deadly mountains there is life here. Rugged and dangerous creatures, both magical and more natural, survive here. To adventurers, these life forms are just another of the things that make the place so deadly.

The Grey

The Grey is a large expanse of vacuum space located in the northwestern hemisphere of Luclin. The terrain is comprised of grey sand that presumably is the same sand that can be found in the Scarlet Desert but was changed by the vacuum of The Grey, leaching the color from it. Many sand dunes still exist here just as they did hundreds of years ago. The absence of moving air has left them in a perpetual state of calm, only occasionally disturbed by the rumbling passage of the native worms. The Grey remains largely unexplored...

The Scarlet Desert

The Scarlet Desert is a large desert valley permeated by a reddish hue. Vegetation here is sparse, and similar to that found in most desert regions. The bed of the dried up river Ripflow meanders through the desert, before ending in the Twilight Sea. Sheer mountainous cliffs border the northern and southern edge of the desert. These cliffs are dotted with natural cave systems. One of these provides shelter to the source of the Ripflow. A large mesa can be found in the northeastern section of the desert. The Ripflow riverbed runs nearby on its way to the Twilight Sea. There is one small oasis also found here, located in the southeastern part of the desert. This oasis is commonly used as a watering hole by the inhabitants of the desert.

The Twilight Sea

The Twilight Sea is a large body of water completely surrounded by towering cliffs and low, sturdy mountains. The sea contains several islands. These islands nearly fill the sea itself, in some places making it look like a river with many tributaries. The sea itself is calm and pristine, with waves that wash gently upon its shores. The sea gets its name because it exists in the twilight zone, the area that separates the light and dark sides of Luclin.

To the east is a dock, with a road leading to Katta Castellum. There are other man-made structures on the islands of the sea. Not the least of these structures is the tower built by Vornol, considered one of the greatest Magicians to ever live.

The Twilight Regions

These are the places where the darkness and the light mingle. These are the places of shadow. The Twilight Regions are where Luclin's creations rule supreme, where evil and good alike are wary to tread without good cause. No one really knows what can be found in the depths of the Twilight Regions, because no one who has entered it has returned to talk about it.

Optional Patch Zones

From time to time Sony Online Entertainment will make new zones available to players on a "patch only" basis. In other words, to get to these zones, you must download and install a patch to the game. There are currently three zones available by installing the Optional Patch file from the official site.

None of these zones are on Luclin (yet!) but they're included here because they do represent new and different places for players to visit.

The Warrens

On the continent of Odus, entered from Paineel, the Warrens are a low-to-mid-level zones (roughly, levels 5 to 30). They consist of a series of caves inhabited by many, many bad-tempered little kobolds and a lot of bats.

StoneBrunt Mountains

You must pass through the Warrens to get to StoneBrunt; there's no other way in or out. This is a pretty wilderness zone suitable for levels 20 to 40 or thereabouts. It's mostly populated with natural creatures like pandas, gorillas, snakes and panthers. However, watch out for the Titans – supernaturally powerful entities in the form of more natural creatures. There are also a couple of kobold villages and, on a high plateau, a whole city. The city is inhabited by the Kejeks, a feline race related to the Kerrans (and perhaps to the Vah Shir?). The Kejeks' crop of catnip is greatly prized by Druids.

The Hole

A high-level zone (don't even try to visit before you hit level 45, and then stay close to the entrances) with several epic encounters.

Skoriksis' Mission

by Kevin "Skoriksis" Freet

The banging on the thin wooden door was loud enough to raise the dead in the Field of Bone. Slowly, the young Iksar slithered out of his nest and stood upright as he cautiously opened his eyes to try and adjust to the light. Skoriksis, now more awake and familiar with his surroundings, moved to the door to see what the commotion was about.

As he opened the door, a large figure clad in golden armor with the symbol of the Crusaders of the Greenmist across his chest stood in the street. The lights from the nearby torches danced across his blade with a hypnotic pattern. Skoriksis pulled his attention away from the blade and looked up at him with curious yellow eyes and asked the obvious question.

"Yes sir? You wanted to see me?" he quietly asked.

In a loud rumbling voice, the Crusader spoke to the young Iksar. "The Arch Duke wants to see you … immediately."

"Yes sir," Skoriksis responded, "I'll head there right away."

Without another word, the Crusader turned, moved down the street and vanished into an alley. Skoriksis knew it was not proper to keep the Arch Duke waiting, and if Skoriksis ever wanted to become a full member of the Shadow Knights of Cabilis, this was his chance. He quickly grabbed his khukri and a backpack of supplies and headed off to the Temple.

In moments, Skoriksis was kneeling before the Arch Duke. Arch Duke Xog peered down at the young Iksar and began to make his intent clear.

"I have an important mission for you, young one. It's a mission of the highest importance and you might not finish it alive. If you choose to deny my request, the penalties will be severe. However, if you take the mission and succeed, your name will be written in the journals of the Greenmist for all eternity."

Without second of thought, he replied to the Arch Duke. "I will gladly give my life to the Crusaders of the Greenmist and our home of Cabilis. Just give me your instructions and I will carry them out at once."

The Arch Duke's voice dropped to almost a low whisper as he stared at the young one. "Excellent. I knew we could count on you. Tell me young one, do you know of the moon that rises at night?"

"Yes sir. I believe that moon has been called Luclin by the soft-skins." replied the eager Iksar.

"That is correct." The Arch Duke peered around to make sure no one was hiding in the shadows listening. "It's come to our attention that the great Combine Portal in the Dreadlands has become active. Within the last few days, many soft-skins have been traveling through our lands of Kunark and heading that way. There have even been rumors of a strange cat-like race coming out of the great portal. The rumors we are hearing from our undercover agents in Firiona Vie say that this Great Portal is actually a gateway to the moon that rises in the night sky."

Skoriksis's eyes widened. "And what do you need me to do?"

The Arch Duke leaned closer to Skoriksis as he whispered, "We must know what is going on at the portal. We must be certain that the vile Venril Sathir does not have his undead hands in this. Pack what you can, and head to the Lake of Ill Omen. From there, find your way through the treacherous Frontier Mountains to the wastelands of the Dreadlands, the home of Venril's defiled castle. Find the ice tunnel that buries itself into the heart of the mountain and you will find the portal. Be wary, young one! For the path from our city to the portal is filled with many dangers. Creatures that can run faster than you and can see through the shadows are at every turn. Be careful where you step and watch for the dagger that you cannot see."

"I will not fail you, Arch Duke. I will return with news of the portal and of Luclin." Skoriksis quickly bowed and dashed off to begin his journey.

After he was out of sight, the Arch Duke slowly turned to look out over Cabilis as he quietly whispered, "You had better come back with news, else you'll not be welcome to come back at all."

Creatures of Luclin

primagames.com

Disclaimer!

These stats only represent those creatures that venture closest to the two more accessible cities, Shadow Haven and Shar Vahl.

In fact, they only represent an initial survey of even those creatures. This chronicler is sure that many more – and much more dangerous – creatures lie beyond the horizon.

When several creatures are listed under one heading (as with different varieties of reishi to be found under "Reishi"), the first stats are those shared by all of that type of creature. For example, all reishi are "Warriors." That stat is listed once and not repeated for each variety of this mushroom. Then, each specific variety lists those stats that are different from other varieties of reishi.

Class. All creatures of Luclin, intelligent or not, can be described by one of the adventuring classes. For example, most of the less intelligent creatures fit the Warrior pattern.

Typical Levels list the probable level of experience for each creature. **Typical Attributes** list the probable stats for the creature. In general, all of the "skills" (especially its ability to fight) are at about the same level, so one general **Typical Level** is listed.

Regeneration is given as *Slowest, Slower, Slow, Average, Fast, Faster, Fastest.*

Typical Base Damage is how much damage the creature can inflict with a single strike. **Typical Base AC** lists how well the creature's skin protects it from damage.

Speed and **Attack Speed** are listed as *Slowest, Slower, Slow, Average, Fast, Faster, Fastest.* A typical Human's Speed and Attack Speed are both Average.

Awareness Range lists from how far away the creature is likely to spot you (*None, Shortest, Shorter, Short, Average, Long, Longer, Longest*). Average awareness range is about 600 feet. **Average Reaction Radius** lists from how far away the creature will Con you (*None, Smallest, Smaller, Small, Average, Large, Larger, Largest*). Average reaction radius is about 60 feet.

Frenzy. If a creature sees it can outnumber a potential target by at least 3-to-1, it might frenzy and attack. The chance that each creature might frenzy is listed next.

In addition, some creatures list special stats, like magical resistances or invulnerability to normal weapons.

Fungal Fiend

These bipedal creatures are made up of colonies of fungus. This is not immediately evident from a distance, as they look very much like a humanoid even when seen from relatively close up. These creatures are not very smart, but they have earned the name "fiend."

Known Fungoid Types

Fungoid Sporeling
400-600 HP

Fungoid Worker
700-800 HP

Fungoid
800-900 HP

Mature Fungoid
1100-1200

Known Fungal Fiend Types

Patog Phlarg Fiend
Plerg Phlarg Fiend

Patog phlarg fiend tends to be slightly higher level than plerg phlarg fiend.

Typical Fungoid

Warrior

Typ. Levels	215-225
Typ. Attributes	
STR	75
STA	75
DEX	75
INT	75
AGI	75
WIS	75
Typ. Skill Lvl.	110
Slowest Regen. Rate	
Typical Base Damage	20-25
Average Attack Speed	
Average Speed	
Typical Base AC	64
Average Awareness Range	
Average Reaction Radius	
Won't Frenzy	
Can Walk	

Typical Fungal Fiend

Warrior

Typical Levels	12-17
Typical HP	330-450
Typical Attributes	
STR	100
STA	90
DEX	80
INT	50
AGI	80
WIS	60
Typical Skill Levels	65-80
Typical Base Damage	17
Typical Base AC	24
Average Regeneration	
Average Attack Speed	
Average Speed	
Shorter Awareness Range	
Average Reaction Radius	
Won't Frenzy	
Walks, Swims	
Disease/Poison Resist	15
Fire Vulnerability	5

Grimling

These Gnome-sized humanoids tend to have dark skin and dark hair. Their society is as complex as any of the tribal races on Norrath, and their skills reflect this. Grimlings protect their own, and will come to each other's aid when needed. The depths of their societies have not been explored, and their hostile dislike for strangers makes approaching them difficult.

Known Types

Bodyguard. Can be Shaman or Warrior.

Fisherman

Grunt. Regenerates faster than most Grimlings, and is less likely to frenzy. Can be hit by normal weapons.

Guard

Herder

Invader. Can be Shaman or Warrior.

Lookout

Mystic. Is a Shaman.

Pickpocket. Is a Rogue.

Recruit. Regenerates faster than most Grimlings. Some can only be hit by magic weapons; others have Magic, Fire, Cold & Disease Resistance 20.

Typical Grimling

Warrior

Typical Levels	10-25
Typical HP	380-730
Typical Attributes	
STR	75-80
STA	80-90
DEX	75-90
INT	20-60
AGI	80-90
WIS	20-60
Typical Skill Levels	70-115
Typical Base Damage	17-24
Typical Base AC	24-52

Fast Regeneration

Average Attack Speed

Fast Speed

Average Awareness Range

Average Reaction Radius

Less Likely to Frenzy

Walks, Swims

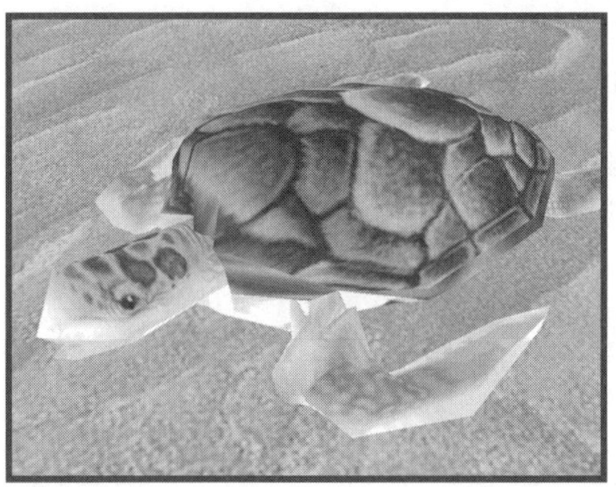

Moor Tortoise

These passive creatures tend to be light brown in color, giving them some camouflage against predators when sunning themselves on the sand. Their hard shells and sharp beaks make them more dangerous than they might appear. And when in the water they are agile enough to avoid most predators.

Typical Moor Tortoise

Warrior	
Typical Levels	14-16
Typical HP	490
Typical Attributes	
STR	75
STA	75
DEX	75
INT	75
AGI	75
WIS	75
Typical Skill Levels	85
Typical Base Damage	21
Typical Base AC	40
Average Regeneration	
Average Attack Speed	
Slow Speed	
Average Awareness Range	
Larger Reaction Radius	
Won't Frenzy	
Walks, Swims	

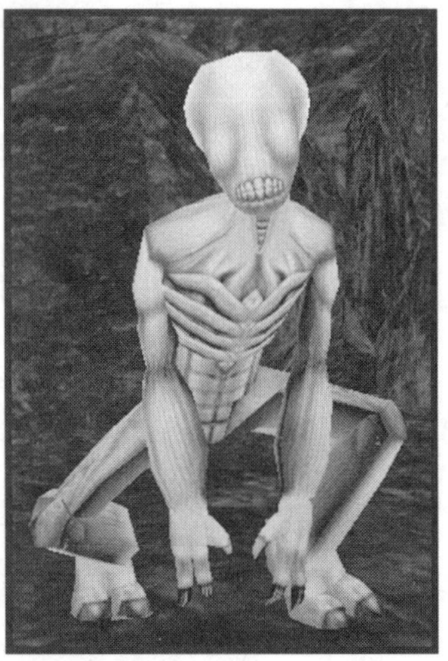

Netherbian

These eyeless creatures vary in form and coloration. Their motivations are completely unknown, but they are believed to be only somewhat intelligent.

Typical Netherbian

Typical Levels	220-230
Typical Attributes	
STR	75
STA	75
DEX	75
INT	75
AGI	75
WIS	75
Typical Skill Levels	110-130
Slowest Regeneration Rate	
Typical Base Damage	20-30
Average Attack Speed	
Average Speed	
Typical Base AC	64
Average Awareness Range	
Average Reaction Radius	
Won't Frenzy	
Can Walk	

Known Types

	HP	Class
Netherbian Drone	500-600	Rogue or Warrior
Netherbian Warrior	800-900	Warrior
Netherbian Swarmcaller	900-1000	Rogue
Swarm Leader	1100-1300	Warrior

Typical Owlbear

Warrior

Typical Levels	10-23
Typical HP	410-650
Typical Attributes	
STR	75-80
STA	80-90
DEX	75-90
INT	20-60
AGI	80-90
WIS	20-60
Typical Skill Levels	70-105
Typical Base Damage	16-22
Typical Base AC	40

Fast Regeneration

Average Attack Speed

Fast Speed

Average Awareness Range

Average Reaction Radius

Average Chance to Frenzy

Walks, Swims

Owlbear

Most commonly found in the Hollowshade Moor, where they breed their young, these huge bear-shaped creatures are strong and much quicker than they appear. Their owlish heads have sharp piercing beaks that can rip through flesh with ease. These creatures can also be found in the Grimling Forest and the Paludal Caverns, but in smaller numbers.

Known Types

Bonegrinder

Cub. Usually has lower base AC than most owlbears, but it regenerates faster. It has a larger reaction radius than most.

Fleshrender. Inflicts higher base damage than most owlbears. Can only be hit by magic weapons.

Furious Owlbear. Less likely to frenzy than other owlbears, has a larger reaction radius than most, and regenerates faster.

Gatherer

Grappler. Less likely to frenzy than other owlbears, has a larger reaction radius, inflicts more base damage, and regenerates faster. Magic, Fire, Cold and Disease Resistance 20.

Grimling Herder

Owlbear Lookout

Patrolling Owlbear

Ravager

Ravenous Owlbear. Shorter awareness radius than most owlbears.

Razorclaw

Spurclaw

Reishi

These large, stationary mushrooms are semi-intelligent and have a wide variety of abilities that they can use to defend themselves from predators. Generally these creatures are passive, and a lot of trouble can be avoided by careful travelers who just keep their distance.

Sensate Reishi Life Cycle

Reishi tend to get more powerful as they grow older. In some cases, their typical stats stay the same, but in other cases they steadily progress. **Typical Stats** for all Reishi are listed first, followed by **Progressive Stats** for their five life stages.

Typical Stats

Warrior

Typical Attributes

STA	100
DEX	50
INT	15
AGI	90

Typical Base AC

Faster Regeneration

Average Attack Speed

Slow Speed

Shorter Awareness Range

Small Reaction Radius

Less Likely to Frenzy

Walks, Swims

Progressive Stats

Stage	Level	HP	STR	WIS	Skill	Dam.	AC
Sensate Reishi Sprout	5-7	130	50	20	30	7	0
Sensate Reishi Juvenile	8-10	210	50	25	45	10	0
Sensate Reishi	11-13	300	70	35	60	13	8
Mature Sensate Reishi	14-16	410	80	45	75	16	20
Sensate Reishi Elder	17-19	530	90	65	90	19	32

Rhinoceros Beetle

These colossal beetles use their huge, sharp mandibles to crush and cut the giant fungus that they feed on. They also have a massive horn atop their heads, which they use only for defense. These creatures are generally docile, but they will fight if attacked.

Typical Rhinobeetle

Rogue or Warrior

Typical Levels	8-22
Typical HP	400-900
Typical Attributes	
STR	75
STA	75
DEX	75
INT	75
AGI	75
WIS	75
Typical Skill Levels	55-100
Typical Base Damage	12-21
Typical Base AC	4-40

Average Regeneration
Faster Attack Speed
Average Speed
Average Awareness Range
Larger Reaction Radius
Won't Frenzy
Walks, Swims

Known Types

Rhinobeetle. Magic and Disease Resistance 5, Poison Resistance 10.

Rhinobeetle Hatchling. Poison Resistance 10.

Cht'Thk Ash Beetle

Cht'Thk Bloodling

Cht'Thk Brood Mother. Has no skills, and is usually around level 10.

Cht'Thk Broodling. Has no skills.

Cht'Thk Swarmer

Cht'Thk rhinobeetles cannot swim.

Queen Cht'Thk. Base damage and AC are significantly higher than those of other rhinobeetles, but she is slower. Magic, Fire, Cold, Disease and Poison Resistance 5.

Life Stages

As might be expected, the youngest stages of these beetles have only minimal attributes of any sort. As a beetle progresses through its life cycle, it becomes stronger, faster and more skilled, with higher levels and hit points. The stages are:

- broodling/hatchling
- bloodling
- swarmer
- full grown (rhinobeetle, ash beetle)

Rockhopper

These reptilian creatures use their powerful legs to propel themselves up and down mountains and rocky terrain. They use their powerful claws to dig small prey out of cracks and crevices. They are found primarily on or near mountains and within caves. These creatures are not terribly aggressive, but they are often found in small groups and they do tend to aid each other when attacked. The smallest types tend to be scavengers, while the larger ones are predatory.

Known Types

Rockhopper

Young Rockhopper. Has fewer HP, lower skills, less base damage and lower level than adult hopper.

Blood Drenched Hopling. Cannot swim.

Frost Covered Hopling. Much more powerful than other rockhoppers — *not* a typical hopper.

Needle Clawed Hopper. Cannot swim.

Rockhopper Scavenger. Significantly more dangerous than the average hopper.

Saurek Claw Beast. Aggressive — attacks all within range. Cannot swim.

Typical Rockhopper

Warrior

Typical Levels	8-15
Typical HP	550-620
Typical Attributes	
STR	75
STA	75
DEX	75
INT	75
AGI	75
WIS	75
Typical Skill Levels	45-70
Typical Base Damage	10-15
Typical Base AC	4-16

Average Regeneration
Average Attack Speed
Average Speed
Average Awareness Range
Larger Reaction Radius
Won't Frenzy
Walks, Swims

Magic and Disease Resistance	5
Poison Resistance	10

Saurek Rockhoppers

The Saurek hoppers (except for the claw beast) share a few similarities. They are stronger, more dexterous and agile than most other hoppers, but they cannot swim, have no special resistances, and have a smaller reaction radius than other hoppers. Their other average stats include:

Saurek	Level	HP	Skill	Damage
Hopper	5-7	130	25	6
Darkclaw	6-8	160	35	8
Shredder	7-9	190	40	9
Deathmaw	8-10	210	45	10

Scorpion

Luclin scorpions are similar, but not identical to, their Norrath counterparts. The whiptail scorpion is especially interesting — it is more of a "Rogue" than a "Warrior."

Typical Scorpion

Warrior

Typical Levels	1-4
Typical HP	30-55
Typical Attributes	
STR	85
STA	95
DEX	90
INT	70
AGI	125
WIS	20
Typical Skill Levels	10-15
Typical Base Damage	3-4
Typical Base AC	15-20

Attacks all PCs within range
Average Regeneration
Average Attack Speed
Average Speed
Average Awareness Range
Average Reaction Radius
Average Chance to Frenzy
Walks

Typical Whiptail Scorpion

Rogue

Typical Levels	1-3
Typical HP	28
Typical Attributes	
STR	85
STA	95
DEX	90
INT	70
AGI	125
WIS	20
Typical Skill Levels	10
Typical Base Damage	3
Typical Base AC	25

Average Regeneration
Average Attack Speed
Average Speed
Average Awareness Range
Average Reaction Radius
Average Chance to Frenzy
Walks

Shik'Nar

These insectoids inhabit the cavernous underground of Luclin, one of those places being the Paludal Caverns. These beetle-like creatures are reasonably intelligent and can even use their mandibles for manual tasks. Their wings don't allow them to fly, but they give the Shik'Nar a little more agility.

Known Types

Ch'ktok

Outcast Shik'Nar. The typical outcast is a bit weaker and of lower level than other Shik'Nar.

Typical Shik'Nar (Ch'ktok)

Warrior

Typical Levels	19-21
Typical HP	610
Typical Attributes	
STR	90
STA	120
DEX	70
INT	50
AGI	80
WIS	60
Typical Skill Levels	100
Typical Base Damage	21
Typical Base AC	40

Average Regeneration

Average Attack Speed

Average Speed

Shorter Awareness Range

Average Reaction Radius

Won't Frenzy

Walks, Swims

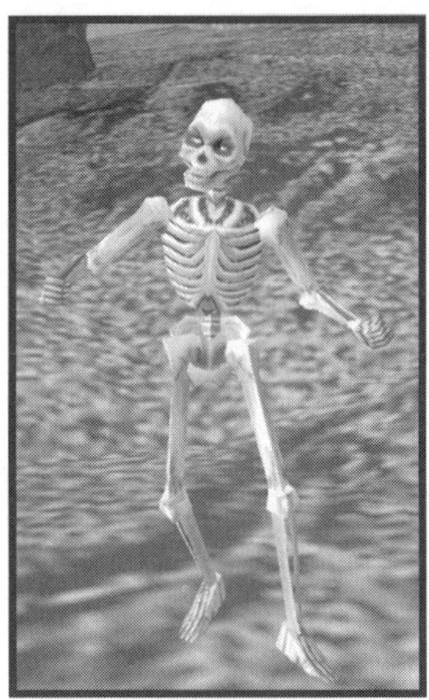

Skeleton

Like similar creatures on Norrath, skeletons aren't bound together by genetic or family relationships, which means we shouldn't expect their stats to be closely related, either. They haven't changed much, and as always will attack you without provocation, in many cases without considering your level. Their misplaced self-preservation means they will never run from a fight, no matter how hopeless the outcome. Some skeletal stats are similar, others aren't. Stats that tend to be similar are listed under **Typical Skeleton**. Stats that vary, depending on the skeleton that happens to be attacking you, are listed for each type of skeleton. **Grimling skeletons** and **nuisances** are different enough that they have separate listings here, on the next page.

Typical Skeleton

Typical Attributes

STR	75-80
STA	75-80
DEX	80-90
INT	75-80
AGI	75-90
WIS	75-80

Average Regeneration
Average Attack Speed
Average Speed
Average Awareness Range
Average Reaction Radius
Won't Frenzy
Walks
Disease and Poison Resistance 250

Known Types

Corpse. It might actually frenzy, and can only be hit by magic weapons. Fire Resistance 20.

Lesser Shade. Large reaction radius.

Skeletal Brigand. Attacks all PCs within range.

Skeletal Hunter. Attacks all PCs within range.

Skeletal Thug. Attacks all PCs within range.

Smelly Corpse. No Disease or Poison Resistance.

Skeleton	Level	HP	Skill	Damage	AC
Corpse	18–22	710	100	30	50
Lesser Shade	3–7	100	25	6	0
Skeletal Brigand	6–8	160	35	8	0
Skeletal Hunter	5–7	130	30	7	0
Skeletal Thug	8–10	210	45	10	0
Smelly Corpse	23–27	810	125	26	60

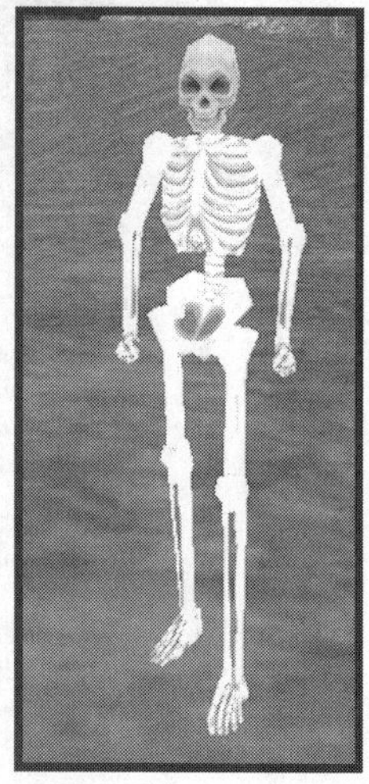

Grimling Skeleton

Warrior

Typical Levels	1-4
Typical HP	30-60
Typical Attributes	
STR	90
STA	90
DEX	85
INT	10
AGI	90
WIS	10
Typical Skill Levels	10-15
Typical Base Damage	3-4
Typical Base AC	0

Shortest Awareness Range

Small Reaction Radius

Won't Frenzy

Walks

Disease and Poison Resistance 10

Nuisance

Tiny skeletons of an unknown origin. These undead (if they are indeed undead) tend to not be aggressive, which alone makes them different than the usual undead. They also have spell casting ability.

Cleric

Typical Levels	3-5
Typical HP	30
Typical Attributes	
STR	75
STA	75
DEX	75
INT	75
AGI	75
WIS	75
Typical Skill Levels	20
Typical Base Damage	5
Typical Base AC	0

Average Regeneration

Average Attack Speed

Average Speed

Average Awareness Range

Average Reaction Radius

Won't Frenzy

Walks

Disease and Poison Resistance 250

Sonic Wolf

These beasts are only wolfish in their appearance when seen at a distance. When viewed closely (if one dares), it can be seen that these creatures have no eyes. Instead they have enormous ears that they use in much the same fashion as bats. They can emit sounds for use in combat as well as navigation. Their foreclaws are long and sharp, making these creatures very lethal.

Typical Sonic Wolf

Warrior

Typical Levels	14-23
Typical HP	530-750
Typical Attributes	
STR	80
STA	80-90
DEX	75-90
INT	20-60
AGI	80-90
WIS	20-60
Typical Skill Levels	70-90
Typical Base Damage	17-22
Typical Base AC	25-50

Average Regeneration
Average Attack Speed
Fast Speed
Average Awareness Range
Smaller Reaction Radius
Average Chance to Frenzy
Walks, Swims
Can only be hit by magic weapons
Can "see" Invisible-to-Undead creatures

Known Types

Patrolling Sonic Wolf

Sonic Devourer

Sonic Hunter

Sonic Pup. Slightly lower-than-average level and hit points.

Sonic Ravager

Sonic Stalker. Can be a Shaman.

Sonic Tracker

Sonic Wolf Fiend

Sonic Wolfling. Magic, Fire, Cold and Disease Resistance 20.

Sonic pup, wolfling and wolf fiend share a few characteristics. They regenerate a bit faster than other sonic wolves, have a slightly larger reaction radius, and are less likely to frenzy. They can all be hit by normal weapons.

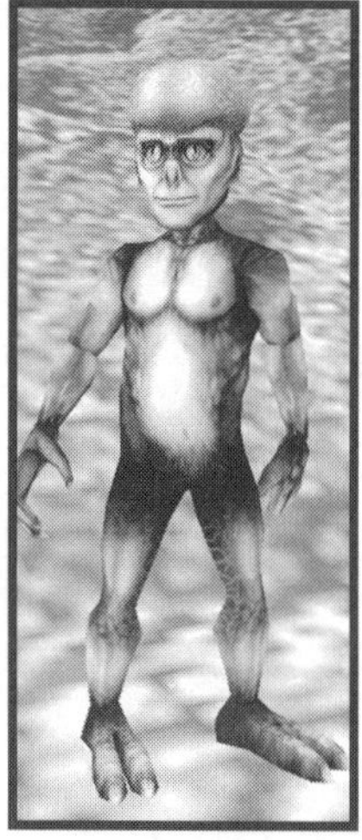

Tegi

This small humanoid race is native to Luclin. They are known for their attunement to the elemental spirits. Their society is broken up into clans, each clan usually made up of Tegi with the same elemental attunement. The affinity of any individual Tegi is usually apparent in their coloration; Fire Tegi are reddish, Rock Tegi are tan or brown, Water Tegi are blue, Shadow Tegi are dark grey to black, and Air Tegi can be nearly transparent. It seems likely that there exist other types of Tegi that have yet to be discovered.

Typical Tegi

The closest creatures in this chapter to a civilized (that is, player character) race, there is no such thing as a "typical tegi." They have a wide range of skills and attributes; some have a bit of magic, cold, fire, disease or poison resistance. However, most of them seem to share a few characteristics:

Average Regeneration

Average Attack Speed

Average Speed

Average Awareness Range

Average Reaction Radius

Won't Frenzy

Walks

Known Types

Fire

Air

Water

Rock

Shadow

Shadecaller (Necromancer)

Earth Caller (Magician)

Spiritweaver (Shaman)

Shadeweaver (Shaman)

Beastlord

Cleric

Rogue

Warrior

Known Clans

Shak Dratha

Firefall Guardians

Gor Taku

Firefall Guardians

Firefall Guardians are the Tegi elite. (Well, they're not so bright, but other than that ....) Typical stats include:

Typical HP	7000
Typical Attributes	
STR	50
STA	100
DEX	50
INT	15
AGI	90
WIS	10
Typical Skill Levels	220
Typical Base Damage	100
Typical Base AC	120
Faster Regeneration	
Faster Attack Speed	
Slow Speed	
Shorter Awareness Range	
Small Reaction Radius	
Less Likely to Frenzy	
Walks, Swims	
Fire Resistance	120

The following four Firefall types are known:

Firefall Caller (Magician)
Firefall Guardian (Warrior)
Firefall Seer (Shaman)
Firefall Sentry (Rogue)

Tiger

There are a few actual tigers on Luclin, including a couple of prides in Shadeweaver's Thicket, the Pasha and Raji.

Typical Tiger

Typical Attributes	
STR	75
STA	75
DEX	75
INT	75
AGI	75
WIS	75
Typical Base AC	
Average Regeneration	
Average Attack Speed	
Average Speed	

Known Types

Tiger	Level	HP	Skill	Damage	AC
Pasha Pride Tigress	8-12	240	50	11	0
Pasha Pride Cub	4-8	130	30	7	0
Raji Pride Tigress	13-17	410	75	16	20
Raji Pride Cub	8-12	240	50	11	20

Troglodytes

Given this name by others, they refer to themselves as Galorians. These humanoids have a very limited intellect, and tend to live in small crude tribes. There skin tends to be reddish, and their hair dark.

Known types - Trog Bull and Trog Hunter.

Typical Troglodyte

Typical Levels	120-130
Typical Attributes	
STR	75
STA	75
DEX	75
INT	75
AGI	75
WIS	75
Typical Skill Levels	120
Slowest Regeneration Rate	
Typical Base Damage	20-30
Average Attack Speed	
Average Speed	
Typical Base AC	64
Average Awareness Range	
Average Reaction Radius	
Won't Frenzy	
Can Walk	

Known Types

	HP	Class
Troglodyte	500-700	Warrior
Trog Hunter	800-900	Shaman
Trog Bull	950-1050	Warrior
The Trog King	1400-1500	Warrior

Underbulk

These large and powerful creatures have beetle-like exoskeletons, with pincers on their forelimbs as well as a pincer for a maw. Their bulk makes them slow, and they possess no more intelligence than the beetles they resemble.

Known Types

Underbulk	Level	HP	Skill	Damage	AC
Cht'Thk Blood Bulk	13-15	340	70	15	16
Glowing Muck Digger	12-14	380	70	15	16
Grime Tunneler	11-13	300	60	13	8
Muck Digger	8-10	210	45	10	0
Mud Burrower	5-7	130	30	7	0
Sediment Delver	13-15	380	70	15	16
Stoneclaw Burrower	10-14	300	60	13	8
Stoneclaw Digger	9-11	240	50	11	0

Glowing muck dweller, **grime tunneler** and **sediment delver** share a few similarities. All three have a slower regeneration, but faster speed, than most other underbulks, and have a larger reaction radius. None of them will frenzy.

Cht'Thk blood bulk is like these last three, but also has a larger awareness radius and cannot swim. Its basic stats and skills are all near 75.

Typical Underbulk

Warrior

Typical Attributes

STR	50-70
STA	100
DEX	50
INT	15
AGI	90
WIS	10

Typical Base AC

Faster Regeneration

Average Attack Speed

Slow Speed

Shorter Awareness Range

Small Reaction Radius

Less Likely to Frenzy

Walks, Swims

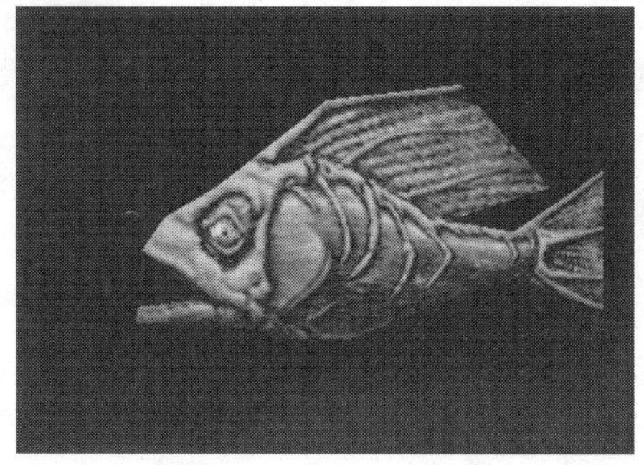

Wetfang Minnow

These aggressive fish reside in many of the waters of Luclin, varying slightly from river to river or lake to lake. However, all variations of this fish are equally aggressive and dangerous. Their needle-sharp teeth can easily rip flesh.

Typical Wetfang

Warrior

Typical Levels	10-14
Typical HP	300
Typical Attributes	
STR	95
STA	120
DEX	70
INT	15
AGI	150
WIS	60
Typical Skill Levels	60
Typical Base Damage	13
Typical Base AC	8

Average Regeneration
Average Attack Speed
Average Speed
Shorter Awareness Range
Average Reaction Radius
Won't Frenzy
Swims

Typical Blackfin Minnow

Warrior

Typical Levels	12-16
Typical HP	530
Typical Attributes	
STR	75
STA	75
DEX	75
INT	75
AGI	75
WIS	75
Typical Skill Levels	90
Typical Base Damage	21
Typical Base AC	32

Average Regeneration
Average Attack Speed
Average Speed
Average Awareness Range
Larger Reaction Radius
Won't Frenzy
Swims

Xakra Silkworm (Vacuum Worm)

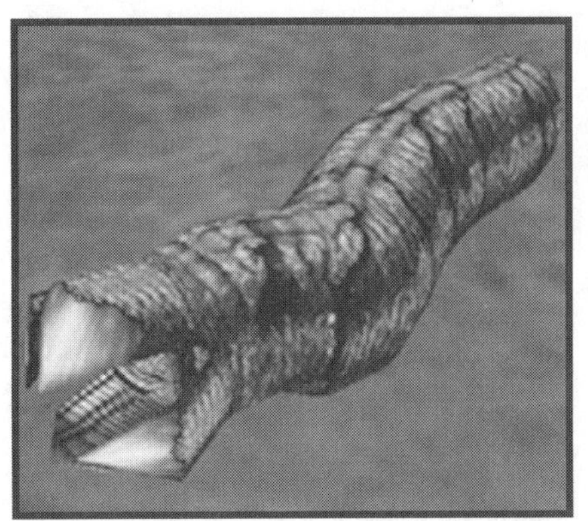

These creatures are very strong, with thick hides that protect them from even the mightiest blows. They have large worm-like bodies, with huge beaks for mouths. They can spin silk from the ethereal realm. They can survive in any atmosphere (or none at all), hence the common name "vacuum worm."

Typical Worm

Warrior	
Typical Levels	1-3
Typical HP	32-40
Typical Attributes	
STR	75
STA	75
DEX	75
INT	75
AGI	75
WIS	75
Typical Skill Levels	10
Typical Base Damage	3
Typical Base AC	0

Average Regeneration

Average Attack Speed

Average Speed

Average Awareness Range

Average Reaction Radius

Won't Frenzy

Walks

Known Types

Xakra Silkworm

Xakra Larva. Larger reaction radius.

Zones

Grimling Forest

Grimling, Owlbear, Rockhopper, Sonic Wolf

Hollowshade Moor

Grimling, Moor Tortoise, Owlbear, Rhinoceros Beetle, Rockhopper, Sonic Wolf, Wetfang Minnow

Netherbian Lair

Fungal Fiend, Grimling, Netherbian, Troglodytes

Paludal Caverns

Fungal Fiend, Owlbear, Shik'Nar, Reishi, Underbulk, Wetfang Minnow

Bandits

Bandits have taken up residence in the Paludal Caverns. These folk can appear as any other person (or Gnome, or Elf ...), but their desires are usually contrary to those of travelers.

Shadeweaver's Thicket

Nuisance, Rhinoceros Beetle, Rockhopper, Skeleton, Tegi, Tiger, Underbulk, Vacuum Worm

Loda Kai Brigands

These brigands constantly raid the trade routes between Shar Vahl and Shadow Haven. This band will accept any race, as long as they are cutthroats at heart.

Shar Vahl

Rhinoceros Beetle, Rockhopper, Scorpion, Skeleton, Vacuum Worm

Nearby Factions

Shadeweaver's Thicket

Guardians of Shar Vahl: Vah Shir, occasional other people, tigers

Lodikai: Bandits (some skeletons)

Gor Taku: Tegi Clan

Shak Dratha: Tegi Clan

Paludal Caverns

Lake Recondite Bandits

Deepwood Owlbears

Hollowshade Moor

Grimlings of the Moor: Grimlings and sonic wolves

Sonic Wolves of the Moor

Sonic Wolf Invaders

Owlbears of the Moor

Owlbear Invaders

Gnoll: Rhinobeetles and rockhoppers

Grimling Invaders

Grimling Forest

Pack of the Great Moon: Sonic wolves

Grimlings of the Forest

Dark Forest Denizens: Rhinobeetles, rockhoppers

Netherbian Lair

Netherbians

Troglodytes: Haven (Recuso) Smugglers

Spells

Spell Definitions

Another several hundred spells have been added to *EverQuest* since the last strategy guide, when *Ruins of Kunark* was released. As before, we've detailed spells up to level 25, and also listed the casters' levels and skills and the target's reaction for higher level spells. Also as before, most spells, but not all, are listed here – there are a few that require a bit more effort to find.

However, this chapter's organization is significantly different from the *Kunark* strategy guide spell chapter. In that book, since so many spells could be cast by multiple classes, we listed each spell just once, organized alphabetically. In contrast, nearly all of these new spells can only be cast by one class, so we've listed these spells by class, and in order of increasing level. Let's discuss the notation used, and then dive into the spells themselves.

Please note that several of the spells in this chapter were added to *EverQuest* before *The Shadows of Luclin*. In some cases, old spells are now new Beastlord spells, so we've listed them again, for the Beastlord. In other cases, spells have been added since *The Ruins of Kunark* (with *The Scars of Velious*, or at other times). So that you'd have access to a complete spell list, between the *Kunark* guide and this one, those spells are included here as well.

Casters is pretty obvious. This class of caster has access to the spell once he or she reaches the level in parentheses. For example, *Cure Disease* (Beastlord 9, p. 145) is available at level 9 for Beastlords, level 5 for Clerics, and so forth. **Mana Cost** and **Casting Skill** are also obvious.

Casting Time is how long it takes to cast the spell. **Casting Delay** is how long you must wait after casting this spell before you can cast another spell. If a **Recasting Delay** is listed, you must wait that long until you can cast *this* spell again. *Flash of Light* (Beastlord 9, p. 145) has a recasting delay – it takes 1.5 seconds to cast, after which you must wait another 2.5 seconds before you can cast any other spell. However, you must wait 5.5 seconds after casting it before you can cast *it* again.

Duration is how long the spell lasts. Sometimes this is based on the level of the caster. For example, if *Inner Fire* (Beastlord 9, Shaman 1, p. 145) is cast by a level 6 Shaman, it will last 21 minutes: 3 + (3 x 6) = 21. (Note that targets have occasional chances to prematurely dispel a spell.)

Sometimes, a caster reaches the maximum possible duration as soon as he learns a spell. For example, a Beastlord gets *Inner Fire* at level 9. According to the formula, the spell lasts 30 minutes at level 9 (3 + 3 x 9 = 30), but the maximum duration for the spell is just 27 minutes. When a spell's maximum duration immediately applies to the listed class (but not all of them), the maximum duration is marked in **bold**, to indicate that you don't have to bother with any calculations.

Range is how far away the spell can be cast, in feet. **Radius of Effect** is how large an area the spell affects, also in feet. In some cases, such as *Song of Sustenance* (Bard 15, p. 144), the spell affects creatures or even your own group, within that area. In those cases, the spell affects all the people or creatures listed, who are in the radius of effect.

Target tells who you can cast the spell on. If it's "Anyone," you can also cast it on yourself.

Resistance Invoked lists the resistance a target uses to counter the spell. In some cases (especially with beneficial spells), there's no resistance listed, because the target usually *wants* the spell.

Effects are wide-ranged. We won't mention the obvious, but a few need further explanation.

Damage. A common measure of time in *EverQuest* is 6 seconds. For example, if a spell continues to inflict damage (DoT), the damage is usually inflicted every 6 seconds. Some spells inflict an immediate burst of damage, then continue inflicting more damage. For example, *Sicken* (Beastlord 15, p. 147) strikes with 8 HP of damage immediately, then deals another 2 HP every 6 seconds. If a spell lists only continuing damage (no immediate damage), it inflicts the listed amount immediately, and then again every 6 seconds.

Disease. Diseases come in a range of powers, as do their curatives. The lower the numerical rating for a disease, or a curative, the less power it has. Sending a 1 curative spell to heal a 7 disease isn't likely to produce a complete cure, but it might improve your patient's condition. If a spell lists multiple chances (like *Counteract Disease's* "2 chances, 4") (Beastlord 49, p. 152), then the disease or curative has two chances to work its wonder. That means you can be infected by multiple diseases, and some spells might cure multiple diseases. If you only have one disease, a multiple curative has twice the opportunity to cure what ails you.

Poison spells (both inflictive and curative) work just like disease spells.

Magic dispelling spells, along with **Charm** and **Fear** spells, also work like disease spells, but the range of powers is expressed as *lowest* level, *low-level, mid-level, high-level* and *highest* level. Again, don't send a boy out to do a man's job – a low-level Dispel is unlikely to crack a high-level Charm.

HP buffs are special HP that temporarily boost your total. If you're hit during the duration of a Bonus HP spell, you first reduce your Bonus HP before taking any actual damage.

Target's Reaction is what you see the spell's target do when hit with the spell. Anything given here in parentheses is what *you* feel or do. If you do the same thing as any other target, we don't list both reactions. And sometimes you can't tell if a spell has hit someone else, so the only reaction given here is in parentheses, to describe what *you* do.

Bard

Magical Monologue

Casters	Bard (9)
Casting Skill	Singing
Casting Time	3 sec.
Casting Delay	None
Duration	18 sec.
Range	None
Target	Yourself
Resistance Invoked	None
Effect	
Caster can hit "magical-weapon-only" creatures with non-magical weapons	
Target's Reaction	Target's weapons glow.

Song of Sustenance

Casters	Bard (15)
Casting Skill	Stringed Instruments
Casting Time	3 sec.
Casting Delay	None
Duration	12 sec. + 6 sec / 2 levels (max. 90 sec.)
Range	None
Radius of Effect	100 feet
Target	Your Group
Resistance Invoked	None
Effect	
Group doesn't need food or drink during song	
Target's Reaction	Target is sustained.

Cassindra's Chant of Clarity

Casters	Bard (20)
Casting Skill	Singing
Casting Time	3 sec.
Casting Delay	None
Duration	Instantaneous
Range	None
Radius of Effect	30 feet
Target	Your Group
Resistance Invoked	None
Effect	
Mana buff	2
Target's Reaction	(Your mind clears.)

Amplification

Casters	Bard (30)
Casting Skill	Singing
Target's Reaction	Target's voice booms.

Cantata of Soothing

Casters	Bard (34)
Casting Skill	Stringed Instruments
Target's Reaction	(You feel replenished.)

Katta's Song of Sword Dancing

Casters	Bard (39)
Casting Skill	Percussion Instruments
Target's Reaction	Target's weapons whir with a magical rhythm.

Selo's Accelerating Chorus

Casters	Bard (49)
Casting Skill	Percussion Instruments
Target's Reaction	(Your feet move faster.)

Shield of Songs

Casters	Bard (49)
Casting Skill	Stringed Instruments
Target's Reaction	Target is surrounded by a shield of song.

Melody of Ervaj

Casters	Bard (50)
Casting Skill	Brass Instruments
Target's Reaction	(A song of inspiration fills your weapon arm with strength.)

Battlecry of the Vah Shir

Casters	Bard (52)
Casting Skill	Brass Instruments
Target's Reaction	(Your attacks accelerate.)

Elemental Chorus

Casters	Bard (54)
Casting Skill	Percussion Instruments

Occlusion of Sound

Casters	Bard (55)
Casting Skill	Percussion Instruments
Target's Reaction	Target reels in pain and loses concentration. (You reel in pain as every bone in your body vibrates.)

Purifying Chorus

Casters	Bard (56)
Casting Skill	Percussion Instruments

Chorus of Replenishment

Casters	Bard (58)
Casting Skill	Stringed Instruments

Composition of Ervaj

Casters	Bard (60)
Casting Skill	Brass Instruments
Target's Reaction	(A song of inspiration fills your weapon arm with strength.)

Warsong of the Vah Shir

Casters	Bard (60)
Casting Skill	Brass Instruments
Target's Reaction	(Your attacks accelerate.)

Beastlord

Cure Disease

Casters	Beastlord (9), Cleric (5), Druid (5), Necrom. (16), Paladin (15), Sham. (1)
Mana Cost	20
Casting Skill	Alteration
Casting Time	2 sec.
Casting Delay	2.5 sec.
Recasting Delay	5.5 sec.
Duration	Instantaneous
Range	100 feet
Target	Anyone
Resistance Invoked	None
Effect	
Disease Reduction	1

Endure Cold

Casters	Beastlord (9), Cleric (14), Druid (9), Necromancer (4), Ranger (22), Shadow Knight (15), Shaman (1)
Mana Cost	20
Casting Skill	Abjuration
Casting Time	2.5 sec.
Casting Delay	2.5 sec.
Duration	3 min/level (max. **27 min.**)
Range	100 feet
Target	Anyone
Resistance Invoked	None
Effect	
Resist Cold buff	10 + 1/level (max 20)
Target's Reaction	Target is protected from cold.

Flash of Light

Casters	Beastlord (9), Clr. (1), Pal. (9), Shm. (1)
Mana Cost	12
Casting Skill	Divination
Casting Time	1.5 sec.
Casting Delay	2.5 sec.
Recasting Delay	5.5 sec.
Duration	12 sec.
Range	200 feet
Target	Anyone
Resistance Invoked	Magic
Effect	
Blindness	
Attack skill debuff	5
Target's Reaction	Target is blinded by a flash of light.

Inner Fire

Casters	Beastlord (9), Shaman (1)
Mana Cost	10
Casting Skill	Abjuration
Casting Time	3 sec.
Casting Delay	2.5 sec.
Duration	3 min. + 3 min/level (max. **27 min.**)
Range	100 feet
Target	Anyone
Resistance Invoked	None
Effect	
AC buff	5 + 1 / 2 levels (max 10)
HP buff	10 + 1/level (max 20)
Target's Reaction	Body pulses with energy.

Minor Healing

Casters	Beastlord (9), Cleric (1), Druid (1), Paladin (9), Ranger (9), Shaman (1)
Mana Cost	10
Casting Skill	Alteration
Casting Time	1 sec.
Casting Delay	2.5 sec.
Duration	Instantaneous
Range	100 feet
Target	Anyone
Resistance Invoked	None
Effect	
Healing (HP)	10
Target's Reaction	Target feels a little better.

Sharik's Replenishing

Casters	Beastlord (9)
Mana Cost	15
Casting Skill	Alteration
Casting Time	2 sec.
Casting Delay	2.5 sec.
Duration	Instantaneous
Range	100 feet
Target	Your Pet
Resistance Invoked	None
Effect	
HP buff	24 + 1 / 2 levels (max 33)
Target's Reaction	Target feels better.

Spirit of Sharik

Casters	Beastlord (9)
Mana Cost	100
Casting Skill	Alteration
Casting Time	2 sec.
Casting Delay	2.5 sec.
Recasting Delay	12.5 sec.
Duration	Instantaneous
Range	100 feet
Target	Your Pet
Resistance Invoked	None
Effect	

Transforms ordinary pet into appropriately buffed warder.

Cure Poison

Casters	Beastlord (15), Cleric (1), Druid (5), Paladin (9), Ranger (15), Shaman (5)
Mana Cost	20
Casting Skill	Alteration
Casting Time	2 sec.
Casting Delay	2.5 sec.
Recasting Delay	5.5 sec.
Duration	Instantaneous
Range	100 feet
Target	Anyone
Resistance Invoked	None
Effect	
Poison Reduction	1

Endure Fire

Casters	Beastlord (15), Cleric (9), Druid (1), Ranger (9), Shaman (5)
Mana Cost	20
Casting Skill	Abjuration
Casting Time	2.5 sec.
Casting Delay	2.5 sec.
Duration	3 min/level (max. **27 min.**)
Range	100 feet
Target	Anyone
Resistance Invoked	None
Effect	
Resist Fire buff	10 + 1/level (max **20**)
Target's Reaction	Target is protected from fire.

Fleeting Fury

Casters	Beastlord (15), Shaman (5)
Mana Cost	10
Casting Skill	Abjuration
Casting Time	0.5 sec.
Casting Delay	2.5 sec.
Recasting Delay	6.5 sec.
Duration	18 sec.
Range	100 feet
Target	Anyone
Resistance Invoked	None
Effect	
Restores Fatigue	1 point
STR buff	15
AC buff	20
DEX buff	20
Target's Reaction	Target simmers with fury.

Keshuval's Rejuvination

Casters	Beastlord (15)
Mana Cost	30
Casting Skill	Alteration
Casting Time	3 sec.
Casting Delay	2.5 sec.
Duration	Instantaneous
Range	100 feet
Target	Your Pet
Resistance Invoked	None
Effect	
Healing (HP)	70 + 1/level (max 100)
Target's Reaction	Target feels much better. (You feel much better.)

Scale Skin

Casters	Beastlord (15), Shaman (5)
Mana Cost	25
Casting Skill	Abjuration
Component	Snake Skin
Casting Time	2.5 sec.
Casting Delay	2.5 sec.
Recasting Delay	7 sec.
Duration	3 min/level (max. **27 min.**)
Range	100 feet
Target	Anyone
Resistance Invoked	None
Effect	
AC buff	11 + 1/level (max **20**)
Target's Reaction	Target grows scales.

Sense Animals

Casters	Beastlord (15), Druid (1), Shaman (9)
Mana Cost	5
Casting Skill	Divination
Casting Time	2 sec.
Casting Delay	2.5 sec.
Recasting Delay	6.5 sec.
Duration	Instantaneous
Range	None
Radius of Effect	240 feet
Target	Yourself
Resistance Invoked	None
Effect	
Detect animals within range	

Sicken

Casters	Beastlord (15), Shaman (5)
Mana Cost	30
Casting Skill	Conjuration
Casting Time	2 sec.
Casting Delay	2.5 sec.
Duration	1 min. + 6 sec./level (max. **2.1 min.**)
Range	200 feet
Target	Anyone
Resistance Invoked	Disease
Effect	
Disease	1
Immed. HP Dam.	8
Subseq. HP Dam.	2 / 6 sec.
Target's Reaction	Target sweats and shivers, looking feverish.

Spirit of Khaliz

Casters	Beastlord (15)
Mana Cost	150
Casting Skill	Alteration
Casting Time	3 sec.
Casting Delay	2.5 sec.
Recasting Delay	12.5 sec.
Duration	Instantaneous
Range	100 feet
Target	Your Pet
Resistance Invoked	None
Effect	
Transforms pet into appropriately buffed warder.	

Spirit of Lightning

Casters	Beastlord (15)
Mana Cost	50
Casting Skill	Alteration
Casting Time	3 sec.
Casting Delay	2.5 sec.
Recasting Delay	8.5 sec.
Duration	20 min.
Range	100 feet
Target	Your Pet
Resistance Invoked	None (Magic for spell proc)
Effect	
Gives pet chance to proc spell effects:	
Immed. HP Dam.	30 + 1 / 2 levels
Reduces Target's Hate	
Target's Reaction	Target is imbued with the spirit of lightning.

Strengthen

Casters	Beastlord (15), Enchanter (1), Shaman (1)
Mana Cost	10
Casting Skill	Alteration
Casting Time	2 sec.
Casting Delay	2.5 sec.
Duration	3 min. + 3 min/level (max. **27 min.**)
Range	100 feet
Target	Anyone
Resistance Invoked	None
Effect	
STR buff	4 + 1/level (max 10)
Target's Reaction	Target looks stronger. (You feel stronger.)

Drowsy

Casters	Beastlord (22), Shaman (5)
Mana Cost	20
Casting Skill	Alteration
Casting Time	2.5 sec.
Casting Delay	2.5 sec.
Recasting Delay	7.5 sec.
Duration	12 sec. + 6 sec/2 levels
Range	200 feet
Target	Anyone
Resistance Invoked	Magic
Effect	
Attack Sp. debuff	10% - 1% / 4 levels
Target's Reaction	Target yawns. (You feel drowsy.)

Endure Poison

Casters	Beastlord (22), Cleric (9), Druid (19), Paladin (22), Shaman (14)
Mana Cost	20
Casting Skill	Abjuration
Casting Time	2.5 sec.
Casting Delay	2.5 sec.
Duration	27 min.
Range	100 feet
Target	Anyone
Resistance Invoked	None
Effect	
Resist Poison buff	10 + 1/level (max **20**)
Target's Reaction	Target is protected from poison.

Light Healing

Casters	Beastlord (22), Cleric (5), Druid (9), Paladin (15), Ranger (22), Shaman (9)
Mana Cost	25
Casting Skill	Alteration
Casting Time	2 sec.
Casting Delay	2.5 sec.
Duration	Instantaneous
Range	100 feet
Target	Anyone
Resistance Invoked	None
Effect	
Healing (HP)	24 + 1 / 2 levels (max **33**)
Target's Reaction	Target feels better.

Spirit of Bear

Casters	Beastlord (22), Shaman (9)
Mana Cost	40
Casting Skill	Abjuration
Casting Time	5 sec.
Casting Delay	2.5 sec.
Duration	3 min/level (max. 36 min.)
Range	100 feet
Target	Anyone
Resistance Invoked	None
Effect	
STA buff	8 + 1 / 2 levels (max **15**)
Target's Reaction	Target is surrounded by a brief ursine aura. (You feel the spirit of bear enter you.)

Spirit of Keshuval

Casters	Beastlord (22)
Mana Cost	200
Casting Skill	Alteration
Casting Time	4 sec.
Casting Delay	2.5 sec.
Recasting Delay	12.5 sec.
Duration	Instantaneous
Range	100 feet
Target	Your Pet
Resistance Invoked	None
Effect	

Transforms ordinary pet into appropriately buffed warder.

Spirit of the Blizzard

Casters	Beastlord (22)
Mana Cost	50
Casting Skill	Alteration
Casting Time	3 sec.
Casting Delay	2.5 sec.
Recasting Delay	8.5 sec.
Duration	20 min.
Range	100 feet
Target	Your Pet
Resistance Invoked	None
Effect	
Gives pet chance to proc spell effects:	
Immed HP Dam.	30 + 1 / 2 levels
Reduces Target's Hate	
(Resistance: Cold)	
Target's Reaction	Target is imbued with the spirit of an ancient blizzard.

Summon Drink

Casters	Beastlord (22), Cleric (5), Druid (14), Magician (1), Shaman (5)
Mana Cost	10
Casting Skill	Conjuration
Casting Time	4 sec.
Casting Delay	2.5 sec.
Duration	Instantaneous
Range	None
Target	Yourself
Resistance Invoked	None
Effect	
Create Item	1 globe of water

Tainted Breath

Casters	Beastlord (22), Shaman (9)
Mana Cost	40
Casting Skill	Conjuration
Casting Time	2 sec.
Casting Delay	2.5 sec.
Duration	42 sec.
Range	200 feet
Target	Anyone
Resistance Invoked	Poison
Effect	
Poison	5
Immed. HP Dam.	10
Subseq. HP Dam.	8 / 6 sec.
Target's Reaction	Target has been poisoned.

Herikol's Soothing

Casters	Beastlord (30)
Casting Skill	Alteration
Target's Reaction	Target feels much better.

Shrink

Casters	Beastlord (30), Shaman (19)
Mana Cost	50
Casting Skill	Alteration Indoors only
Casting Time	4 sec.
Casting Delay	2.5 sec.
Duration	Instantaneous
Range	200 feet
Target	Anyone
Resistance Invoked	None
Effect	
Shrinks Target	66% of original size
Target's Reaction	Target shrinks. (You feel smaller.)

Spirit of Herikol

Casters	Beastlord (30)
Casting Skill	Alteration

Spirit of Inferno

Casters	Beastlord (30)
Casting Skill	Alteration
Target's Reaction	Target is imbued with the spirit of a blazing inferno.

Spirit of Wolf

Casters	Beastlord (30), Druid (14), Ranger (30), Shaman (9)
Mana Cost	40
Casting Skill	Alteration Outdoors only
Casting Time	4.5 sec.
Casting Delay	2.5 sec.
Recasting Delay	6 sec.
Duration	3 min/level (max. 36 min.)
Range	100 feet
Target	Anyone
Resistance Invoked	None
Effect	
Speed buff	30% + 1% / 2 levels (max 55%)
Target's Reaction	Target is surrounded by a brief lupine aura. (You feel the spirit of wolf enter you.)

Spirit Sight

Casters	Beastlord (30), Shaman (9)
Mana Cost	20
Casting Skill	Divination
Casting Time	2 sec.
Casting Delay	2.5 sec.
Duration	27 min.
Range	100 feet
Radius of Effect	60 feet
Target	Anyone
Resistance Invoked	None
Effect	
See Invisible	
Target's Reaction	Target's eyes tingle.

Spirit Strength

Casters	Beastlord (30), Shaman (19)
Mana Cost	40
Casting Skill	Alteration
Casting Time	5 sec.
Casting Delay	2.5 sec.
Duration	36 min.
Range	100 feet
Target	Anyone
Resistance Invoked	None
Effect	
STR buff	7 + 1 / 2 levels (max **18**)
Target's Reaction	Target looks stronger. (You feel stronger.)

Spirit Strike

Casters	Beastlord (30), Shaman (14)
Mana Cost	75
Casting Skill	Evocation
Casting Time	2.5 sec.
Casting Delay	2.5 sec.
Duration	Instantaneous
Range	200 feet
Target	Anyone
Resistance Invoked	Cold
Effect	
Immed. HP Dam.	60 + 1/level (max **81**)
Target's Reaction	Target staggers as spirits of frost slam against them.

Summon Food

Casters	Beastlord (30), Cleric (9), Druid (14), Magician (1), Shaman (9)
Mana Cost	10
Casting Skill	Conjuration
Casting Time	4 sec.
Casting Delay	2.5 sec.
Duration	Instantaneous
Range	None
Target	Yourself
Resistance Invoked	None
Effect	
Create Item	1 black bread

Turtle Skin

Casters	Beastlord (30), Shaman (14)
Mana Cost	50
Casting Skill	Abjuration
Casting Time	5 sec.
Casting Delay	2.5 sec.
Recasting Delay	10 sec.
Duration	36 min.
Range	100 feet
Target	Anyone
Resistance Invoked	None
Effect	
AC buff	17 + 1/level (max **35**)
Target's Reaction	Target's skin looks greener. (Your skin becomes as hard as turtle shell.)

Endure Magic

Casters	Beastlord (39), Cleric (19), Druid (34), Enchanter (20), Paladin (30), Shaman (19)
Mana Cost	40
Casting Skill	Abjuration
Casting Time	2.5 sec.
Casting Delay	2.5 sec.
Duration	27 min.
Range	100 feet
Target	Anyone
Resistance Invoked	None
Effect	
Resist Magic buff	20
Target's Reaction	Target is protected from magic.

Envenomed Breath

Casters	Beastlord (39), Shaman (24)
Mana Cost	100
Casting Skill	Conjuration
Casting Time	3 sec.
Casting Delay	2.5 sec.
Duration	42 sec.
Range	200 feet
Target	Anyone
Resistance Invoked	Poison
Effect	
Poison	3
Immediate Dam.	30 HP
Subsequent Dam.	27 HP/6 sec.
Target's Reaction	Target has been poisoned.

Healing

Casters	Beastlord (39), Cleric (14), Druid (19), Paladin (30), Ranger (39), Shaman (19)
Mana Cost	60
Casting Skill	Alteration
Casting Time	3 sec.
Casting Delay	2.5 sec.
Duration	Instantaneous
Range	100 feet
Target	Anyone
Resistance Invoked	None
Effect	
Healing (HP)	70 + 1/level (max **100**)
Target's Reaction	Target feels much better. (You feel much better.)

Spirit of Monkey

Casters	Beastlord (39), Shaman (24)
Mana Cost	40
Casting Skill	Alteration
Casting Time	5 sec.
Casting Delay	2.5 sec.
Duration	36 min.
Range	100 feet
Target	Anyone
Resistance Invoked	None
Effect	
DEX buff	20
Target's Reaction	Target is surrounded by a brief simian aura. (You feel the spirit of monkey enter you.)

Spirit of Ox

Casters	Beastlord (39), Shaman (24)
Mana Cost	60
Casting Skill	Alteration
Casting Time	5 sec.
Casting Delay	2.5 sec.
Duration	45 min.
Range	100 feet
Target	Anyone
Resistance Invoked	None
Effect	
STA buff	9 + 1 / 2 levels (max **23**)
Target's Reaction	Target is surrounded by a brief bovine aura. (You feel the spirit of ox enter you.)

Spirit of the Scorpion

Casters	Beastlord (39)
Casting Skill	Alteration
Target's Reaction	Target is imbued with the spirit of a scorpion.

Spirit of Yekan

Casters	Beastlord (39)
Casting Skill	Alteration

Summon Companion

Casters	Beastlord (39), Enchanter (44), Magician (39), Necromancer (44), Shadow Knight (52), Shaman (44)
Casting Skill	Conjuration
Target's Reaction	Target summons a companion to their side.

Yekan's Quickening

Casters	Beastlord (39)
Casting Skill	Alteration

Yekan's Recovery

Casters	Beastlord (39)
Casting Skill	Alteration
Target's Reaction	Target feels much better.

Counteract Disease

Casters	Beastlord (49), Cleric (29), Druid (29), Necr. (39), Paladin (56), Sham. (24)
Mana Cost	50
Casting Skill	Alteration
Casting Time	4 sec.
Casting Delay	2.5 sec.
Duration	Instantaneous
Range	100 feet
Target	Anyone
Resistance Invoked	None
Effect	
Disease Reduction	2 chances, 4

Frenzy

Casters	Beastlord (49), Shaman (19)
Mana Cost	35
Casting Skill	Abjuration
Casting Time	2 sec.
Casting Delay	30 sec.
Duration	1 min. + 18 sec/level
Range	None
Target	Yourself
Resistance Invoked	None
Effect	
DEX buff	25
STR buff	15 + 1 / 4 levels (max **28**)
AC buff	15 + 1 / 2 levels (max **35**)
AGI buff	10 + 1 / 2 levels (max **25**)
Target's Reaction	Target goes berserk.

Invigor

Casters	Beastlord (49), Cleric (9), Druid (14), En. (24), Pal. (22), Ran. (30), Sham. (24)
Mana Cost	20
Casting Skill	Alteration
Casting Time	3.5 sec.
Casting Delay	2.5 sec.
Recasting Delay	6 sec.
Duration	12 seconds
Range	100 feet
Target	Anyone
Resistance Invoked	None
Effect	
Restores Fatigue	35
Target's Reaction	Target looks energized. (Your body zings with energy.)

Invisibility

Casters	Beastlord (49), Enchanter (4), Magician (8), Shaman (29), Wizard (16)
Mana Cost	30
Casting Skill	Divination
Casting Time	5 sec.
Casting Delay	2.5 sec.
Duration	20 min.
Range	100 feet
Target	Anyone
Resistance Invoked	None
Effect	
Invisibility	
Target's Reaction	Target fades away. (You vanish.)

Listless Power

Casters	Beastlord (49), Enchanter (29), Shaman (29)
Casting Skill	Alteration
Target's Reaction	Target looks frail.

Protect

Casters	Beastlord (49), Shaman (24)
Mana Cost	75
Casting Skill	Abjuration
Casting Time	6 sec.
Casting Delay	2.5 sec.
Recasting Delay	14.5 sec.
Duration	36 min.
Range	100 feet
Target	Anyone
Resistance Invoked	None
Effect	
AC buff	17 + 1/level (max **45**)
Target's Reaction	Target is covered in a protective aura.

Raging Strength

Casters	Beastlord (49), Shaman (29)
Casting Skill	Alteration
Target's Reaction	Target looks stronger.

Spirit of Kashek

Casters	Beastlord (49)
Casting Skill	Alteration
Target's Reaction	Target has been buffed!

Spirit of Vermin

Casters	Beastlord (49)
Casting Skill	Alteration
Target's Reaction	Target is imbued with the spirit of vermin.

Vigor of Zehkes

Casters	Beastlord (49)
Casting Skill	Alteration

Sha's Lethargy

Casters	Beastlord (50)
Casting Skill	Alteration
Target's Reaction	Target yawns. (You feel drowsy.)

Ultravision

Casters	Beastlord (51), Enchanter (29), Shaman (29)
Casting Skill	Divination
Target's Reaction	Target's eyes glow violet. (Your eyes tingle.)

Aid of Khurenz

Casters	Beastlord (52)
Casting Skill	Alteration

Health

Casters	Beastlord (52), Shaman (34)
Casting Skill	Alteration
Target's Reaction	Target looks healthy.

Spirit of Wind

Casters	Beastlord (52)
Casting Skill	Alteration
Target's Reaction	Target is imbued with the spirits of the four winds.

Venom of the Snake

Casters	Beastlord (52), Necromancer (34), Shaman (39)
Casting Skill	Conjuration
Target's Reaction	Target has been poisoned.

Deftness

Casters	Beastlord (53), Shaman (39)
Casting Skill	Alteration
Target's Reaction	Target looks dexterous.

Resist Poison

Casters	Beastlord (54), Cleric (34), Druid (44), Shaman (39)
Casting Skill	Abjuration
Target's Reaction	Target is resistant to poison.

Spirit of Omakin

Casters	Beastlord (54)
Casting Skill	Alteration

Spirit of the Storm

Casters	Beastlord (54)
Casting Skill	Alteration
Target's Reaction	Target is imbued with the spirit of an ancient storm.

Strength of Stone

Casters	Beastlord (54), Druid (34)
Casting Skill	Alteration
Target's Reaction	Target looks stronger.

Chloroplast

Casters	Beastlord (55), Druid (44), Ranger (55), Shaman (39)
Casting Skill	Alteration
Target's Reaction	Target begins to regenerate.

Omakin's Alacrity

Casters	Beastlord (55)
Casting Skill	Alteration

Sha's Restoration

Casters	Beastlord (55)
Casting Skill	Alteration
Target's Reaction	Target feels rejuvenated.

Incapacitate

Casters	Beastlord (56), Enchanter (44), Shaman (44)
Casting Skill	Alteration
Target's Reaction	Target looks frail.

Shifting Shield

Casters	Beastlord (56), Shaman (34)
Casting Skill	Abjuration
Target's Reaction	Target is surrounded by a shifting spirit shield.

Spirit of Zehkes

Casters	Beastlord (56)
Casting Skill	Alteration

Greater Healing

Casters	Beastlord (57), Cleric (24), Druid (29), Paladin (39), Ranger (57), Shaman (29)
Mana Cost	150
Casting Skill	Alteration
Casting Time	4 sec.
Casting Delay	2.5 sec.
Duration	Instantaneous
Range	100 feet
Target	Anyone
Resistance Invoked	None
Effect	
Healing (HP)	240 + 2/level (max **300**)
Target's Reaction	Target feels much better. (You feel much better.)

Nullify Magic

Casters	Beastlord (58), Cleric (39), Druid (44), Enchanter (29), Magician (34), Necromancer (39), Paladin (58), Ranger (58), Shadow Knight (58), Shaman (44), Wizard (34)
Casting Skill	Abjuration
Target's Reaction	Target feels dispelled.

Spirit of Khurenz

Casters	Beastlord (58)
Casting Skill	Alteration

Talisman of Altuna

Casters	Beastlord (58), Shaman (44)
Casting Skill	Alteration
Target's Reaction	Target looks tougher. (You feel tough.)

Blizzard Blast

Casters	Beastlord (59), Shaman (44)
Casting Skill	Evocation
Target's Reaction	Target staggers as spirits of frost slam against them.

Sha's Ferocity

Casters	Beastlord (59)
Casting Skill	Alteration

Spiritual Purity

Casters	Beastlord (59)
Casting Skill	Alteration
Target's Reaction	Target is enveloped by an aura of spiritual purity.

Alacrity

Casters	Beastlord (60), Enchanter (24), Shaman (44)
Mana Cost	115
Casting Skill	Alteration
Casting Time	4 sec.
Casting Delay	2.5 sec.
Duration	1 min. + 12 sec/level (max. **11 min.**)
Range	100 feet
Target	Anyone
Resistance Invoked	None
Effect	
Attack Speed buff	22% + 1% / 2 levels (max 40%)
Target's Reaction	Target feels much faster.

Spirit of Kati Sha

Casters	Beastlord (60)
Casting Skill	Alteration

Spiritual Strength

Casters	Beastlord (60)
Casting Skill	Alteration
Target's Reaction	Target looks tougher. (You feel tough.)

Cleric

Sanctuary

Casters	Cleric (9)
Mana Cost	25
Casting Skill	Divination
Casting Time	2.5 sec.
Casting Delay	2.5 sec.
Recasting Delay	7.5 sec.
Duration	10 hours
Range	None
Radius of Effect	40 feet
Target	Location
Resistance Invoked	None
Effect	
You are notified of anything entering the area	
Target's Reaction	Target is at peace.

Celestial Remedy

Casters	Cleric (19)
Mana Cost	190
Casting Skill	Alteration
Casting Time	4 sec.
Casting Delay	2.5 sec.
Duration	24 sec.
Range	100 feet
Target	Anyone
Resistance Invoked	None
Effect	
Heals HP every 6 sec. (HoT)	35 + 1/level (max 65 / 6 sec.)
Target's Reaction	Target's body is covered with a soft glow. (Celestial light pumps through your body.)

Imbue Amber

Casters	Cleric (29), Shaman (29)
Casting Skill	Alteration

Imbue Black Pearl

Casters	Cleric (29)
Casting Skill	Alteration

Imbue Black Sapphire

Casters	Cleric (29)
Casting Skill	Alteration

Imbue Diamond

Casters	Cleric (29)
Casting Skill	Alteration

Imbue Emerald

Casters	Cleric (29), Druid (29)
Casting Skill	Alteration

Imbue Opal

Casters	Cleric (29)
Casting Skill	Alteration

Imbue Peridot

Casters	Cleric (29)
Casting Skill	Alteration

Imbue Plains Pebble

Casters	Cleric (29), Druid (29)
Casting Skill	Alteration

Imbue Rose Quartz

Casters	Cleric (29)
Casting Skill	Alteration

Imbue Ruby

Casters	Cleric (29)
Casting Skill	Alteration

Imbue Sapphire

Casters	Cleric (29), Shaman (29)
Casting Skill	Alteration

Imbue Topaz

Casters	Cleric (29)
Casting Skill	Alteration

Sermon of the Righteous

Casters	Cleric (29)
Casting Skill	Evocation
Target's Reaction	Target shrieks in pain.

Armor of Protection

Casters	Cleric (34)
Casting Skill	Abjuration
Target's Reaction	Target looks protected.

Sacred Word

Casters	Cleric (39)
Casting Skill	Evocation
Target's Reaction	Target is stunned.

Celestial Healing

Casters	Cleric (44)
Casting Skill	Alteration
Target's Reaction	Target's body is covered with a soft glow. (Celestial light pumps through your body.)

Armor of the Faithful

Casters	Cleric (49)
Casting Skill	Abjuration
Target's Reaction	Target looks protected.

Improved Invis to Undead

Casters	Cleric (50), Necromancer (50)
Casting Skill	Divination
Target's Reaction	Target fades a little. (You feel your skin tingle.)

Epitaph of Life

Casters	Cleric (52)
Casting Skill	Evocation
Target's Reaction	Target staggers under the weight of divine words. (You stagger as the light of divine words enter your mind.)

Heroic Bond

Casters	Cleric (52)
Casting Skill	Abjuration
Target's Reaction	Target's eyes gleam with heroic resolution. (You feel heroic.)

Mark of Retribution

Casters	Cleric (54)
Casting Skill	Abjuration
Target's Reaction	Target's skin gleams with a dull red aura.

Stun Command

Casters	Cleric (55)
Casting Skill	Evocation
Target's Reaction	Target is stunned.

Judgement

Casters	Cleric (56)
Casting Skill	Evocation
Target's Reaction	Target has been struck by the judgement of the gods. (You have been struck down by the judgement of the gods.)

Blessed Armor of the Risen

Casters	Cleric (58)
Casting Skill	Abjuration
Target's Reaction	Target looks protected.

Naltron's Mark

Casters	Cleric (58)
Casting Skill	Abjuration
Target's Reaction	Target is cloaked in a shimmer of glowing symbols. (A mystic symbol flashes before your eyes.)

Aegolism

Casters	Cleric (60)
Casting Skill	Abjuration
Target's Reaction	Target's eye gleams with the power of Aegolism.

Blessing of Aegolism

Casters	Cleric (60)
Casting Skill	Abjuration
Target's Reaction	Target's eye gleams with the power of Aegolism.

Druid

Tangling Weeds

Casters	Druid (1), Ranger (9)
Mana Cost	15
Casting Skill	Alteration
Casting Time	2 sec.
Casting Delay	2.5 sec.
Recasting Delay	6.5 sec.
Duration	10 min. + 1 min/level
Range	200 feet
Target	Anyone
Resistance Invoked	Magic
Effect	
Speed debuff	-40% - 1% / level (max -45%)
Target's Reaction	Target's movements slow as their feet are covered in tangling weeds.

Protection of Wood

Casters	Druid (9)
Mana Cost	25
Casting Skill	Abjuration
Casting Time	4.5 sec.
Casting Delay	2.5 sec.
Recasting Delay	8.5 sec.
Duration	27 min.
Range	100 feet
Radius of Effect	65 feet
Target	Your Group
Resistance Invoked	None
Effect	
AC buff	10 + 1 / 2 levels (max 15)
HP buff	10 + 1/level (max 20)
(must heal to get HP buff)	
Target's Reaction	Target's skin turns hard as wood.

Protection of Rock

Casters	Druid (19)
Mana Cost	150
Casting Skill	Abjuration
Casting Time	6.5 sec.
Casting Delay	2.5 sec.
Recasting Delay	10.5 sec.
Duration	27 min.
Range	100 feet
Radius of Effect	65 feet
Target	Your Group
Resistance Invoked	None
Effect	
AC buff	25
HP buff	40 + 1/level
Target's Reaction	Target's skin turns hard as stone.

Ring of Surefall Glade

Casters	Druid (19)
Mana Cost	150
Casting Skill	Alteration
Casting Time	7 sec.
Casting Delay	2.5 sec.
Recasting Delay	12.5 sec.
Duration	Instantaneous
Range	None
Target	Yourself
Resistance Invoked	None
Effect	
	Teleports you to Surefall Glade
Target's Reaction	Target fades away.

Ring of the Combines

Casters	Druid (24)
Mana Cost	150
Casting Skill	Alteration
Casting Time	7 sec.
Casting Delay	2.5 sec.
Recasting Delay	12.5 sec.
Duration	Instantaneous
Range	None
Target	Yourself
Resistance Invoked	None
Effect	
Teleports you to The Dreadlands	
Target's Reaction	Target fades away.

Imbue Emerald

Casters	Cleric (29), Druid (29)
Casting Skill	Alteration

Imbue Plains Pebble

Casters	Cleric (29), Druid (29)
Casting Skill	Alteration

Circle of Surefall Glade

Casters	Druid (29)
Casting Skill	Alteration
Target's Reaction	Target creates a mystic portal.

Protection of Steel

Casters	Druid (29)
Casting Skill	Abjuration
Target's Reaction	Target's skin turns hard as steel.

Circle of Iceclad

Casters	Druid (34)
Casting Skill	Alteration
Target's Reaction	Target creates a mystic portal.

Fury of Air

Casters	Druid (34)
Casting Skill	Evocation
Target's Reaction	Target has been struck by lightning. (Lightning surges through your body.)

Ring of Great Divide

Casters	Druid (34)
Casting Skill	Alteration
Target's Reaction	Target fades away.

Ring of Iceclad

Casters	Druid (34)
Casting Skill	Alteration
Target's Reaction	Target fades away.

Circle of Great Divide

Casters	Druid (39)
Casting Skill	Alteration
Target's Reaction	Target creates a mystic portal.

Protection of Diamond

Casters	Druid (39)
Casting Skill	Abjuration
Target's Reaction	Target's skin turns hard as diamond.

Ring of Cobalt Scar

Casters	Druid (39)
Casting Skill	Alteration
Target's Reaction	Target fades away.

Ring of Wakening Lands

Casters	Druid (39)
Casting Skill	Alteration
Target's Reaction	Target fades away.

Ro's Fiery Sundering

Casters	Druid (39)
Casting Skill	Evocation
Target's Reaction	Target is immolated by blazing flames.

Circle of Cobalt Scar

Casters	Druid (44)
Casting Skill	Alteration
Target's Reaction	Target creates a mystic portal.

Circle of Wakening Lands

Casters	Druid (44)
Casting Skill	Alteration
Target's Reaction	Target creates a shimmering portal.

Fixation of Ro

Casters	Druid (44)
Casting Skill	Alteration
Target's Reaction	Target is surrounded by an outline of cold flame.

Protection of Nature

Casters	Druid (49)
Casting Skill	Abjuration
Target's Reaction	Target's skin shimmers with divine power.

Improved Superior Camouflage

Casters	Druid (50)
Casting Skill	Divination
Target's Reaction	Target fades away. (You vanish.)

Foliage Shield

Casters	Druid (52)
Casting Skill	Divination
Target's Reaction	Target is surrounded by mystical foliage.

Spirit of Eagle

Casters	Druid (54)
Casting Skill	Alteration
Target's Reaction	Target's body pulses with an avian spirit.

Chloroblast

Casters	Druid (55), Shaman (55)
Casting Skill	Alteration
Target's Reaction	Target is blasted with chlorophyll.

Nature Walkers Behest

Casters	Druid (55)
Casting Skill	Conjuration
Target's Reaction	Target summons a spirit of nature.

Ro's Smoldering Disjunction

Casters	Druid (56)
Casting Skill	Alteration
Target's Reaction	Target is surrounded by an outline of cold flame.

Circle of Seasons

Casters	Druid (58)
Casting Skill	Abjuration
Target's Reaction	Target is surrounded by a swirling seasonal haze.

Nature's Recovery

Casters	Druid (60)
Casting Skill	Alteration
Target's Reaction	Target begins to regenerate.

Nature's Touch

Casters	Druid (60)
Casting Skill	Alteration
Target's Reaction	Target feels much better.

Protection of the Glades

Casters	Druid (60)
Casting Skill	Abjuration
Target's Reaction	Target's skin shimmers.

Enchanter

Enchant Clay

Casters	Enchanter (8)
Mana Cost	60
Casting Skill	Alteration
Component	Large Block of Clay
Casting Time	6 sec.
Casting Delay	2.5 sec.
Duration	Instantaneous
Range	None
Target	Yourself
Resistance Invoked	None
Effect	
Summons Enchanted Large Block of Clay	

Intellectual Advancement

Casters	Enchanter (12)
Mana Cost	35
Casting Skill	Alteration
Casting Time	4 sec.
Casting Delay	2.5 sec.
Recasting Delay	4.5 sec.
Duration	27 min.
Range	100 feet
Target	Anyone
Resistance Invoked	None
Effect	
Raises caster's level when checking for fizzle	3 levels
Target's Reaction	Target's mind sharpens. (Your mind sharpens.)

Intellectual Superiority

Casters	Enchanter (20)
Mana Cost	70
Casting Skill	Alteration
Casting Time	4 sec.
Casting Delay	2.5 sec.
Recasting Delay	4.5 sec.
Duration	27 min.
Range	100 feet
Target	Anyone
Resistance Invoked	None
Effect	
Raises caster's level when checking for fizzle	6 levels
Target's Reaction	Target's mind sharpens. (Your mind sharpens.)

Haunting Visage

Casters	Enchanter (29)
Casting Skill	Conjuration
Target's Reaction	Target takes on a threatening visage.

Gift of Magic

Casters	Enchanter (34)
Casting Skill	Alteration
Target's Reaction	Target appears to be staring into nothingness. (Your thoughts begin to race and flow faster.)

Calming Visage

Casters	Enchanter (39)
Casting Skill	Conjuration
Target's Reaction	Target takes on a non-threatening visage.

Wandering Mind

Casters	Enchanter (39)
Casting Skill	Conjuration
Target's Reaction	Target stares off into space. (You forget what you were supposed to be ....)

Summon Companion

Casters	Beastlord (39), Enchanter (44), Magician (39), Necromancer (44), Shadow Knight (52), Shaman (44)
Casting Skill	Conjuration
Target's Reaction	Target summons a companion to their side.

Boon of the Garou

Casters	Enchanter (44)
Casting Skill	Divination
Target's Reaction	Target's face contorts and stretches, the skin breaking and peeling. (You feel ... strange.)

Enchant Velium

Casters	Enchanter (44)
Casting Skill	Alteration

Enchant Adamantite

Casters	Enchanter (49)
Casting Skill	Alteration

Enchant Brellium

Casters	Enchanter (49)
Casting Skill	Alteration

Enchant Mithril

Casters	Enchanter (49)
Casting Skill	Alteration

Enchant Steel

Casters	Enchanter (49)
Casting Skill	Alteration

Illusion: Imp

Casters	Enchanter (49)
Casting Skill	Divination
Target's Reaction	Target's image shimmers. (You feel different.)

Improved Invisibility

Casters	Enchanter (50), Wizard (55)
Casting Skill	Divination
Target's Reaction	Target fades away. (You vanish.)

Tricksters Augmentation

Casters	Enchanter (52)
Casting Skill	Divination

Beguiling Visage

Casters	Enchanter (54)
Casting Skill	Conjuration
Target's Reaction	Target takes on a beguiling visage.

Illusion: Vah Shir

Casters	Enchanter (54)
Casting Skill	Divination
Target's Reaction	Target's image shimmers. (You feel different.)

Gift of Insight

Casters	Enchanter (55)
Casting Skill	Alteration
Target's Reaction	Target appears to be staring into nothingness. (Your thoughts begin to race and flow faster.)

Horrifying Visage

Casters	Enchanter (56)
Casting Skill	Conjuration
Target's Reaction	Target takes on a threatening visage.

Glamorous Visage

Casters	Enchanter (58)
Casting Skill	Conjuration
Target's Reaction	Target takes on a non-threatening visage.

Spellshield

Casters	Enchanter (58)
Casting Skill	Abjuration
Target's Reaction	Target is surrounded by a barrier of magical energies.

Gift of Brilliance

Casters	Enchanter (60)
Casting Skill	Alteration
Target's Reaction	Target appears to be staring into nothingness. (Your thoughts begin to race and flow faster.)

Koadic's Endless Intellect

Casters	Enchanter (60)
Casting Skill	Alteration
Target's Reaction	Target's mind expands beyond the bounds of space and time.

Magician

Summon Elemental Defender

Casters	Magician (12)
Mana Cost	40
Casting Skill	Conjuration
Casting Time	6 sec.
Casting Delay	2.5 sec.
Recasting Delay	8.5 sec.
Duration	Instantaneous
Range	None
Target	Yourself
Resistance Invoked	None
Effect	
Create Item	1 Elemental Defender

Summon Phantom Leather

Casters	Magician (20)
Mana Cost	100
Casting Skill	Conjuration
Casting Time	6 sec.
Casting Delay	2.5 sec.
Recasting Delay	8.5 sec.
Duration	Instantaneous
Range	None
Target	Yourself
Resistance Invoked	None
Effect	
Create Item	Complete leather armor (no rent: it disappears when you log out)
Target's Reaction	(You summon a suit of Phantom Leather armor.)

Expedience

Casters	Magician (29)
Casting Skill	Alteration
Target's Reaction	Target shimmers and blurs.

Summon Phantom Chain

Casters	Magician (29)
Casting Skill	Conjuration
Target's Reaction	(You summon a suit of Phantom Chain armor.)

Monster Summoning I

Casters	Magician (34)
Casting Skill	Conjuration

Summon Shard of the Core

Casters	Magician (34)
Casting Skill	Conjuration

Summon Companion

Casters	Beastlord (39), Enchanter (44), Magician (39), Necromancer (44), Shadow Knight (52), Shaman (44)
Casting Skill	Conjuration
Target's Reaction	Target summons a companion to their side.

Summon Phantom Plate

Casters	Magician (39)
Casting Skill	Conjuration
Target's Reaction	(You summon a suit of Phantom Plate armor.)

Elemental Maelstrom

Casters	Magician (44)
Casting Skill	Evocation
Target's Reaction	Target's skin shreds and tears as bolts of elemental power strike. (Your skin tears and melts as bolts of elemental power strike you.)

Summon Elemental Blanket

Casters	Magician (49)
Casting Skill	Conjuration

Monster Summoning II

Casters	Magician (50)
Casting Skill	Conjuration

Transons Elemental Infusion

Casters	Magician (52)
Casting Skill	Conjuration
Target's Reaction	Target is infused with elemental energy.

Veil of Elements

Casters	Magician (54)
Casting Skill	Divination
Target's Reaction	Target is hidden by a veil of elements. (A veil of elements hides you from sight.)

Burnout IV

Casters	Magician (55)
Casting Skill	Alteration
Target's Reaction	Target goes berserk.

Wrath of the Elements

Casters	Magician (55)
Casting Skill	Evocation
Target's Reaction	Target is assaulted by the wrath of the elements. (Your body is consumed by the wrath of the elements.)

Rod of Mystical Transvergance

Casters	Magician (56)
Casting Skill	Conjuration

Transons Phantasmal Protection

Casters	Magician (58)
Casting Skill	Abjuration
Target's Reaction	Target is surrounded by a phantasmal protection.

Valiant Companion

Casters	Magician (59)
Casting Skill	Alteration
Target's Reaction	Target has become fearless!

Monster Summoning III

Casters	Magician (60)
Casting Skill	Conjuration

Shock of Fiery Blades

Casters	Magician (60)
Casting Skill	Conjuration
Target's Reaction	Target is seared by a thousand fiery blades.

Necromancer

Focus Death

Casters	Necromancer (12)
Mana Cost	35
Casting Skill	Alteration
Casting Time	3 sec.
Casting Delay	2.5 sec.
Recasting Delay	32.5 sec.
Duration	1 min. + 18 sec/level (max. 15 min.)
Range	100 feet
Target	Your Pet
Resistance Invoked	None
Effect	
Attack Speed buff	10% + 1% / 5 levels (max 15%)
STR buff	12 + 1 / 4 levels (max 20)
AC buff	12 + 1 / 4 levels (max 20)
Target's Reaction	Target's eyes gleam with madness.

Shackle of Bone

Casters	Necromancer (20)
Mana Cost	80
Casting Skill	Alteration
Casting Time	2.5 sec.
Casting Delay	2.5 sec.
Recasting Delay	7.5 sec.
Duration	12 sec. + 6 sec/2 levels
Range	200 feet
Target	Undead
Resistance Invoked	Magic
Effect	
Attack Speed debuff	-20% - 1% / 4 levels (max -60%)
Target's Reaction	Target is hindered by a shackle of bone.

Eternities Torment

Casters	Necromancer (29)
Casting Skill	Alteration
Target's Reaction	Target is tortured by a reflection of eternity without rest.

Torbas Acid Blast

Casters	Necromancer (34)
Casting Skill	Conjuration
Target's Reaction	Target is blasted by a jet of acid. (A blast of acid eats at your skin.)

Chilling Embrace

Casters	Necromancer (39)
Casting Skill	Alteration
Target's Reaction	Target is wracked by chilling poison.

Shackle of Spirit

Casters	Necromancer (39)
Casting Skill	Alteration
Target's Reaction	Target is hindered by a shackle of spirit.

Summon Companion

Casters	Beastlord (39), Ench. (44), Mag. (39), Necromancer (44), SK (52), Sham. (44)
Casting Skill	Conjuration
Target's Reaction	Target summons a companion to their side.

Corpal Empathy

Casters	Necromancer (44)
Casting Skill	Alteration
Target's Reaction	Target's wounds disappear.

Dead Man Floating

Casters	Necromancer (44)
Casting Skill	Abjuration
Target's Reaction	Target looks dead. (You become like the dead.)

Incinerate Bones

Casters	Necromancer (44)
Casting Skill	Evocation
Target's Reaction	Target shrieks as their bones are set ablaze.

Insidious Retrogression

Casters	Necromancer (49)
Casting Skill	Conjuration
Target's Reaction	Target's body is pelted by spores.

Improved Invis to Undead

Casters	Cleric (50), Necromancer (50)
Casting Skill	Divination
Target's Reaction	Target fades a little. (You feel your skin tingle.)

Degeneration

Casters	Necromancer (52)
Casting Skill	Alteration
Target's Reaction	Target weakens. (You feel your vitality dwindle.)

Succussion of Shadows

Casters	Necromancer (54)
Casting Skill	Alteration
Target's Reaction	Target shakes violently as their body is assaulted by living shadows.

Augmentation of Death

Casters	Necromancer (55)
Casting Skill	Alteration
Target's Reaction	Target's eyes gleam with madness.

Conglaciation of Bone

Casters	Necromancer (55)
Casting Skill	Evocation
Target's Reaction	Target's bones freezes and crack. (You feel your bones harden and crack from the frost.)

Crippling Claudication

Casters	Necromancer (56)
Casting Skill	Alteration
Target's Reaction	Target begins to have trouble moving their arms. (Your arms become heavy.)

Mind Wrack

Casters	Necromancer (58)
Casting Skill	Alteration
Target's Reaction	Target staggers. (You feel your mana drain away.)

Arch Lich

Casters	Necromancer (60)
Casting Skill	Alteration
Target's Reaction	Target's skin peels away. (You feel the skin peel from your bones.)

Zevfeer's Theft of Vitae

Casters	Necromancer (60)
Casting Skill	Alteration
Target's Reaction	Target staggers as a rush of blood leaves their body. (You feel a rush of blood leave your body.)

Paladin

Cease

Casters	Paladin (9)
Mana Cost	15
Casting Skill	Evocation
Casting Time	1.5 sec.
Casting Delay	2.5 sec.
Recasting Delay	11.5 sec.
Duration	Instantaneous
Range	200 feet
Target	Anyone
Resistance Invoked	Magic
Effect	
Stun	1 sec.
Target's Reaction	Target is stunned.

Desist

Casters	Paladin (15)
Mana Cost	25
Casting Skill	Evocation
Casting Time	2 sec.
Casting Delay	2.5 sec.
Recasting Delay	12.5 sec.
Duration	Instantaneous
Range	200 feet
Target	Anyone
Resistance Invoked	Magic
Effect	
Stun	2.5 sec.
Target's Reaction	Target is stunned.

Instrument of Nife

Casters	Paladin (30)
Casting Skill	Abjuration
Target's Reaction	Target's weapon becomes an instrument of Rodcet Nife. (A brilliant blue aura surrounds your weapon.)

Divine Purpose

Casters	Paladin (39)
Casting Skill	Alteration
Target's Reaction	Target's eyes are filled by the flame of a divine purpose. (A flame of divine purpose compels you.)

Divine Vigor

Casters	Paladin (39)
Casting Skill	Alteration
Target's Reaction	Target begins to radiate with divine favor.

Thunder of Karana

Casters	Paladin (49)
Casting Skill	Evocation
Target's Reaction	Target's ears fill with the deafening roar of Karana's Thunder.

Valor of Marr

Casters	Paladin (49)
Casting Skill	Alteration
Target's Reaction	Target feels the blessing of Mithaniel Marr.

Flame of Light

Casters	Paladin (50)
Casting Skill	Evocation
Target's Reaction	Target's body erupts in a flame of divine light. (A flame of divine light erupts around you.)

Divine Glory

Casters	Paladin (53)
Casting Skill	Alteration
Target's Reaction	Target begins to radiate with divine glory.

Quelious' Words of Tranquility

Casters	Paladin (54)
Casting Skill	Evocation
Target's Reaction	Target is stunned by words of tranquility.

Wave of Healing

Casters	Paladin (55)
Casting Skill	Alteration
Target's Reaction	Target is surrounded by a wave of healing. (A wave of of healing washes over you.)

Breath of Tunare

Casters	Paladin (56)
Casting Skill	Alteration
Target's Reaction	Target is washed over by the breath of Tunare. (You feel the cleansing breath of Tunare surround you.)

Celestial Cleansing

Casters	Paladin (59)
Casting Skill	Alteration
Target's Reaction	Target's body is covered with a soft glow. (Celestial light pumps through your body.)

Brell's Mountainous Barrier

Casters	Paladin (60)
Casting Skill	Alteration
Target's Reaction	Target begins to radiate with divine strength.

Divine Strength

Casters	Paladin (60)
Casting Skill	Alteration
Target's Reaction	Target begins to radiate with divine strength.

Ranger

Tangling Weeds

Casters	Druid (1), Ranger (9)
Mana Cost	15
Casting Skill	Alteration
Casting Time	2 sec.
Casting Delay	2.5 sec.
Recasting Delay	6.5 sec.
Duration	10 min. + 1 min/level
Range	200 feet
Target	Anyone
Resistance Invoked	Magic
Effect	
Speed debuff	-40% - 1% / level (max **-45%**)
Target's Reaction	Target's movements slow as their feet are covered in tangling weeds.

Hawk Eye

Casters	Ranger (15)
Mana Cost	25
Casting Skill	Alteration
Casting Time	3 sec.
Casting Delay	2.5 sec.
Recasting Delay	5.5 sec.
Duration	1 min. + 12 sec/level
Range	None
Target	Yourself
Resistance Invoked	None
Effect	
Archery hit buff	10%
Target's Reaction	Target's eyes sharpen with an aura of avian presence.

Riftwind's Protection

Casters	Ranger (30)
Casting Skill	Abjuration
Target's Reaction	Target's skin glows with a pale greenish tint.

Call of Sky

Casters	Ranger (39)
Casting Skill	Alteration
Target's Reaction	Target's weapons gleam. (The Call of Sky fills your weapons with power.)

Natures Precision

Casters	Ranger (39)
Casting Skill	Evocation
Target's Reaction	Target becomes one with their weapons.

Force of Nature

Casters	Ranger (49)
Casting Skill	Alteration
Target's Reaction	Target becomes a force of nature.

Call of Earth

Casters	Ranger (50)
Casting Skill	Abjuration
Target's Reaction	Target's body is surrounded by the Call of Earth. (The Call of Earth surrounds your body protectively.)

Strength of Nature

Casters	Ranger (51)
Casting Skill	Abjuration
Target's Reaction	Target's body is strengthened by nature. (Nature's strength flows through your muscles.)

Falcon Eye

Casters	Ranger (52)
Casting Skill	Alteration
Target's Reaction	Target's eyes sharpen with an aura of avian presence.

Jolting Blades

Casters	Ranger (54)
Casting Skill	Conjuration
Target's Reaction	Target's weapons buzz with a magical aura.

Call of Fire

Casters	Ranger (55)
Casting Skill	Alteration
Target's Reaction	Target's weapons gleam. (The Call of Fire fills your weapons with power.)

Cinder Jolt

Casters	Ranger (55)
Casting Skill	Alteration
Target's Reaction	Target's head snaps back.

Mark of the Predator

Casters	Ranger (56)
Casting Skill	Abjuration
Target's Reaction	Target growls as a whisper of the predator pervades the air. (The spirit of the predator strengthens your attacks.)

Eagle Eye

Casters	Ranger (58)
Casting Skill	Alteration
Target's Reaction	Target's eyes sharpen with an aura of avian presence. (Your eyes sharpen with an aura of avian presence.)

Call of the Predator

Casters	Ranger (60)
Casting Skill	Abjuration
Target's Reaction	Target growls as a whisper of the predator pervades the air. (The spirit of the predator strengthens your attacks.)

Warder's Protection

Casters	Ranger (60)
Casting Skill	Abjuration
Target's Reaction	Target's skin glows with a vibrant greenish tint.

Shadow Knight

Despair

Casters	Shadow Knight (9)
Mana Cost	12
Casting Skill	Alteration
Casting Time	2 sec.
Casting Delay	2.5 sec.
Recasting Delay	5 sec.
Duration	1 min. + 6 sec./level
Range	100 feet
Target	Anyone
Resistance Invoked	Magic
Effect	
Attack Skill debuff	-5
Target's Reaction	Target is lost in a fit of despair.

Scream of Hate

Casters	Shadow Knight (15)
Mana Cost	85
Casting Skill	Alteration
Casting Time	1.5 sec.
Casting Delay	2.5 sec.
Recasting Delay	8.5 sec.
Duration	10 min.
Range	200 feet
Target	Drain
Resistance Invoked	Magic
Effect	
Drain ATK to caster	8
Target's Reaction	Target is washed over by a wave of shadows. (You feel a gutwrenching hatred.)

Strengthen Death

Casters	Shadow Knight (29)
Casting Skill	Alteration
Target's Reaction	Target's eyes gleam with madness.

Scream of Pain

Casters	Shadow Knight (30)
Casting Skill	Alteration
Target's Reaction	Target is engulfed in a seething mass of darkness.

Scream of Death

Casters	Shadow Knight (39)
Casting Skill	Alteration
Target's Reaction	Target's hands are covered by a nimbus of deathly darkness.

Shroud of Hate

Casters	Shadow Knight (39)
Casting Skill	Alteration
Target's Reaction	Target is washed over by a wave of shadows. (You feel a gutwrenching hatred.)

Shroud of Pain

Casters	Shadow Knight (50)
Casting Skill	Alteration
Target's Reaction	Target is engulfed in a seething mass of darkness.

Summon Corpse

Casters	Necromancer (39), Shadow Knight (51)
Casting Skill	Conjuration

Summon Companion

Casters	Beastlord (39), Enchanter (44), Magician (39), Necromancer (44), Shadow Knight (52), Shaman (44)
Casting Skill	Conjuration
Target's Reaction	Target summons a companion to their side.

Abduction of Strength

Casters	Shadow Knight (52)
Casting Skill	Alteration
Target's Reaction	Target weakens. (You feel your strength dwindle.)

Mental Corruption

Casters	Shadow Knight (52)
Casting Skill	Alteration
Target's Reaction	Target is surrounded by a sickly green nimbus.

Torrent of Hate

Casters	Shadow Knight (54)
Casting Skill	Alteration
Target's Reaction	Target is washed over by a wave of shadows. (You feel a gutwrenching hatred.)

Shroud of Death

Casters	Shadow Knight (55)
Casting Skill	Alteration
Target's Reaction	Target's hands are covered by a nimbus of deathly darkness.

Torrent of Pain

Casters	Shadow Knight (56)
Casting Skill	Alteration
Target's Reaction	Target is engulfed in a seething mass of darkness.

Torrent of Fatigue

Casters	Shadow Knight (58)
Casting Skill	Alteration
Target's Reaction	Target weakens. (You feel your vitality dwindle.)

Cloak of the Akheva

Casters	Shadow Knight (60)
Casting Skill	Conjuration
Target's Reaction	Target is surrounded by the chilling protection of a living shadow. (Your body is encased by a living shadow.)

Death Peace

Casters	Shadow Knight (60)
Casting Skill	Abjuration
Target's Reaction	Target dies.

Shaman

Talisman of the Beast

Casters	Shaman (9)
Mana Cost	25
Casting Skill	Alteration
Casting Time	3 sec.
Casting Delay	2.5 sec.
Duration	27 min.
Range	100 feet
Target	Your Group
Resistance Invoked	None
Effect	
STR buff	10
Target's Reaction	Target looks stronger. (You feel stronger.)

Grow

Casters	Shaman (19)
Mana Cost	50
Casting Skill	Alteration
Indoors only	
Casting Time	4 sec.
Casting Delay	2.5 sec.
Duration	Instantaneous
Range	200 feet
Target	Anyone
Resistance Invoked	None
Effect	
Increase Size	33% larger than normal
Target's Reaction	Target grows taller. (You feel bigger.)

Imbue Amber

Casters	Cleric (29), Shaman (29)
Casting Skill	Alteration

Imbue Sapphire

Casters	Cleric (29), Shaman (29)
Casting Skill	Alteration

Form of the Bear

Casters	Shaman (29)
Casting Skill	Alteration
Target's Reaction	Target turns into a bear. (The spirit of the bear blesses you.)

Imbue Ivory

Casters	Shaman (29)
Casting Skill	Alteration

Imbue Jade

Casters	Shaman (29)
Casting Skill	Alteration

Shock of the Tainted

Casters	Shaman (34)
Casting Skill	Conjuration
Target's Reaction	Target screams in pain. (Your body is wracked by shocks of poison.)

Spirit of Bih'Li

Casters	Shaman (39)
Casting Skill	Alteration
Target's Reaction	Target is surrounded by a brief lupine aura. (You feel the spirit of wolf enter you.)

Tumultuous Strength

Casters	Shaman (39)
Casting Skill	Alteration
Target's Reaction	Target looks stronger.

Summon Companion

Casters	Beastlord (39), Enchanter (44), Magician (39), Necromancer (44), Shadow Knight (52), Shaman (44)
Casting Skill	Conjuration
Target's Reaction	Target summons a companion to their side.

Blast of Poison

Casters	Shaman (44)
Casting Skill	Conjuration
Target's Reaction	Target screams in pain. (Your body is wracked by shocks of poison.)

Harnessing of Spirit

Casters	Shaman (49)
Casting Skill	Alteration
Target's Reaction	Target looks tougher. (You feel tough.)

Spirit Quickening

Casters	Shaman (50)
Casting Skill	Alteration
Target's Reaction	Target foams at the mouth.

Disinfecting Aura

Casters	Shaman (52)
Casting Skill	Alteration
Target's Reaction	Target is bathed in a cleansing aura. (You feel a cleansing aura wash over your body.)

Plague of Insects

Casters	Shaman (54)
Casting Skill	Conjuration
Target's Reaction	Target's motions slow as a plague of insects chews at their skin.

Chloroblast

Casters	Druid (55), Shaman (55)
Casting Skill	Alteration
Target's Reaction	Target is blasted with chlorophyll.

Form of the Great Bear

Casters	Shaman (55)
Casting Skill	Alteration
Target's Reaction	Target turns into a bear. (The spirit of the great bear blesses you.)

Regrowth of Dar Khura

Casters	Shaman (56)
Casting Skill	Alteration
Target's Reaction	Target begins to regenerate.

Cannibalize IV

Casters	Shaman (58)
Casting Skill	Alteration
Target's Reaction	Target winces. (Your body aches as your mind clears.)

Talisman of Epuration

Casters	Shaman (58)
Casting Skill	Abjuration
Target's Reaction	Target has been protected by the Talisman of Epuration.

Focus of Spirit

Casters	Shaman (60)
Casting Skill	Alteration
Target's Reaction	Target looks focused. (You feel focused.)

Khura's Focusing

Casters	Shaman (60)
Casting Skill	Alteration
Target's Reaction	Target looks focused.

Wizard

O'Keils Embers

Casters	Wizard (12)
Mana Cost	35
Casting Skill	Abjuration
Casting Time	3 sec.
Casting Delay	2.5 sec.
Recasting Delay	8.5 sec.
Duration	10 min. + 1 min/level
Range	100 feet
Target	Anyone
Resistance Invoked	Fire
Effect	
Reflect Damage	3
Resist Fire buff	10
Target's Reaction	Target begins to radiate.

Garrisons Mighty Mana Shock

Casters	Wizard (20)
Mana Cost	90
Casting Skill	Evocation
Casting Time	3 sec.
Casting Delay	2.5 sec.
Duration	Instantaneous
Range	200 feet
Target	Anyone
Resistance Invoked	Magic
Effect	
Immed.HP Dam.	102 + 2/level (max 148)
Target's Reaction	Target's skin blisters as it is consumed by pure mana.

Combine Gate

Casters	Wizard (24)
Mana Cost	150
Casting Skill	Alteration
Casting Time	7 sec.
Casting Delay	2.5 sec.
Recasting Delay	12.5 sec.
Duration	Instantaneous
Range	None
Target	Yourself
Resistance Invoked	None
Effect	
Teleports you to The Dreadlands	
Target's Reaction	Target fades away.

Imbue Fire Opal

Casters	Wizard (29)
Casting Skill	Alteration

Minor Familiar

Casters	Wizard (29)
Casting Skill	Conjuration
Target's Reaction	Target summons forth a minor familiar.

Great Divide Gate

Casters	Wizard (34)
Casting Skill	Alteration
Target's Reaction	Target fades away.

Iceclad Gate

Casters	Wizard (34)
Casting Skill	Alteration
Target's Reaction	Target fades away.

Iceclad Portal

Casters	Wizard (34)
Casting Skill	Alteration
Target's Reaction	Target creates a shimmering portal.

O'Keils Flickering Flame

Casters	Wizard (34)
Casting Skill	Abjuration
Target's Reaction	Target begins to radiate.

Cobalt Scar Gate

Casters	Wizard (39)
Casting Skill	Alteration
Target's Reaction	Target fades away.

Elnerick Entombment of Ice

Casters	Wizard (39)
Casting Skill	Evocation
Target's Reaction	Target is entombed by elemental ice.

Great Divide Portal

Casters	Wizard (39)
Casting Skill	Alteration
Target's Reaction	Target creates a shimmering portal.

Invisibility to Undead

Casters	Wizard (39)
Casting Skill	Divination
Target's Reaction	Target fades a little. (You feel your skin tingle.)

Translocate: Combine

Casters	Wizard (39)
Casting Skill	Alteration
Target's Reaction	Target fades away.

Translocate: Fay

Casters	Wizard (39)
Casting Skill	Alteration
Target's Reaction	Target fades away.

Translocate: North

Casters	Wizard (39)
Casting Skill	Alteration
Target's Reaction	Target fades away.

Translocate: Tox

Casters	Wizard (39)
Casting Skill	Alteration
Target's Reaction	Target fades away.

Wakening Lands Gate

Casters	Wizard (39)
Casting Skill	Alteration
Target's Reaction	Target fades away.

Cobalt Scar Portal

Casters	Wizard (44)
Casting Skill	Alteration
Target's Reaction	Target creates a shimmering portal.

Enticement of Flame

Casters	Wizard (44)
Casting Skill	Evocation
Target's Reaction	Target succumbs to the enticement of flame.

Translocate: Cazic

Casters	Wizard (44)
Casting Skill	Alteration
Target's Reaction	Target fades away.

Translocate: Common

Casters	Wizard (44)
Casting Skill	Alteration
Target's Reaction	Target fades away.

Translocate: Nek

Casters	Wizard (44)
Casting Skill	Alteration
Target's Reaction	Target fades away.

Translocate: Ro

Casters	Wizard (44)
Casting Skill	Alteration
Target's Reaction	Target fades away.

Translocate: West

Casters	Wizard (44)
Casting Skill	Alteration
Target's Reaction	Target fades away.

Wakening Lands Portal

Casters	Wizard (44)
Casting Skill	Alteration
Target's Reaction	Target creates a shimmering portal.

Lesser Familiar

Casters	Wizard (49)
Casting Skill	Conjuration
Target's Reaction	Target summons forth a lesser familiar.

Translocate: Cobalt Scar

Casters	Wizard (49)
Casting Skill	Alteration
Target's Reaction	Target fades away.

Translocate: Great Divide

Casters	Wizard (49)
Casting Skill	Alteration
Target's Reaction	Target fades away.

Translocate: Iceclad

Casters	Wizard (49)
Casting Skill	Alteration
Target's Reaction	Target fades away.

Translocate: Wakening Lands

Casters	Wizard (49)
Casting Skill	Alteration
Target's Reaction	Target fades away.

Translocate

Casters	Wizard (50)
Casting Skill	Alteration
Target's Reaction	Target fades away.

Firetrees Familiar Augment

Casters	Wizard (52)
Casting Skill	Alteration
Target's Reaction	Target is covered in a red glow.

Translocate: Group

Casters	Wizard (52)
Casting Skill	Alteration
Target's Reaction	Target fades away.

Familiar

Casters	Wizard (54)
Casting Skill	Conjuration
Target's Reaction	Target summons forth a familiar.

Improved Invisibility

Casters	Enchanter (50), Wizard (55)
Casting Skill	Divination
Target's Reaction	Target fades away. (You vanish.)

Decession

Casters	Wizard (56)
Casting Skill	Alteration
Target's Reaction	Target fades away.

Greater Familiar

Casters	Wizard (60)
Casting Skill	Conjuration
Target's Reaction	Target summons forth a greater familiar.

Hsagra's Wrath

Casters	Wizard (60)
Casting Skill	Evocation
Target's Reaction	Target 's soul is assaulted by the ages.

Ice Spear of Solist

Casters	Wizard (60)
Casting Skill	Evocation
Target's Reaction	Target is struck down by Solist's spear of ice.

Porlos' Fury

Casters	Wizard (60)
Casting Skill	Evocation
Target's Reaction	Target's soul is assaulted by the ages.

Wolves and Mammoths

by Cryth Thistledown, Preserver of Tunare

Snow crunched loudly under the wolf's padded feet. Her gray-white fur bristled as a chill wind picked up force across the Plains of Everfrost. With her face lifted to the moonlit sky, Cryth began a full-throated howl to warn all on the tundra that a wolf hunted tonight. Her sensitive nose tingling with the scent of a fresh trail, she began pursuit of the night's prey.

On a small rise above the tundra, Cryth hunkered down in the snow to study the wooly mammoth herd grazing below her. Near the edge of the herd was an older male, just past his prime, and an easy target for the wolf to take down on her own. As the herd drifted across the tundra in search of food, the wolf began the careful work of isolating her target from the rest of the mammoth herd. As she abruptly charged in and nipped at the creature's heels, the mammoth discovered it no longer had the safety of the herd to protect it. The wooly mammoth was left with little choice but to run further out onto the Plains of Everfrost and away from the safety of the herd.

Satisfied with their location, the wolf began to cast a spell, calling up roots from the earth to entwine the fleeing mammoth. The entrapped mammoth began to trumpet in fear as the wolf again cast a spell, this time using the slow acting Drifting Death which would eventually tire the wooly mammoth until it died. Panting heavily from her exertions and the excitement of the hunt, the wolf rested nearby as she waited for the wooly mammoth she had chosen to die.

Cryth's fur-tipped ears swiveled as she heard another wolf's howl echoing across the tundra. The mammoth was dead now and she had taken the hide and as much of the meat as she could reasonably carry, so there was no need to linger here. Stretching her legs for the long run back to Halas, the wolf's paws barely touched upon the snow as she ran.

Cryth slowed as she approached the Everfrost Peaks and moved to a point just below the pass through the mountains. Hidden from view, she began chanting another spell. The cold air shimmered about the wolf's form as the body elongated and stood upright. Forepaws became shapely hands, thick fur faded into warm leather clothing, the muzzle with sharp canines retracted into the youthful face of a Wood Elf maiden. Tossing her reddish brown hair out of her eyes and tucking part of it behind one sharply pointed ear, Cryth scooped up her backpack and walked past the two Barbarians guarding the pass, looking just like any other adventurer that traveled through the region.

Upon reaching Halas, Cryth boarded the small ferry that transported folks across the small lake to Halas proper. As she disembarked, Cryth turned to the right and made her way directly to Mcdaniel's Smokes & Spirits, her favored tavern for a bit to drink and a bite to eat. She nodded to the bartenders as she passed through the doorway, then made her way upstairs to barter with the merchants there.

A short while later, Cryth returned downstairs and picked up a bottle of Frozen Toe Rum from the bartenders, then left the building. Nearby was a small outdoor oven. Opening her backpack, Cryth removed the mammoth meat and began to prepare steaks using the jug of sauces and bag of spices she had just purchased from the merchants inside.

When the steaks were done she gathered her belongings and carried the meal over to the sled dog pens, making a comfortable seat for herself in the snow. Tossing a couple of steaks for the dogs to enjoy, she uncorked the bottle of Frozen Toe Rum and began to eat, enjoying the antics of the dogs as much as she enjoyed the warm feeling from a hot meal and rum coursing through her body. Dropping the rest of the scraps to the dogs, Cryth waved farewell as she gathered her cloak around her tightly, heading back to Mcdaniel's to sleep for the night. Tomorrow would bring its own adventures, and she would need her rest.

Words to the Wise

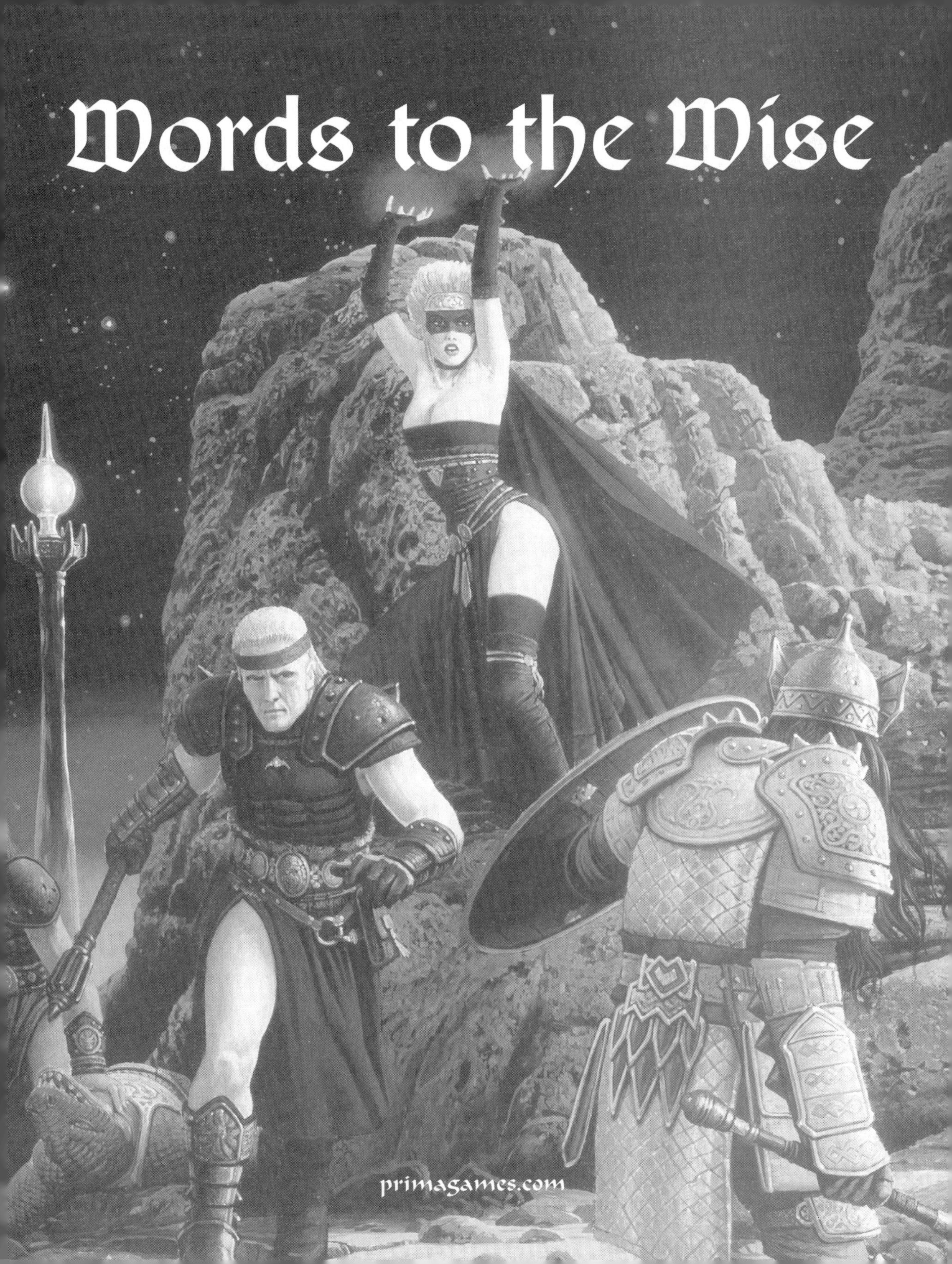

primagames.com

In the case of an online game as massive and complex as EverQuest, *it is impossible to write a book that tells a player what to do. What to do? We assembled a panel of players who are intimately familiar with the game and asked them what they thought a player new to the Luclin area should know. Things may change after this book is printed, but if you're looking from advice from worn and weary adventurers, you need look no further.*

Beastlord/Vah Shir

If you want to wrap your head around the idea of Beastlord, think of a cross between a Monk and a Shammy. The spells that are given are mainly a complement to your basic hand-to-hand melee fighting ability and not a primary method of damage. The Warder is also a supplemental form of damage and is not to be used as a traditional mage pet. Let's say that again: *don't use the Warder as your tank.*

You'll find that about half of the spells are a variety of pet buffs. There are some nice, well-balanced self buffs, such as *Turtle Shell* and *Spirit Strength*. Learn to love and use them.

The fact that the Beastlord gets *Spirit of Wolf* makes sense and is a major plus to the class. Of course there is the same drawback that the Rangers have – i.e., that you only get it at later levels.

Handling Warders

Beastlords are fighters more than spellcasters; consider the warder to be a weapon, and learn to fight well with it.

Know the aggro. Know how much your aggro you pet gives. Sometimes it may tank several blues critters while you just stand back and heal it. That's great until something aggros on you ... you're not *supposed* to be able to do that, but sometimes it works ... and that's a wonderful, beautiful thing.

Not your first class. Pet classes are not for the *EverQuest* novice. Get experience with another class before you try out pets.

First off, Warders are not very powerful. Secondly, they don't do that much damage. Also, be aware that summoning pets is an ability gained at ninth level ... it's not a spell you scribe. That can be confusing to those new to the class.

That being said, the fact that you can call the Warder without a mana expenditure – combined with the fact that the button re-pops automatically – just may allow for some enterprising players to make more use of the Warder than its designers intentioned, but that is more a likeliness than a suggestion or recommendation.

Don't abandon it. While it may be tempting, Beastlords cannot afford to leave the fighting to the pet. They must stand beside their warder and get directly involved with the combat. In fact, Beastlords should be tanking for their pets for the low- to mid-level game. Until you've achieved a high level, your pet's job is to assist you in your fighting.

If your hit points get low, step back and let your pet tank long enough for you a quick heal.

Know the commands. Learn all the pet commands and setup macro keys for them. Some of the important ones are: /pet guard here, /pet guard me, /pet follow me, /pet kill <target> , /pet back off, and /pet get lost. These will be things you use often when managing your warder's actions.

Keep it close. Warders tend to get into trouble fast if you do not keep a short leash on them. When fighting it is best to have your pet guard an area and pull the NPC to your camp spot. Once you get within range of your camp spot, your warder will jump to your aid.

Let's say that one again ... don't let your pet get out of sight, they'll only pick fights with more creatures than they can kill, and there's a good chance that you'll get involved in the fatal battle.

If for some reason your warder gets lost, do not worry. The easiest thing to do is zone into a new area – that will reunite you. It also works for you to leave the game entirely and log back in – he will be at your side when you reappear. If for some reason your warder seems to be confused, get close to him and use the /pet follow me command.

Use spells wisely. Given the choice, use your hitpoint/ac buff line of spells rather than the pet heals ... at least at lower levels. They serve the same purpose – your pet's long term survival – and are more mana efficient. As you progress and learn more healing arts, the healing line of spells get better and more efficient, so use them in the mid to high end part of the game.

All buff spells that can be cast on other players can be used on your warder. He's your ally; treat him like one. You should buff him up whenever mana permits. This is, of course, in *addition* to your spells that are made just for your warder.

Learn your foe's weaknesses. Some are more immune to fire than lightning. Make sure you buff your warder with the most effective battle enhancements for what you are fighting.

Let it die. Warders are very loyal beasts. They are willing to die for their masters. Don't get sentimental. If things get dire, allow your warder to do just that ... die in order that you may live. Leave him to fight to the death, while you seek a safe place to plan your revenge.

Beastlord Training

Pierce? The newbie weapon for a Beastlord is a piercing weapon. That means you could get a bit of a bump if you put a few, if not all, of your training points in piercing. Your first few kills still won't be easy, but after level 2 you'll have a much better time.

Hand-to-Hand? On the other hand, putting your five points into Hand-to-Hand. The logic behind this choice is that a Beastlord is actually designed to fight that way. If you do so, you'll notice that your kills will get easier once you have worked your way up to a 10 defense and a 10 offense.

Just plain fight? It actually works very well to avoid using weapons until teens to mid 20's. Hand-to-Hand works far better –this is, of course, up to personal preference.

Buy extra food and drink. These kitties have a high metabolism, and they go through food faster than most other races.

Loot everything you kill. You never know what may be useful. But you knew that, didn't you?

Don't destroy your acrylia slate. That little guy comes in handy on quests.

Don't get stuck in a rut. As a Beastlord, explore the different fighting abilities open to you and don't ignore Hand-to-Hand.

Go on quests. The Vah Shir have some of the best newbie quests in the game; take advantage of them.

Learn to sew. Tailoring is a really useful skill for a Vah Shir because the world has loads of silk and pelts.

Feed yourself. Hunt. Pick up fruit. Fish for food and sell the extra fish for water. If you live off the land you never have to buy food.

Stay away from sticky foods; they're murder on the fur.

Safe Fall

The innate safe fall of the Vah Shir is incredible. They have to fall a long way before they take damage. If you *do* manage to break the safe fall barrier, you can easily take 100+ damage and kill yourself

Cat Styles

So have you figured out the kinds of cats the various Vah Shir are based on?

Tiger	White Tiger
Panther	Siamese
Cougar	Leopard
Black Jaguar	Lynx

Lost and Found

In the newbie areas you can find some red/blue or red/black things lying on the ground. If you find them, pick them up and turn them into the Shaman who is just left of the palace stairs. At the very least you'll get some experience points, which is a good deal for something that was essentially effortless and free. You'll probably also get some other goodie, which you can use or sell as you prefer.

This is what happens when your pet wanders off ...

... and brings back a load of Frogloks.

Porting to Luclin

by Gnish, Mage of Death

The night was dark and stormy as Gnish made his way to the wizard spires in the Dreadlands. Silently he moved… passing by others within a hand's width, yet no one saw him. A few may have thought the shadows moved, but none were aware of his presence.

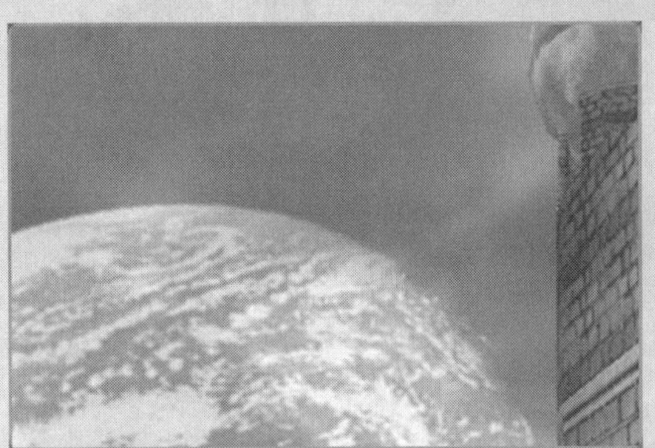

The power emanating from the spires was making the hair around his neck begin to stand up.

"Ah, soon," Gnish thought, as he gazed at the gradient disc of Luclin, the moon that orbits Norath.

So named after the goddess Luclin, the moon was a land of unusual creatures, including the Kerran cats and some Gnome colonies that were thought to have been blown into oblivion by the Erudites. It seemed appropriate that Gnomes would be one of the earlier races to settle the new land. After all, their heritage was one of exploration and discovery. They engineered the ship that discovered Velious, so it was only fitting that they be among the first to the moon.

Suddenly, a deep voice boomed, "Porting to Luclin, Porting to Luclin! Please get your ticket if you haven't already, and step up within the spires. Porting in one minute!"

Eagerly, Gnish stepped up to the corner of one spire and stiffened with anticipation.

This night, his work was to be done in secret. This night, Bertoxxulus's plans would begin to unfold ....

Not for "Real" Newbies

You might want to think twice about playing a Vah Shir if you are brand-new to *EverQuest*. It may look fun – in fact it *is* fun – but it's kind of tough. The quests, mobs and city are different from the rest of Norrath. If you're an absolute newbie, you're probably better off with an easier first experience. Vah Shir are moderate to difficult to play. If you don't feel comfortable with your character, it's possible to become fatally frustrated.

Quests

The team has put a lot of excellent work into the design of this zone. It's absolutely full of quests ... probably the most interactive zone in the game to date. Talk to people! Go on quests!

Don't sneer at the newbie quests! They give you a chance to explore the city and talk to people, and build up experience points.

There may be quests waiting in odd places. These are felines, they are cunning and devious and always where you don't expect them.

The Note

The little hand-in note that you get at the outset is *not* something to be ignored or lost! This is a trip-up for the more experienced players, because none of the old school race/classes had newbie notes that did much besides give a small amount of XP, and maybe a tunic or a weapon. The Vah Shir newbie starts off in a similar situation as the Iksar newbie: the note is key to beginning of a line of valuable and fun quests. If you blow off the newbie quests and ditch the note, you'll be kicking yourself for sure later on.

General Etiquette

By Kevin Freet (Skoriksis)

Never Beg

If there's one thing that drives players crazy, it's people begging for free handouts. Some high-level players dread going into a city because of the mass of tells they might get from lower-level characters looking for free items, free money, powerlevels, or whatever else they think they can get. This is a bad practice to get into. If you think you've come up with the greatest excuse as to why you deserve free stuff ... forget about it, because chances are the person you are begging from has already heard it. Kindness, good conversation, clever roleplaying, being polite, and generally being pleasant will get you a lot further in this game than begging ever will.

Do Your Research

Just because you've never been in a certain situation before doesn't mean you have to be ignorant. It goes back to the Boy Scout motto: "Always be prepared." Many people have taken their own personal time to create web sites about *EverQuest* (which we've listed in **Words to the Wise: Sites** on p. 202) in order to help their fellow *EQ* players. These sites can give you almost anything you ever wanted to know: items, spells, zone locations, maps, monster lists, and much more! Go to these sites and find out about a place before you go there. Keep the maps by your computer. Take some time to learn about the area you're in and where you are going before you go there. Everyone else around you will be thankful for it.

Play For Fun

Sometimes people forget that *EverQuest* is a game. People log in to have fun, but they lose sight of that and become obsessed with a goal, or will go out of their way to be rude to other players. Always remember that there are other real people on the other side of the Wood Elf you're looking at, or that Wizard who's fighting in your group. Real feelings can get hurt, and people will get offended from time to time. Keep in mind that *EQ* is a game. Spend more time choosing a race and class that you will enjoy, and less time trying to figure out the exact combination of equipment, race, class, and stats that will be the most powerful character you can create.

Be Polite

Situations always come up where you find yourself wondering about a spell, a skill, a quest, or just where to go next. Sometimes you find yourself in a bad situation and need a little bit of help from a fellow player, perhaps a stranger. Take this advice from a high-level player: "I'm more apt to help someone who is polite, patient, and doesn't want to be a bother over someone who is rude, pushy, and demands I help them." If you find yourself stumped on something or just want some friendly advice, find someone who can help you. If you are in a guild, ask some of your guildmates. Or maybe you need to ask a player who is higher level than you if they've been in that situation and what they did or would do. If you find yourself wondering something and must ask a total stranger, make sure you are polite when you ask. Start off with a simple, "Hello. I'm sorry to trouble you but I have a question if you aren't terribly busy." Most of the time, people will take a moment to answer your question if they can. If you don't get a response from them, don't keep sending them tells. They could be terribly busy and don't have time to chat. Simply move on to ask someone else. As your mother might have always told you, remember your manners. Remember "please" (not plz), "thank you", and "you're welcome."

Soloing Isn't Always Best

Many people feel they need to pick a class that's a good "solo" class so they can level as fast as possible with as little human contact as is achievable. While this might be one of the fastest ways to get to level 50, it's not always the best choice. Much of the joy that comes from playing *EverQuest* comes from the interaction with your friends and other players in the game. If you spend your entire career playing solo, avoiding groups, and being anti-social, you're going to find it a very lonely existence at the top. *EverQuest* is a group-oriented game. It's meant to be played by working together to achieve a common goal. As the game progresses and you progress in levels, things will change. The game that was so easy for you from 1 to 50 isn't the same game from 50 to 60. Spend time in your character's youth to get to know people. Make friends and hunt with a variety of people. After a while, you'll find that your friends list is always full and people enjoy your company. You can log in, send a tell to one of your friends, and be off and grouping in no time. Some of the best groups in the game are made up of people who've been hunting for 20 levels or more! Just because you can solo doesn't mean you should.

Group Etiquette

By Gnish, Mage of Death

In the lower levels, soloing is a viable option, but eventually you'll find yourself needing to group in order to bring in experience. But why would anyone want to group? Well, for starters, a group brings together different classes that will be beneficial. For instance, a group might choose Enchanters for crowd control and mana regen, tanks to take the damage and pull, Clerics for healing, Druids/Shamans for buffs and damage, etc.

So, what is the proper etiquette for a group?

Use your assist key. If you don't have an assist key, then make one. What you want is a hotkey that directly assists the main puller/tank (e.g., */assist Jietoh*). If you don't know who the main assist is, ask and find out. Nothing makes your Enchanter as mad as when a group member wakes up their mezzed mobs because he or she doesn't know how to or who to assist.

Use aggro management. Only the main tank should be taking a beating from the pulled mob. If you're getting beat on, you need to figure out what you're doing to get the aggro transferred to you. Are you casting high damage spells too soon? Are hitting your taunt key when you shouldn't be? If you aren't doing anything out of the ordinary, then it may be best to let the main tank build aggro by "soloing" the mob for a little bit before anyone else steps in to assist.

Take care of your Cleric. If the Cleric is buffing group members with symbol (which requires a component), then donate a portion of the loot intake to the Cleric. At the upper levels, some groups will designate that any dropped gems or other similar high platinum items (sapphires, ruby crowns, etc.) go to the Cleric. After all, it's a group's responsibility to make sure that their Cleric is reimbursed for the money he or she has to spend in order to properly buff the group.

Forgo the use of offending language. Be it cursing or "Dude" speak ("Phat L33T"). It is just not necessary.

Buff your group. If you are a buffer class, then buff your group. A buffed group is a lethal group. In order to keep track of your buffs, its also good practice to buff yourself first, then other group members. That way, you will see your buff fading first and will then be able to rebuff the rest of the group without them always asking for buffs.

Know your group role. Are you a backup healer? Are you the snarer? Are you supposed to watch for and handle additional mobs (aka "adds")? For instance, there will be times when the Cleric needs help in healing. So, if you are the backup healer, keep a spell loaded. After all, it might be your heal that saves the Enchanter that the Cleric couldn't heal because he had 3 mobs beating on him.

Determine the chain of command. This may seem like a small thing, but there will be times in which you have several people shouting conflicting orders to you. If you know your chain of command, then you know whose orders to follow. A prime example of this would be a pull where you have 5 or so things and one person is telling you to evacuate, while another telling you it's ok, you guys can handle it.

Share the loot. Nothing upsets a group more than one person taking all or most of the loot. Most groups these days will assign a "master looter" to do all the looting. Then, at the end of the night, he will split all the cash and handle the rolls for items that dropped (the 1k and up items, that is).

Call what you have incoming and what you're killing. This is for your main tank and puller. Both should have hotkeys set up that tells the group what they have incoming (/g incoming %T). For those instances where you have several mobs in camp, it's really necessary for the main tank to call out what he is killing (/g Killing %T, please assist), since sometimes, the assist button may not function properly and will return the wrong target.

Have fun. I know, it may be a small thing, but have fun. It *is* a game after all.

Raid Etiquette

By Gnish, Mage of Death

What is the proper etiquette for a raid? Some things are the same:

Use aggro management.

Take care of your Cleric.

Forgo the use of offending language.

Buff your group.

Know your group role.

Share the loot.

Call what you have incoming and what you're killing.

Use your assist key only when asked. In raids do *not* assist until the assist is called. On raids, there will usually be one main tank that fights the mob for 30 seconds or so to build up aggro, before shouting for everyone to get in and assist. Don't assist until told to do so.

Listen to the Raid Leader. It's their raid and their rules, so listen up. Also keep in mind that they are probably receiving a ton of tells, so don't get bent out of shape if your question isn't answered right away.

Bring your fee to the raid. If the raid calls for you to bring 10 peridots and 50 pp, then bring it. If you don't, then the odds are high you won't be coming back. The Raid Leader puts a fee out to make sure that all Clerics are reimbursed for their symbols as well as Enchanters and other additional raid costs (Sky, for example, will require coffins for summoning).

Know the possible loot drops. Look up the possible loot drops on the Internet prior to attending the raid, that way when something drops, you can look it up on your printout instead of asking ten times what the stats are.

Need before greed. Quite simply, this means that those who can actually use a loot item get precedence over those who just want the item to sell. Once an item drops, determine if it is an upgrade to your existing equipment or not. If it's not an upgrade, then it's not a "needed" item.

Don't go to the raid expecting to win something. If you do, you'll be sorely disappointed.

Don't go to the raid expecting to get experience. Once again, if you do, you'll be sorely disappointed.

Get to the raid at least 15 minutes early. There is nothing worse than an entire raid waiting on one person to arrive, who logs in at the raid time and then needs to find a port and run to the meet point.

Minimize the use of emotes and talks. The raid is about having fun, but if you spam everyone with emotes, they'll miss important raid information. Also, don't do a lot of talking in the raid channel (either /ooc, /shout, or /auction).

Put the raid before yourself. This isn't about you and your group, but about many groups coming together to accomplish a common goal.

Communicate. If you need to leave early, tell the Raid Leader at the start, and then remind him about 30 minutes before you have to leave. By doing so, you give him ample time to find a replacement for you.

Additional Notes for Raid Leaders

Communicate. It's your responsibility to communicate to the raid so that they know what is going on. Also along these lines, be sure to go over raid rules and loot rules once you have all groups set.

Be prepared for a "Worst Case Scenario." If you're going into a dangerous area, how will corpse recovery be handled in case of a total raid wipeout?

Delegate a Loot Master. You'll be much too busy with the raid to handle loot as well.

Know your destination/purpose and make sure your raid knows it as well. Pick a destination for your raid and stick to it. When people join up to go to a particular destination, it's usually because they actually want to go there. If you want to change your destination, make sure to discuss it in the raid channel to get a feel for what everyone else thinks. You don't want to switch gears and have 50% of your raid leave because they don't wish to go the new place.

Guild Creation and Management

By Brandon de la Cruz

Guilds in *EverQuest* are much more than just a large group of players: they are an extension of the game itself. Guilds give you ways to explore and enjoy the social aspects of an online RPG, make it easy to interact with other players with similar interests, encourage you to host events from newbie gatherings to raids. Guilds are a great way to progress in the game and worth the time investment.

How to Make the Most of Your Guild

Here are some basic tips that will keep your guild growing and contented:

1. Get a web page. This is probably the most important thing you can do for your guild. If you can set up an e-mail list or message board, that's even better. The idea is to provide a meeting place for your guild members where they can find the latest news and be able to propose event ideas.

2. Write a charter. Creating a charter is part of the process of guild creation anyway, but writing out a good charter will help you determine the focus and policies of your guild. Do you want to have a raiding guild, a role-playing guild, or some of both? Do you want your members to be above or below a certain level? Do you want to exclude certain classes or races? (This is primarily done for role-playing reasons.) A charter posted on your guild website will also give you something to refer to in resolving disputes (and there are *always* disputes). Don't be afraid to change it as your guild's ideas and policies develop.

3. Establish a hierarchy or ruling system. This is an important thing to consider when forming your guild. Will it be run by one guildleader as a dictatorship? Will there be other officers, or a council, that will have input? Maybe you want to have a truly democratic guild where each member's vote counts equally. There are many successful guild models – you can make anything work as long as the guild members are in general agreement and support the leadership decision.

4. Work with other guilds. This is true for any type of guild, for any number of reasons. A raiding guild may need additional members for difficult encounters. A role-playing guild can greatly benefit from having an enemy guild to taunt and harass. (Let's not forget the fun of an all-out guild war!) The best way to accomplish these things is to have good inter-guild relations. Go out of your way to help other guilds by volunteering your members for role-playing scenarios, or offer assistance in raids (*always* get their permission, of course). Appoint a Guild Ambassador to be in contact with other guilds and to help plan multi-guild events. You'll find that if you treat other guilds with the respect you give your own members, then great things will be sure to follow.

Spellbook Organization

By Gnish, Mage of Death

One of the more important aspects of playing *EverQuest* is efficiency: being able to do things fast with minimal effort. For a spellcaster, efficiency comes in many forms, but one of the most important forms is within the spellbook. Due to the fact that only 8 spells can be memorized at one time, many casters spend a bit of time going to their spellbook for new spells to swap out.

So, how do you increase your spellbook efficiency? By placing similar spells side by side in a spellbook, then setting up hotkeys for spells. To do this, you must first determine what kind of spells you have.

Utility

All spellbooks have 50 pages / 5 spells each.

Move "old" spells to the back. First, move any spells that you no longer use to page 30 or higher. These would be spells that you've upgraded (*Endure Magic* for instance, when you have *Resist Magic*). The main purpose of this is to keep those spells out of your way. In the event you do forget where you placed a spell, then you'll know that you only need to search pages 1-30 since pages 31+ are old spells.

Organize page by page. When placing spells on a page, try to place the most used ones close together to make it easier on you. The only exception to this would be for Druids and Wizards. For your port spells, alphabetize them. It will save you time there too.

Hotkeys

Once your spellbook is done, the next step is setting up hotkeys. For example, you could choose hotkey banks 5 and 6 for your spells.

To set up a hotkey:

1. Hit Alt and M at same time.

2. Click on *Socials*.

3. Page ahead until you find a social page with nothing filled in. You can expect to fill up one or two pages with spellbook hotkeys.

4. Right-click on a box on the Socials page.

5. Enter a name for this hotkey (top left corner). Try to be descriptive, like using "Gbuffs" for group buffs.

6. Select a color for the hotkey name. For instance you could use blue for all your buff spells/hotkeys.

7. Enter /book # (with "#" being the number of the page) so that when the hotkey is hit, you'll jump to the correct book page. For instance, if you're doing Clerical buffs, you'll want to jump to page one. So, enter "/book 1" (no quotes). Now, you'll notice that you have several other lines available. Feel free to enter emotes there for the book if you want, but try to keep the number of emotes down as it will drive other players nuts.

8. Repeat until you have a hotkey for each of your spell book pages.

9. Copy the spellbook social hotkeys to the hotkey bank. Simply click-and-hold on a spellbook social hotkey until you see the icon/gem appear on your cursor. Then move over to the hotkey bank and drop the icon/gem there.

Spell Types (Examples)

Class-specific websites often have examples of useful spell groupings.

Spell Type	Cleric	Druid	Enchan.	Mag.	Necro.	Shaman	Wiz.
Crowd Control	Yes (Roots, Stuns)	Yes Roots	Yes (Mezz, Stuns)	–	Yes (Fear, Roots)	Roots	Roots
Cure	Yes	Yes	–	–	Yes	Yes	–
Dmg Over Time	Yes (Undead)	Yes	Yes	–	Yes	Yes	–
Debuffs	Yes (Nullify Magic)	–	Yes	Yes	Yes	Yes	Yes
Direct Damage	Yes	Yes	Yes	Yes	Yes	Yes	Yes
Area Effect Dmg	–	Yes	–	Yes	Yes	–	Yes
Evacuations	–	Yes	–	Yes (Self-only)	–	–	Yes
Group Buffs	Yes	Yes	Yes (Clarity, C2, Runes, Haste)	–	Yes	Yes	–
Group Ports	–	Yes	–	–	–	–	Yes
Heals	Yes	Yes	–	–	Yes	Yes	–
Pet & Pet Buffs	Yes (Hammer)	Yes (Charms)	Yes (Charms)	Yes	Yes	Yes	–
Resistance Buffs	Yes	Yes	Yes	Yes (Self-only)	Yes	Yes	–
Self-Only Buffs	Yes	Yes	Yes	Yes	Yes	Yes	Yes
Translocates	–	–	–	Yes	–	–	Yes
Travel	Yes	Yes	Yes	–	Yes	Yes	Yes

Sample of Organized Spellbooks

With the generals done, let's go through a few spellbooks and see how we could organize them.

Cleric

Spell Type	Page	Spells
Group Buffs	1	AC/HP: Heroism, Group Heroism Symbol: Marzin, Group Symbol AC: Bulwark of Faith, Aegolism (Hero/Symbol combo)
Heals	2	Highest Rezz spell (in case your heal fails), Complete Heal, Divine Light, Celestial Healing, Remedy
Buffs	3	Death Pact, Self-only AC buff, Mark of Karn, Nullify Magic, Hammer Pet
Crowd Control	4	Stuns, Roots
Resistance Buffs	5	Resist Magic, Resist Disease, Resist Poison
Cures	6	Cure Disease, Cure Blindness, Cure Poison, etc
DD and DoTs	7	Reckoning, Turning of the Undead, Earthquake
Travel	8	Invisibility to Undead, Bind, Gate

Druid

Spell Type	Page	Spells
Group Buffs and Heals	1	AC/HP: Skin Like Nature Regen (Chloroplast/Regrowth), Strength: (Strength of Stone) Damage Shield Highest Healing Spell
Group Buffs and Self-only Buffs	2	Spirit of Wolf, Group SoW,, Group Wolf Form, Self-Only Shield buff, Self-only Wolf Form
Damage Over Time	3	
Crowd Control/Movement Spells	4	Snare, Ensnare, Grasping Roots
Direct Damage (Single Target)	5	
Direct Damage (Area of Effect)	6	
Resistance Buffs	7	Resist Magic, Resist Disease, Resist Cold (Circle spell), Resist Fire (Circle Spell)
Cures	8	Cure Disease
Travel	9	Superior Camo, See Invis, Bind
Self-Only Ports	10-12	All of them including Gate (leaving room for more spells so page 12 may be empty)
Group Ports	13-15	All of them (leaving room as well)
Group Evacuations	16-19	All of them (leaving room as well)

Necromancer

Spell Type	Page	Spells
Self-only Buffs and Utility	1	Manaskin, AC/HP Shield, Feign Death, Harmshield
Group Buffs	2	Dead Man Floating
Damage Over Time	3	Bond of Death, Ignite Blood, Envenomed Breath
Crowd Control /Movement Spells	4	Darkness, Roots, Screaming Terror, Invoke Fear
Direct Damage (Single Target)	5	Life Drain, Ignite Bones, Undead Nukes, etc.
Direct Damage (Area of Effect)	6	Yes, I keep them here, although they are virtually useless.
Resistance Buffs	7	Resist Disease
Cures	8	Cure Disease
Travel	9	Bind, Gate, Levant, Invis to Undead, Gather Shadows
Pets	10	Summon Pet spell (L49, L53, L56, L59), Reclaim Energy
Pets and Pet Buffs	11	Undead Charm, Pet Buff

The Exploration

by Andrea Silva (Cryth Thistledown, Bristlebane)

Having picked themselves up from the fall down the tunnel, the party gathered their wits and looked around. The musky smell of the caverns invaded their senses. Cryth began a whispered chant, the air in front of her beginning to attain a slight glow as she whispered. But, just as the shadows began to fade, Zandar gave Cryth a shake to interrupt her spell.

Don't!" he whispered harshly. "Create no additional light until we've had a minute to scout around. In this darkness, the light would other alert others to our presence."

A quick survey of their surroundings showed them to be underground in some sort of hidden cavern. The way they had come down was all but obscured now, and an immediate escape no longer seemed an option. Occasionally, a shuffling could be heard ahead on the dusty path, but it sounded distant, as did the occasionally moans ... or perhaps the wind whispering amongst the stalagmites.

"Save the lights for an emergency. Wherever we are, it appears to have seen very little of light. Perhaps that will work in our favor."

And with that, Gnish glanced around quickly and disappeared. His voice carried upon the wind that originated from seemingly nowhere.

"Wait here, and I'll scout ahead to see what we have fallen into."

As Gnish crept ahead, he could see a variety of creatures. He had almost climbed on top of a mushroom for a better look, when suddenly it moved. And further ahead, he saw what appeared to be prisoners.

The further he went, the louder the moans became. His Gnomish eyes picked out a path, but it seemed to be leading him further into the depths. Then, he spotted the most hideous creatures he had ever witnessed ....

His blood ran cold. These beings appeared to be marching on some kind of patrol. But, when Gnish looked down at their feet, he noticed that they had none. Instead, their legs ended just around the calves. "What kind of creature is this?" he began to think to himself.

Suddenly, the beings looked up as if searching for something felt, but not heard.

"Come hither, trespasser," he heard. "Come to us."

Against his will, Gnish began to slowly move. His eyes locked in horror on the creatures that summoned him to them.

Horses

Note: All aspects of online games are liable to change. Horses are such a recent addition at the time of this book's printing that they are more likely than other elements to change without warning. However, this should be close to the way horses will work.

Bridles. There are sixteen types of bridle, split into four categories: rope, leather, silk and chain. These correspond to the speed of the horses, with rope being roughly equivalent to the speed of *Journeyman's Boots* and Chain being slightly slower than *Spirit of the Cheetah*. Sizes vary depending on your race. The color of the bridle corresponds to the color of the horse: tan, brown, white and black.

Summoning. Once you have purchased a bridle you need to place it in one of your main inventory slots and summon your magical steed by right-clicking on the bridle. After a few seconds your mount will arrive and you will be placed upon its back. When you no longer require the services of your steed, click the icon in your buff window and your mount will disappear until you call again.

Variations. Just like the transportation we use in the real world, horses range widely in cost and speed, from relatively affordable to insanely expensive. The summoning whips are No Drop, so you'll have to buy your own pony, but they are not lore, so if you're really rich you can buy a horse to match each outfit. The two of you share HP, so mobs can't kill your horse without killing you at the same time. The animations are beautiful, and there are impressive little touches, such as it taking a while for your horse to hit running speed: it walks a few steps, trots a few steps, then speeds up and races like the wind. The view is very realistic in first-person view — so targeting may be a challenge — and the different sizes mean the different racial heights are even more noticeable.

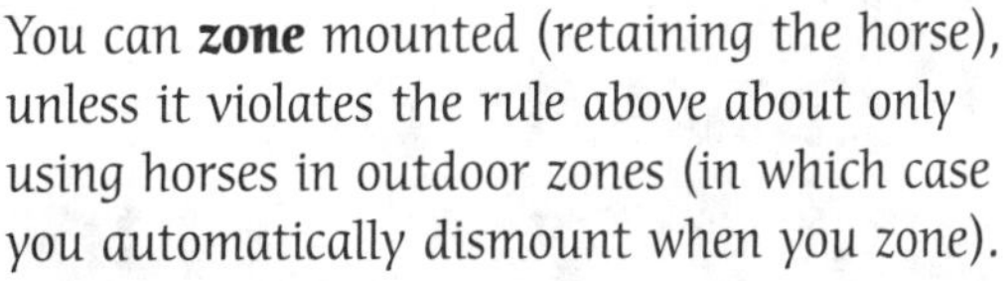

Restrictions

Players are not **invisible** (in any form) while mounted. Mounting removes invisibility. This includes Hide and Sneak.

Players cannot **levitate** while mounted. Mounting removes levitation, and spells with a levitation component will fail to take hold while mounted.

Rogues cannot **backstab** while on a horse. Use of the "backstab" key basically produces an additional attack, but it is not an actual backstab.

Change-form spells work while mounted (as long as the new form can also ride a horse), including *Shrink*. Changed forms cancel upon mounting.

Getting **stunned** while on a horse has a percentage chance of dismounting you.

Getting **summoned** (same zone) dismounts you if you travel more than 15ft or so. This includes voluntary teleportation, including spells like Shadowstep and Gate.

Horses can only be used **outdoors**, not in dungeons (indoor or outdoors or underground). You'll lose your horse upon transition to these locations. Horses cannot get to Planes, either.

You can **zone** mounted (retaining the horse), unless it violates the rule above about only using horses in outdoor zones (in which case you automatically dismount when you zone).

You can't **submerge** while mounted. You'll be forced to swim on the surface.

Speed buffs are cancelled upon mounting, and anything that adds positive movement rate will fail to take hold while mounted. Anything that adds negative movement rate will still slow down the horse.

You can't **feign death** while on a horse. You'll have to purposefully dismount before feigning death.

Several **special combat maneuvers** are unavailable to you when on horseback, such as flying-kick and round-kick.

Skills Usable on Horses

Apply Poison (must be still)	Alchemy
Archery (must be still)	Baking
Bash	Tailoring
Kick	Tradeskills
Mend	Begging
Sense Heading	Intimidation (you can look very scary on a war horse!)
Throwing	Bind Wounds (Self-only)
Tracking	Meditate (they'd have to be standing still; still under debate at time of printing)
Fishing	
Make Poison	
Tinkering	
Research	

Magician Pets and Focus Items

The mainstay of the Magician's arsenal are pets. What follows is some more detailed information about them.

Focus. A pet's power can be increased through the use of focus items.

Focus items only function on pets from level 4 to 49.

The four focus items available from the Temple of Solusek Ro enhance particular attributes of a pet. Because each pet has inherent natural attributes, each focus object works differently on each pet type.

The quests to obtain the focus items can be obtained from Vira in the Temple of Solusek Ro. (Do not attempt to obtain these items until you are at least level 30 or have plenty of friends helping you.)

Each elemental becomes more powerful than the one before it when you use the focus objects. Some receive more hit points, while others receive more stat boosts. Simply put, a pet summoned with a focus object will be more powerful than a pet summoned without one, and it is certainly worth accomplishing the quests to obtain the items.

Mage focus items must be held during summoning in order to be effective. There are rumored to be more powerful versions of these items known as the Staves of Elemental Mastery ....

Earth Elementals

The Earth Elemental is the elemental that you want to be using for serious battles. It has the most Hit Points of any pet. It also has a massive Strength (about equal to that of an Ogre). Earth Elementals deal the most damage of any pet. Their weakness is that they have low Agility. Anything swinging at them will hit them.

Level 50+ Earth Elementals now have the ability to cause damage through their *Root* spell.

Focus Object: Shovel of Ponz. These pets have the most Hit Points of any pet. Because of this, the focus objects do not add any extra Hit Points to the pets. Rather, the pets get extra Strength, Agility and other stats to help them dodge a little better and hit for higher damages.

Water Elementals

Water Elementals are the composite elemental – they combine a little bit of the best of all of the other elementals. Their Strength is second only to an Earth Elemental (again, about equal to that of a Troll), their Agility is good (about as good as an Elf) and their Hit Points are just under that of an Earth Elemental. They are the most balanced elemental. Water Elementals also heal faster than any other elemental.

Focus Object: Stein of Ulissa. A Water Elemental summoned with a focus object obtains the same number of Hit Points as an Earth Elemental of the same level summoned with no focus object. They also receive boosted stats.

Air Elemental

The Air Elemental is the elemental that you want tanking for you. It has an incredibly high Agility, making it much harder to hit than any other elemental. It has good Strength (about equal to that of a Barbarian). It deals good damage, is hard to hit, and has the ability to turn invisible. This means you can use the "/pet back off" command to good effect. The Air Elemental backs off and, assuming that the monster does not follow (i.e., goes after another party member), the Air Elemental turns invisible, guaranteeing that it will not be hit while it heals.

At Level 50+ its Stun causes damage.

Focus Object: Broom of Trilon. An Air Elemental summoned with a focus object gets a Hit Point bonus, giving it about the same number of Hit Points as a Water Elemental of the same level, summoned without a focus object. However, they receive less stat buffs than the Water Elemental.

Fire Elemental

The Fire Elemental is the elemental you want to use against creatures with very quick attacks (Griffawns) or against massive amounts of smaller creatures (dungeon "hall trash"). They have good Strength (like a Barbarian) and good Agility (like an Elf). They have the least Hit Points of any elemental, but compensate with an innate Fire Shield that damages an attacker. This means that each time an attacker hits your pet, he or she takes damage.

Level 50+ Fire Elementals cast a variety of Wizard-based spells, including *Force Shock*, *Flame Shock*, *Shock of Lightning*, *Shieldskin*, *O'Keils Radiation* and *Dispel Magic*.

The level 50+ Fire Elementals will also buff any pets or charmed creatures nearby with *O'Kiels Radiation* and dispel any Damage Shields on its attackers.

Focus Object: Torch of Alna. A Fire Elemental summoned with a focus object gets a Hit Point bonus, giving it about the same number of Hit Points as an Air Elemental of the same level summoned without a focus object. It receives about the same stat buffs as the Air Elemental.

General Pet Information

Weapons. Giving weapons to pets only gives them the Dual Wield skill—it does not alter their Damage or Attack Speed. However, pets that inherently do less damage than a weapon will benefit from receiving weapons (true if the weapon's damage is greater than half of the pet's maximum damage). This means that for pets up to level 16, a weapon can increase its overall damage.

When pets receive weapons, they'll use the weapon with the lowest attack delay.

XP Share. When you group, the pet might take a minimal experience share from your party. This is different from soloing – when you solo, your pet gets a percentage of the experience that you would ordinarily have received. Also, soloing pets take half of the XP from any kill in which they delivered over half of the damage to the monster.

When the "/pet guard here" command is used on a pet, it will always turn to face the nearest monster.

General Commands

... with thanks for new entries to James Lewis (Ronaldor Vladimir) and The Mage Compendium (http://www.magecompendium.com)

/anon or /a (On or Off)

Makes you Anonymous in /who and /who all, preventing other players from seeing your class, level and current location.

/afk <text>

When activated, all private tells sent to the user will auto-respond with the following text, "You told <players name>, 'Sorry, I am A.F.K. (Away from keyboard) right now.'" If you add some text after the /afk command it will appear as "AFK Message: <text>"

/assist

Assists the targeted PC or mob.

/assist <target> or <player name>

Targets the player or monster that <target> or <player name> is currently targeting, to a range of 200 feet.

/assist (On or Off)

Enables or disables auto attack when assisting a player.

/attack (On or Off)

Toggles auto attack on or off.

/auction <text>

Allows users to send auction messages throughout the current zone.

/autosplit

Splits any loot you get with the rest of your party. Each member must do this to split all loot.

/bazaar (Welcome, Search, List and Help)

For additional information about commands, please purchase the appropriate documentation located in the central building in the Bazaar.

/book <#> (1 to 50)

Takes you to the corresponding page of your spell book. Type in a number for <#>.

/bug or /b

Takes you to a bug-reporting screen.

/camp (Server or Desktop)

Causes player to camp out of the game, either to the server selection screen or his desktop.

/cast # (1 to 8)

Casts the spell memorized in the corresponding slot.

/charinfo

Display your current Bind Point.

/chatfontsize (0 to 5)

Allow players to adjust the size of the font in the chat window.

/consent <player name>

Gives <player name> permission to drag all your current corpses.

/consider or /con

Gives vital statistics of a targeted PC or NPC. (However, be careful not to consent by mistake. You can just press [C] on the keyboard to consider your target.)

/corpse

Will summon a character's corpse if it's within a 50 foot radius of the player.

/doability # (1 to 10)

Fires the specified ability. Abilities 1-6 are those that are set on the "Abilities" page. Numbers 7-10 represent those that are set on the "Combat Skills" page.

/disband

Causes a player to disband from a group or decline a group invitation.

/duel or /d

Challenges targeted PC to a duel. To accept, they type /d with you targeted as well. Duel is in effect until one "dies" (is knocked unconscious) or flees the zone.

/decline

Allows the user to decline a duel.

/fastdrop (On, Off or Never)

Enables/disables a confirmation box for dropping items onto the ground. Does not allow you to drop Items at all.

/feedback

Takes you to the feedback/comments screen.

/filter

Toggles the profanity filter on and off.

/follow

When this command is used while targeting another player, the user will automatically follow the targeted character as long as you are grouped with them.

/friend <player name>

Adds or removes a "friend" from your friends list.

/gems

Toggles the mini-game Gems on screen or off screen.

/gsay or /g

Text is seen by all in your group.

/help <topic> (Normal, Emote and Guild)

Displays emotes, guild commands, and normal commands separately.

/hidecorpses (None, All or Allbutgroup)

Draws all corpses. Hides all corpses. Hides all corpses except group's.

/hotbutton <name> <color> <text>

This command is used to create a hotkey.

<name> The hotkey will automatically be created with this name.

<color> This is optional. Uses this color number for the color of the text.

<text> Up to 60-character macro to be used for the hotkey.

/inspect (On or Off)

Toggles the ability to inspect players using the right click.

/invite

Invites a player to group with you.

/invwinlabels

This command toggles the inventory slot descriptions on or off.

/language help

Displays a list of available languages and their corresponding number.

/language #

Selects the chat language to use in general communication.

/language

Displays the current language.

/lfg (On or Off)

Toggles the Looking For Group flag. /lfg without on or off gives you an error.

/ignore <player name>

Turns off all text from that player.

/location

Displays the user's current coordinates.

/lootnodrop (Always, Sometimes or Never)

Always (Default) You will be presented with a yes/no confirmation box when attempting to loot any nodrop item.

Sometimes You will be presented with a yes/no confirmation box when attempting to loot any No Drop items that your race and/or class cannot use.

Never No Drop items will be looted without confirmation.

/loot

Allows the user to loot a corpse from a short distance. The corpse must be targeted when performing this command.

/log

Logs all text locally to the user's machine. The log.txt file which is generated can be found in the *EverQuest* directory.

/mcicontrol

Allows a player to control sound devices such as cdaudio or mp3s to play when in-game. This command will be further developed in the future to be more user friendly. Until that point, the following are some commands you can use to play audio CDs:

Before using any other of these commands, use the following to open up communications:

/mcicontrol open cdaudio
/mcicontrol play cdaudio
/mcicontrol pause cdaudio
/mcicontrol stop cdaudio
/mcicontrol step cdaudio
/mcicontrol back cdaudio
/mcicontrol eject cdaudio

Note: Though ejecting itself should not cause any gameplay problems, putting in a new disk may. If you have AutoPlay enabled on your computer (which is windows' default), it may start your CDaudio program and possibly switch out of *EverQuest*, causing *EverQuest* to likely crash, or at the least may cause a phantom cursor to appear.

If you have AutoPlay disabled, putting in a disk should not cause any problems.

/filter
Toggles the profanity filter on and off.

/microphone
Toggles the microphone on or off.

/mousespeed (1, 2, 3 or 4)
Sets the mouse movement multiplier.

/motd
Allows you to view the Message of The Day.

/note <text>
This puts what you wrote after /note in a "note.txt" file in your EQ directory. Do this when you need to write down a note and don't have (or don't want to use) pencil and paper.

/ooc
Allows you to say something as yourself, not as your character, heard throughout the zone.

/pause
Inserts a pause in a social command.
For example:

/sit Off
/cast 1
/pause 100
/sit On

This would cause you to stand up, cast the spell in slot 1, wait 10 seconds after you've started casting the spell, and sit down.

/petition <msg>
Used to request assistance from a GM. The more detailed <msg> is, the quicker the assistance can be rendered.

/played
Gives you the birthdate & hours played w/ your character.

/random (# to #)
Generates a random number between # and #.

/reply <text>
If a "/tell" is received, the user may respond by using this command.

/report <name>
Logs the text currently displayed in the text area and the name you typed after /report, used for reporting abuse and bad behavior to the GM/Guides.

/reverb (On or Off)
Toggles the reverb (echo) sounds on or off.

/roleplay
This command activates the "/anonymous" flag along with changing the user's display name to purple, leaving your guild tag visible.

/reversesound
This command should be very useful for those who have had to place their speakers backwards due to cable lengths.

/safelock <password>
This command will lock the *EverQuest* interface with the password that you supply to the command. You must use this command a second time, supplying the same password, to unlock the interface.

/serverfilter (On or Off)
Enables and disables server side filtering for channels not listed here: O.O.C., Shout, Auction, Guild Chat, Damage Shields or any form of combat miss.

/shout
Text is seen across entire zone.

/shownames (On or Off)
Turns on or off visible names above PC's and NPC's heads. Red names are PvP, Blue names are –PvP.

/showspelleffects (On or Off)
Enables/disables particle effects for spells only.

/sit (On or Off)
Causes your character to sit.

/sit Off
Causes your character to stand.

/split # # #
Splits a defined amount of money with your group: plat, gold, silver and copper respectively.

/split 4 3 2 0
Splits 4 plat, 3 gold, 2 silver, and 0 copper with the rest of the group. All numbers must be present; use 0 for coins to not be split.

/stopsong
Enables Bards to stop their songs.

/surname <last name>

Players over level 20 may use this command to assign a last name to their character.

/target <name>

The command can be used to target other players by name. Please note that this ability is subject to the range to the target.

/targetgroupbuff (On or Off)

When on, all group buff spells you cast will require a target but will affect everyone within range of your target, even if it is not your own group. When it is off, your group buff spells will act normally. This will only work with group buffs that have a duration, and will not affect heals, portals or change form spells.

/tell <player name> <text>

Text is seen by named player anywhere in the game.

/trader (Edit, Delete, New, Quit, List, Help, Add and Welcome)

For additional information about commands, please purchase the appropriate documentation located in the central building in the Bazaar.

/trackplayers (Group, On or Off)

The command will work for all players with the tracking skill. It enables you to turn your player tracking on and off, or use as a group.

/tracksort (Normal, Distance, Consider, Rconsider or Rdistance)

The command sorts the tracking list. Options beginning with R are reverse order. Ranger-only tracking command.

/trackfilter (Red, Yellow, White, Blue or Green)

Filters out monsters of that consider color. Ranger-only tracking command.

/usercolor <chat type> <redvalue> <greenvalue> <bluevalue>

Changes the color of the chat text.
For example:
/usercolor 3 255 255 0
Changes guild chat to yellow.
This is the same as editing the TextColor portion of your eqclient.ini file. For a list of the chat type or common color values, see p. 201.

/voice

Toggles the voice recognition system on or off; *EverQuest* requires a restart for this to be effective. Also see /microphone command.

/vrdelay <delay in milliseconds>

Allows the user to set how long *EverQuest* will sleep in the main rendering loop in order to improve voice recognition response.

/time

Gives you the time of day in Norrath.

/wincolor <window name> <redvalue> <greenvalue> <bluevalue> <transparency>

This command allows players with the *Velious* expansion or later to change the color and transparency of the background for all of the window boxes for the updated user interface.
Values :
<window name>
(Chat, Spell, Player, Party, Target, Buff, Data, Main, Inv, Track, or Hotbox)
<transparency>
(0, 1, 2, 3 or 4)

/wincolor <window name> RESET

Resets the color and transparency to default settings.

/who

Lists all player characters in your zone.

/who corpse

Lists all the corpses a player has in the current zone.

/who all

Lists all player characters in the world.

/who all <Guild>

Lists all player characters in your guild, even if they have /roleplay command active.

/whotarget

Can be typed to do a /who on the targeted PC.
Note:
/who and /who all are also usable with masks to look for certain players or classes online.
For example:

/who wiz all

Generates a list of all Wizards online in all zones.

/who wiz 30 50 lfg

Generates a list of Wizards looking for a group between levels 30 and 50 in your current zone. /who wiz 30 50 lfg all Generates a list of Wizards looking for a group between levels 30 and 50 in all zones. If you put "all" at the end of your /who command, you get all who are currently logged in for the entire world, not just your current zone.

/who 1 5 all

Generates a list of all players online who are between levels 1 and 5.

/who Ae all

Generates list of all players whose names begin with Ae.

/who GM all

Generates a list of all the GM's that are online.
Note:
GM's are grouped into differing types.
GM-Admins are Sony Administrators that can answer your questions and resolve issues.
GM-Coders and GM-Areas are Sony developers and artists that are resolving game issues and are not available for questions.
Guides are fellow players that are there to answer gameplay questions, and assist in problem resolution due to bugs.

/who friend all

Generates a list of the players in your friends list who are online (see the /friend command).

/yell

Issues a "cry for help" to all players within a 100-foot radius.

Guild Commands

/guildsay

Sends a text message to fellow guild members currently on-line. Each guild has different standards for what is acceptable in /guildsay but you should remember every guild member is listening.

/guildinvite

Guild Leaders and Officers may use this command to invite new guild members. This command only works when both the Officer and the invitee are in the same zone.

/guildremove

Guild Leaders and Officers may use this command to remove guild members. This command now works no matter which zone the Officer and member are in. Only the Guild Leader can remove Officers.

/guilddelete

Guild Leaders may use this command to disband their guild.

/guildstatus <target> or <player name>

When targeting another character or when a character name is added at the end of this command, it will reveal the guild affiliation and status (member, officer, leader) of another PC in your current zone.

/guildmotd <text>

Only Guild Leaders and Officers only can use this command. The message of the day is displayed when characters log on, and stays until a new one is created or the server is rebooted.

/guildmotd

Displays the guild message of the day.

/guildleader

Transfers guild leadership status to a new member.

/guildwar

Allows the Guild Leader to challenge or accept another guild in guild war.

/guildpeace

Allows the Guild Leader to decline the challenge of a guild war.

Pet Commands

/pet <command>

Gives orders to a charmed or summoned pet, including a Beastlord's warder.

Sample pet commands:

/pet sit down

Tells pet to sit down.

/pet stand up

Tells pet to stand up.

/pet hold

This command is only available once you have obtained the Alternate Advancement skill Pet Discipline. It will prevent your pet from attacking anything if you are attacked or if it is attacked.

/pet get lost

Kills pet.

/pet who leader

Pet says who is its master.

/pet guard here

Tells the pet to guard its current location.

/pet guard me

Tells the pet to attack anyone that attacks its master, or that its master attacks.

/pet follow me

Tells the pet to follow you, but ends when you cross a zone line.

/pet attack

Tells the pet to attack the current targeted mob.

/pet kill <target>

Tells the pet to kill the designated <target>.

/pet back off

Tells the pet to stop its attack and return to its /pet guard here point.

/pet as you were

Returns the pet to neutral, belaying all prior orders.

/pet report health

Displays the pet's health as a percentage.

/pet taunt (On or Off)

Tells the pet to stop taunting its attacker.

Bazaar Commands

The team is currently planning to implement a graphical user interface. When this happens, these commands will be obsolete, and possibly removed from the game.

There are two types of commands for use in the bazaar, /bazaar and /trader. The /bazaar commands are for shoppers, the /trader commands are for merchants.

/bazaar welcome

Returns the following text (welcoming you to the bazaar):

Welcome to The Bazaar!

There are currently X traders and Y items for trade.

For a list of commands, type /bazaar help or /trader help.

/bazaar help

Returns a list of commands for both /bazaar and /trader.

Currently it displays the following text:

Format: /bazaar, Commands: welcome, search, list, help.

Format: /trader, Commands: edit, delete, new, quit, list, help, add, welcome.

For additional information about commands, please purchase the appropriate documentation located in the central building.

/bazaar search <player name>

Returns the name of the character and the items he has for sale, along with the price and any comments the seller has about those items.

/bazaar search <item name>

Returns all instances of that item for sale, the character selling them, the price and comments from the seller on the item.

Note that the item name can be a partial match.

/bazaar search <Race> <Class> <Slot> <Stat>

All values are interchangeable and none of the values are required.

Example: /bazaar search BAR warrior neck STR.

Returns all instances of items that a Barbarian Warrior can wear on the neck that has a bonus for strength that are available for sale, the price of those items, the seller, and any comments the seller has made about that item.

/bazaar search race

Returns a list of the possible race options for use with the search command.

/bazaar search class

Returns a list of the possible class options for use with the search command.

/bazaar search slot

Returns a list of the possible slot options for use with the search command.

/bazaar search stat

Returns a list of the possible stat options for use with the search command.

/bazaar search

(Without using any parameters) Returns all items for sale in the bazaar at that moment, including the seller's name, the item name, the price and comments on the item from the seller. This list will often be cut short due to the size of the list. It will almost always be better to use parameters with your search.

/bazaar list

Returns a list of all merchants in the bazaar and how many items they have for sale.

Trader Commands

In order to be a merchant in the bazaar and use most of the /trader commands, you will need to purchase a Trader's Satchel from one of the merchants in the central building of the bazaar.

/trader welcome

Returns the following text (welcoming you to the bazaar):
Welcome to The Bazaar!
There are currently X traders and Y items for trade.
For a list of commands, type /bazaar help or /trader help.

/trader new

Places you onto the list of merchants in the zone. This command will not work if you do not have a Trader's Satchel with items in it. Note: this command will also reset/remove all prices and comments from your wares list, so be sure to only use it when you are first establishing yourself as a trader (or if you want to wipe out your wares list and start fresh).

/trader help

Returns a list of commands for both /bazaar and /trader.
Currently it displays the following text:
Printing help...
Format: /bazaar, Commands: welcome, search, list, help.
Format: /trader, Commands: edit, delete, new, quit, list, help, add, welcome.
For additional information about commands, please purchase the appropriate documentation located in the central building.

/trader list

Gives you a list of all the items that you have for sale (your wares list), including item name, price and your comments about the item.

/trader quit

Removes you from the list of traders and takes your wares off the wares lists.

/trader add

Adds the item on your cursor to your list of items for sale.

/trader edit <price> <description>

Allows you to edit the price and description for the item on your cursor. The item must already be on your list of wares (by use of the /trader add command). The price must be listed in copper pieces, and only the number is needed.
Example: /trader edit 200 Only slightly used
This would set the price to 2 gold pieces (200 copper = 2 gold) and add the description "Only slightly used". Once you've done this you can view the item, along with all your other wares, using the /trader list command.

/trader delete

Removes the item on your cursor from your wares list. Remember: You must have an item on your cursor to add, delete, or edit your wares list. It is also a good idea to use the /trader list command and check your list of wares after making changes.

Emotes

The % codes are:

%M	Returns the name of your pet.
%T	Returns the current target.
%S	Returns the subjective gender-specific pronoun for the target (He, She, It).
%O	Returns the objective gender-specific pronoun for the target (Him, Her, It).
%P	Returns the possessive gender-specific pronoun for the target (His, Her, Its).
%R	Returns the race of the target (only works on Player characters).

For example:

If you have a target of "a gnoll", the following emote:

/point say points at %T indicating that he is ready to kill %O.

This causes your character to execute the /point animation with a text output of "<yourname> points at a gnoll indicating that he is ready to kill it."

Chat Type Values

*For use with **/Usercolor** on page 197.*

1 Say
2 Tell
3 Group
4 Guild
5 OOC
6 Auction
7 Shout
8 Emote
9 Spells
10 You hit other
11 Other hits you
12 You miss other
13 Other misses you
14 Some broadcasts
15 Skills
16 Disciplines/spec. abilities
17 Unused at this time
18 Default/typed text
19 Unused at this time
20 Merchant Offer Price
21 Merchant Buy/Sell
22 Your death message
23 Other's death message
24 Other damage other
25 Other miss other
26 /who command
27 Yell for help
28 Hit for non-melee
29 Spell worn off
30 Money splits
31 Loot message
32 Dice roll
33 Other's spells
34 Spell failures

/em <text> or :<text>

The "/em" command emotes the text you type. Some emotes have animations associated with them, most do not. Sometimes the emote is different depending on whether you have a target. If this is the case, the targeted emote is listed on the first line.

/Agree
/Amaze
/Apologize
/Applaud
/Plead
/Bite
/Bleed
/Blink
/Blush
/Boggle
/Bonk
/Bored
/Bow
/Brb
/Burp
/Bye
/Cackle
/Calm
/Cheer
/Clap
/Comfort
/Congratulate
/Cough
/Cringe
/Cry
/Curious
/Dance
/Drool
/Duck
/Eye
/Gasp
/Giggle
/Glare
/Grin
/Groan
/Grovel
/Happy
/Hungry
/Introduce
/Jk
/Kneel
/Lost
/Massage
/Moan
/Mourn
/Nod
/Panic
/Peer
/Point
/Poke
/Ponder
/Puzzle
/Raise
/Ready
/Roar
/Rofl
/Salute
/Shiver
/Shrug
/Sigh
/Smirk
/Snarl
/Snicker
/Stare
/Tap
/Tease
/Thank
/Thirsty
/Veto
/Welcome
/Whine
/Whistle
/Yawn
/Wave

Common RGB Colors

Black	0,0,0
Red	255,0,0
Orange	255,153,0
Yellow	255,255,0
Green	0,255,0
Light Blue	152,255,255
Blue	0,0,255
Dark Blue	0,0,63
Violet	128,0,128
White	255,255,255

EQ On-Line Sites

These sites were current at the time of publication, but we can't guarantee they will always be there when you need them.

The Official *EverQuest* Site
everquest.station.sony.com/

The one and only official home page. Be sure to try the Newbie Zone message board.

General

Allakhazam everquest.allakhazam.com/
Full service

EQ Stratics eq.stratics.com/
Full service

***EverQuest* Newbie Zone**
pub57.ezboard.com/
btheeverquestnewbiezone OR
newbiezone.freewebspace.com
Masses of newbie information

EQGuide www.eqguide.com/
Good no-spoiler site

EQlizer www.eqlizer.net/index.shtml

EverLore www.everlore.com/
Good spells lists and news section

EverQuest Glossary amtgard.pinkpig.com/everquest/
eqglossary.htm

EverQuest Vault eqvault.ign.com/
Information and forums

The EverQuest Tavern
clubs.yahoo.com/clubs/theeverquesttavern

Illia's EverQuest Bestiary
eqbeastiary.allakhazam.com

EZ Board www.ezboard.com/
EQ-related message boards

PVP pvponline.com
Comic strips only a gamer could love

EQ Items www.pompano.net/~amylynn1

EQ Traders' Corner www.eqtraders.com

EQ Prices.Com www.eqprices.com

EQ Realms eqrealms.com

Gaming Revolution Net.
everquest.gamingrevolution.com/

Companions of the Gate
www.cotg.net

The Long Road Journals
www.longroadjournals.com

Guild Magic www.guildmagic.com
Free guild tracking software

GuildBoss www.guildboss.com
Guild management program

ChrisJerm.com www.geocities.com/chrisjerm/
EverQuest.html

Dragons Art www.dragonsart.com/

EQScreenshots www.geocities.com/eqscreenshots/inside.html

EverQuest Reference gamezportal.com/eqr/

Jibantik's EQ Search Engine
www.jibantik.com

Airo's Favorite Pictures
www.geocities.com/druidelf2/index.html

EqCaster www.eqcaster.com/
Information compendium

Norrath Campgrounds
users.net1inc.net/mr_boffo/spoiler.htm
Spoiler info

Mobhunter www.mobhunter.com/index.jsp
News and links

Seekers of Lore www.loreseekers.com/

Harpy's Head Tavern everquest.station.sony.com/hht/index.jsp

UberQuest www.angelfire.com/games3/EverTry/index.html
Full service

Everquest Neverlost www.everquestneverlost.com/
Forum, news, skills. Atlas for sale

EQ Loot eqloot.gamez.com/

Xegony Alliance www.xegonyalliance.com/
Non-guild group site

Questor's Inn homelessproductions.com/ash/eq/
Fan fiction

Planet EverQuest www.planeteverquest.com/
Full service

Armigers of Mirth www.armigersofmirth.com
Multi-game guild site

EverQuest Widows www.egroups.com/group/EverQuest-Widows
Forum for partners, family, and friends of EQ addicts

Wyndforge's Art of Norrath
reallyswell.com/art/

Bamos' Artwork of Bertox.
home.kscable.com/bertoxart/

Blood and Steel pub5.ezboard.com/bbloodandsteel
EQ forum for tanks

EverQuest Zone Guide
upper.usm.k12.wi.us/Students/
My%20Webs%20SMacD/
EQCompilation3/index.htm

Danimoth's EQ Domain
www.angelfire.com/games3/
danimoth/index.html
Full service

EverQuest Compendium
www.geocities.com/eq_compendium/

EQ Women pub14.ezboard.com/beqwomen
Forum for women who play EQ

EQ Fans	www.geocities.com/amunetpallaton/EQFans.html
EQ Find	www.eqfind.com/ Search engine
EverQuest Central	www.geocities.com/everquestcentral/
EQ Insider	www.eqinsider.com/ Full service
EverQuestRaids.com	www.everquestraids.com/ Event planner
EverQuest, The Community	pub88.ezboard.com/beverquestthecommunity General forum
EverQuesting with Glory	www.glorysite.com/glorysx.html
GuildPortal	www.guildportal.com/ Portal/host site for guilds
Neriak's Library	www.neriak.com/ Dark Elf info
Tales of Norrath	norrath.cjb.net/ Forum
Holger's Guide to Kaladim	www.geocities.com/bruce5674/EQDwarf.html Dwarves
Clan Axepeak	www.axepeak.com Dwarves
The Dwarven Delving	www.delving.addr.com/delving.html Dwarves
Harbingers of Thule	http://turn.to/thule Iksar

Maps

EQ Atlas	www.eqatlas.com/ High quality maps for a large number of areas
EQ Maps	www.eqmaps.com Multiple maps of most locations, plus items database and updates
Outriders of Karana, Kunark Mapping Project	www.tapr.org/~OutridersKarana/kunark/kunark.html
Norrath Map Shop (Questor of Norrath)	www.nx.sakura.ne.jp/~chizuya/indexe.html
Teshia's Maps O' Doom!	www.geocities.com/brcalley82/teshmaps/index.htm

Links

EQ Portal Comm. Housing	www.eqportal.com
EQ Links	www.eqlinks.com/
EQ's Best Link Site	members.home.net/federici2753/MainPage.html
Hibix	www.hibix.com/RPG/Everquest/index.html
EQ's Top Links	www.elessar.iwarp.com/
Father Matt's Tower	www.servantsofmystery.com/fathermatt/fathermatt.htm
GameMaster.com	gamemaster.com/evquest.html

Tradeskills

The Tinkering Compend.	www.eqportal.com/tinkering
Tal Kor Jewelry Academy	www.eqportal.com/jewelry/
Ogre Forj	www.treedcat.com/ogre/ Smithing for Ogres
Belgar's Ultimate Guide to Alchemy (& Shaman)	www.starcrafter.org/alchemy/
EQ Fletching Guide	members.bellatlantic.net/%7Eewj/fletchguide/index.htm
Lokari's Tailoring Guide	www.lokari.net/everquest/tailoring.html
The Smithy	users2.ev1.net/~lyrik/smithy/
Trader's Workshop	www.geocities.com/shadowknight57/ Tradeskills
EverQuest Brewing!	www.nyct.net/~bitsy
Fletcher's Forest	www.amazonsisters.com/fletcher.htm
Unicorn Trading Co.	internettrash.com/users/trading
Simak's EQ Website	www.geocities.com/simak11421

Servers

Ayonae Ro	www.ayonae-ro.net
Ayonae Ro	www.planeteverquest.com/ayonaero
Bertoxxulous Hall	www.berthall.com/
Brell Serilis	pub13.ezboard.com/bbrellserilis
Bristlebane	www.bristlebane.com
Cazic Thule Corner	www.planeteverquest.com/cazicthule/ OR www.cazic-thule.com
Fennin Ro	www.fenninro.com
Firiona Vie	www.firiona-vie.com
Innoruuk	www.innoruuk.com
Lanys T'Vyl	eqasylum.freeservers.com/
Morell-Thule	www.planeteverquest.com/morellthule/
Prexus	prexus.com
Rallos Zek	www.ralloszek.net
Solusek Ro	www.solusekro.com/eq/
Sullon Zek	www.sullonzek.net
Tallon Zek	eqtallonzek.homestead.com/index.html
Tarew Marr	www.tarewmarr.net
Torvonnilous	www.torvonnilous.net
Tunare	www.tunare.com
Xegony	server6.ezboard.com/beverquestxegony
Zebuxoruk	www.2amstudio.com/eq/

Casters

***EverQuest* Realm**	eq.castersrealm.com/ Recommended Database of Official Posts ... plus news, spells, creation guides, and info
Mythiran Tower	mythiran.allakhazam.com Good site for caster research

Bard

Concert Hall	www.attcanada.net/~reaper/
Soerbaird	www.sok.org/soerbaird/
The EverQuesting Bard	amtgard.pinkpig.com/everquest/eqbard.htm
EQ Diva	www.eqdiva.com/
EQ Bard Songs Analysis	www.eqsongs.com/

Beastlord

EQ Beastlord	bcope1.www6.50megs.com/beastlord

Cleric

EQ Cleric	eqcleric.gameglow.com/
Clerics of Hate	www.clericsofhate.com
The White Cross	www.red3.com/eq/index2.htm

Druid

EQ Druids	www.eqdruids.com/
The Druids Grove	server3.ezboard.com/bthedruidsgrove
The Druid Pages	members.tripod.com/thedruidpages/

Enchanter

Xornn's Guide to Ench.	members.tripod.com/xornn/
Enchanters' Realm	pub10.ezboard.com/beqenchantersrealm

Magician

The Mage Compendium	www.magecompendium.com

Monk

Harbingers of Thule	turn.to/thule Iksar Monks
Monkly Business	www.monkly-business.com/index.html
EQ monk forum	kadanit.com/eqmonks/

Necromancer

Necromancer's Hideout	www.geocities.com/Area51/Crater/3074
Necro	necro.eqclasses.com
Brildir Soulterror, Arch Bishop of Necro.	www.geocities.com/brildir/

Paladin

EQ Paladins	paladins.gq.nu
Paladins of Everquest	trump9.tripod.com/paladin.html
Paladins of Norrath	eq.castersrealm.com/pon/

Ranger

***EverQuest* Rangers**	www.geocities.com/eqrangers/
The Ranger's Glade	interealms.com/ranger
Questing Ranger	www.questing-ranger.com/
Ranger's Point	www.geocities.com/rinerdarsmyth/ranger-point.html
The Ranger's Way	www.geocities.com/therangerway/frames.html

Rogue

The Safehouse	pub35.ezboard.com/bthesafehouse
Order of the Black Rose	www.orderoftheblackrose.net
Kiky's Poisonous Pages	kikyara.tripod.com
EQ Addict	pub21.ezboard.com/bramblingsofarogue

Shadow Knight

ShadowKnight	www.sotmesc.org/shadowknight/

Shaman

EQ Shaman	www.eqshaman.com/

Warrior

Swordstrike	www.eqportal.com/Warrior/swordstrike/
The Steel Warrior	www.steelwarrior.org/
The Warrior's Axe	pub73.ezboard.com/bthewarriorsaxe

Wizard

Graffe's Wiz. Compilation	www.graffe.com

EverQuest Newbie FAQ

by Eugen "Ellegon" Weber (Druid, Antonius Bayle)
with contributions from many others (see list on p. 231).
Originally posted on the EverQuest Newbie Zone.

One of our panelists recommended a FAQ from the http://pub57.ezboard.com/btheEverQuestnewbiezone. We're reprinting it with permission because so many new players have found this information to be valuable.

Before You Start to Play

How Do I start?

One of the most important things is to *read* first. Read the manual! [Editor's note: and read this book!] Even if you consider it lame or think you are an experienced player, there are still things that are new or different. Don't you hate people standing in front of a door with a sign "PULL" and they are pushing and whining that it doesn't open? So, do yourself a favor and read the manual. It's not perfect, but a good start.

Ok, so I read the manual, what now?

Run the tutorial. That is *the* most important thing to start. So I say it again: Run the tutorial. To run it, click on the *EverQuest* Tutorial Icon on your desktop. Follow it step by step and learn the basic facts. Facts like talking with NPC's, how to equip items, memorizing spells, using spells, fighting, looting, opening doors, selling and buying things to merchants and much more (ladders!!!). When you have finished it, wait an hour and do it again.... If you skip the tutorial, you will most likely run into troubles... Also the manual might be outdated in certain areas or have typo's (corpse decay times!). It would be wise to check out the file "eqmanual_supplement.txt" in your *EverQuest* folder for corrections/additions.

I read the manual and did the tutorial, can I play now?

Yes, now it's time to enter the world of Norrath. First thing you have to do is to create your account. For that you need a valid credit card (remember the words "Credit Card needed" on the box?). When entering your account number, be sure not to mix up O and 0 (the letter O and zeros). Also a 1 (one) and l (small L) can look similar. If everything works, you're ready to choose your server.

What server is the best?

This question is asked *a lot* on the newbie board. And the opinions vary here. Let us look at the facts first (meaning things everybody agrees to). Four of them are PvP servers (Sullon Vek, Rallos Zek, Tallon Zek and Vallon Zek). All other servers are basic non-PvP servers, with the exception of the new role-play server, Firiona Vie.

Wait, what is PvP?

PvP stands for "Player vs. Player" (as opposed to PvE, which is "Player vs. Environment"). Two players who are *both* PvP can attack, pickpocket, cast detrimental spells on, etc. each other. If only one is PvP, he cannot do anything to the non-PvP. The first (and greatest!) server is Rallos Zek. This server is free-for-all PvP. Everyone automatically starts out in PvP mode and there is no way to become non-PvP. Players on this server may only attack each other if they are within four levels, though. The other three are Sullon Vek, Tallon Zek and Vallon Zek. These servers are PvP-Teams. The races are divided into four teams (Human, Elven, small, and evil). You are automatically PvP with *all three* other teams. You are automatically non-PvP with your own team. The level window on this server is eight levels.

So when I create a char I get killed right away?

No This is thanks to a change that recently got in. You are now "safe" in your first 5 levels. That means you cannot attack nor be attacked. This should help getting started. However, remember that from level 6 it is different than on "non-PvP" servers and you will be in full PvP mode.

But there are still players who only pick "easy" targets, aren't there?

Sure are. As everywhere there are people whose intention is not a "duel" but only to kill easy targets. That might be a player low on health or a much lower level player. However, it's not as easy to find easy targets due to another change, the con system. Other than conning monsters (see below) there are only 3 colors for players: Green (you can't attack as he is too low), black/white (you can attack as he is within PvP range) or red (you can't attack as he is too high). This helps prevent Level 20 players only attacking Level 12 or 13 opponents.

So if I want to fight against other players I have to select one of them?

Not necessarily. You can still duel another player on the "normal" servers, but he has to accept the duel. You can also enter several "Arenas" where everybody is PvP automatically. And last, you can become PvP by giving a book to the Priest of Disorder. From then on you will be PvP. But you will only be able to attack other PvP players, not normal ones. And the decision is final. You can't just switch back and forth. Another thing is that, if you are PvP, no "normal" player can cast spells on you (healing or any other helpful spells).

Ok, now speaking of the normal servers, which is the best?

There are older servers (like Xegony and Bristlebane) and newer servers (like Xev and Firiona Vie). Another important thing is how crowded they are. The more players on a server, the more you will encounter in the game. That means, it's easier to get help, but some zones/point are very crowded and it will become difficult to find critters to attack. The decision is yours.

What's the difference between newer and older servers?

Game-wise: nothing. *But* (and here the opinions vary) the community is different. On newer servers, there are less high level people. So there is less high level equipment around. Money holds a higher value since there is less in circulation. As always, the decision is yours.

Can my character move from one server to another?

Yes, but there are fees associated with transferring characters. For more information visit the official *EverQuest* web sight at www.EverQuest.com.

How many characters can I have?

8 per server, or only 1 on Firiona Vie or Sullon Vek.

I created a character and can no longer find him!

You are most likely on the wrong server. Again: You cannot switch servers and the char will always stay on the server where it was created. So check out the other servers to find him or her.

Selecting Your Race/Class

What is the best race/class?

There is no general best race/class. What to play depends on your personal preferences. You want to be a sole caster? Gnome Wizard could be it. You want to bash things good? Troll Warrior. But there are so many possibilities. However there are certain things that are important when creating your character. Two of them are very important: Vision and Faction.

Humans, Barbarians and Erudites have the very worst vision of any race in the game. This may not seem important until one dies in Everfrost, is bound in Qeynos and has to run through the Blackburrow tunnel to get their body. You quickly learn how to kill fire beetles with your bare hands, just to have something to see by. The world is a dark place. there's no sense in making it any darker until you've mastered some of the fine points of play and learned your way around.

Faction is another consideration. For the most part, this is not a problem for Dwarves, Halflings, Elves and Humans — and in most cases, Gnomes. Depends on where one goes. Barbarians are generally ok, too, but have to be cautious if they go to Faydwer. Erudites, on the other hand, are handicapped in many places by poor faction. Rogues also have some of the same quirks to overcome. Learning how faction works and knowing what to avoid killing is an important lesson in the game.

It's also the faction problem that prompts me to discourage new players from trying the evil races — Trolls, Ogres and Dark Elves can be great fun once you know your way around, but it's just one huge headache if you're still learning. Being evil effectively eliminates about 70% of the cities from your list of support bases.

Wait, what is this faction thing?

There are certain races/communities who don't like each other. Sometimes this "not liking" is just that they won't talk with you. In other cases, they will attack you without asking questions (the term for that is KOS (Kill on Sight)). You can increase or decrease your faction standings by killing things. If one kill affects your faction with a certain group, it will be indicated on the chat window just after you kill an NPC. The message will usually take the form "Your faction with XXX has increased/decreased." For example, if you kill a guard in Freeport, the other guards will like you less and maybe start to attack you, instead of defend you. On the other side, if you kill Gnolls or Orcs in Highpass High, the Guards of Highkeep will like you more (whereas the Gnolls and Orcs will hate you more). Faction is a delicate balance and you have to watch carefully what you do out there.

What happens when I'm KOS in a city and go there?

The guards will attack you and try to kill you. The lower level you are, the bigger the chance that you will die. There are ways to enter a city even when you are KOS, but you have to learn them and some parts will be unavailable for you always.

So what race/class shall I choose to start?

As mentioned before, start to think about what you want to do. From there on, choose your race and class. The game will tell you how difficult the combo is. For example: a Dwarven Warrior might be a good thing to start with. No magic to worry about, no major faction problems on the biggest part of Norrath, no vision problems. The best thing is, you can try multiple chars. If you don't like one, try another. Play them a few levels before you decide. Nobody forces you to play a specific combo. You might notice at level 20 that you no longer like the char. Just create a new one.

How important is the roleplaying?

EverQuest is a roleplay game. Therefore it *should* be very important. Again, nobody forces you to roleplay, but basically you should at least try to do it. If you are an experienced RPG (Role Play Game) Veteran (maybe even with a Pen & Paper RPG background), jump right in. Show others how to do it. If you are new to the concept of RPG, then think about your char. It is more than pixels on the screen. What background does he have? How did he grow up? What does he like, what not? And remember the basic facts: A Paladin shouldn't hunt together with a Dark Elf Necromancer. It just don't fit. Unless the Paladin wants to "turn" the DE on the right side. But then try to do it. Talk with him. Give him advice.

How do I know that I have a good combo/char?

Easy question: If you have fun, then it's ok. It does not matter if you are a weakling Warrior, or a very strong Gnome. But always respect the fun and time of others! Don't have fun at the cost of other people. If your whole group dies, because you weren't in the mood to heal them, you might have fun, but you ruined the fun of others. *EverQuest* is a community where people should care about each other. And there are certain "rules" you should have to agree to when entering the world. You will see more about that in the Etiquette sections (pages 181-184).

I don't like to group. What is the best class/race to solo?

Well, first you should ask yourself if *EverQuest* (as an Online Multiplayer Game) is the right decision for you, if you don't want to group and meet other people. There are other games out there (Diablo II, Half-Life, Quake) that may better suit you. But if you really, really want to solo, then there are several good classes. Again, the opinions vary *very* much here. But a Druid, Mage or even Necro come to my mind.

What about religion?

Religion plays a minor part in *EverQuest*, however it still has several impacts on the gameplay. NPC's consider if they like or hate you based on your race, class and religion. If you worship the god of hate you're definitely making a statement! This is essential for Enchanters. They have the ability to use illusions to change their appearance. However, as much as they can change the "race", they can't change the religion which still "shines through."

The First Steps in Norrath

OK, I did the tutorial, created a char, now what?

Well, to speak with Sony Online Entertainment's words: "You are in our world now." You are a young citizen of Norrath. Depending on your race, you start in one of the major cities. The first steps are important. Look at your inventory. You will find a weapon, a book, a scroll, and maybe (if you are a caster) one or two spells. Equip the weapon (remember the tutorial?), and read the scroll. On the scroll you will find the name of your guildmaster. Search for him in the city you are in and give him your scroll. Don't see this part of the game as wasted. Try to learn the basics of the city. Where is the bank? Where can I buy food? Check out the merchants. If you want, you can make notes. You will be in this city a lot, so the better you know it, the easier it will be for you later. If you are totally lost, try to ask someone for help, showing your guild. If you ask nicely (and if possible roleplay style), the chances are high that someone will help you. When you have given the scroll to your guildmaster, he will give you your newbie tunic, which you can equip too.

What is that book in my inventory?

The book is your way to become PvP on a non-PvP server (see section "Before You Start To Play" for details about PvP). If you don't intend to become PvP, you can destroy the book. Or you can store it in the bank for future use (if you know where the bank is). I'd recommend destroying it over wasting a slot in the bank for that book as PvP basically doesn't exist anymore on non-PvP servers.

I want to sell my weapon, but I can't...

Yes, your newbie weapon (and tunic) is *no drop*. Therefore you can't drop it on the ground, trade it or sell it. That's a good thing as you will not lose it that way.

How do I use my spells?

Do the tutorial. If you did and just forgot: click SPELLS to open your spell book, then click on your spell and it will get attached to your pointer. Drag it to an empty slot in your spell book and click again. You will start to scribe your spell in your book. This will take some time, so be patient. After scribing it, you can memorize it by clicking on it in your spell book, dragging it to an empty slot on the left side of your screen and clicking there again. The memorizing will take some time too. And don't worry, memorizing spells will be *much* faster later in the game.

What can I hunt now?

It is now time to leave your city. You will not find many things to hunt in the cities themselves. When you leave the city, it is very likely that you will *zone* (except for Kelethin, where the city is in the middle of the Greater Faydark Zone). To *zone* means that you will leave one zone and enter another. This will take some time (based on your configuration and Internet Connection Speed, but mostly on your RAM). You will recognize the zoning when the screen freezes and you will see the words "LOADING, PLEASE WAIT..." appear on your screen. After you finished the zoning, you will stand in a new zone. Don't just run mindlessly away. You might never find your way back! Try to stay close to the zone point first. The zone point is a way to flee from trouble.

Enemies cannot follow you through the zone, so if you are fleeing and make it to the zone point, you're as good as saved. Look around to find things to hunt. Good starting critters are Bats, or Decaying Skeletons.

How do I fight?

Do the tutorial. But there are a few other important things. First, *always* consider a target before attacking it. If you don't know what considering is, then go and read the manual. In short it means to check about the critter. To consider something, select it by clicking on it and type "/con." You will see a message.

The most important thing is the color:

Green: You will most likely win

Light Blue: The safest fight that will still yield experience.

Blue: There is a good chance that you'll win

Black The chances are more or less equal

Yellow: There is a good chance that you will die

Red: You will most likely die

You can also tell more from the message. If the enemy looks at you "amiably", it will never attack you, regardless of the color. Wolves to Druids are an example of that. If it looks at you "indifferently", there is a chance that it will attack you, especially if it is blue, black/white or yellow.

After you did a "/con", you can attack by selecting it (if not still selected) and then press "A" (to attack). A good thing would be to re-set your attack key to something you will normally not use when talking (e.g. ~) (details about remapping keys can be found in the section "Hotkeys"). Why? Well, if you stand in front of an NPC and want to talk with him (for example "What is the ....?"), you have to press ENTER first. If you forget that, you will come as far as "Wha" and with the "a" you attack the NPC which will very likely kill you. Trust me on that. It is such a common problem for most players of *EverQuest*, that it is almost a right of passage. After pressing "A" (or better "~") you will switch into Auto-Attack and start to attack and hopefully defeat your enemy. Watch your health bar. If you are about to die, run to a guard or to the zone point.

Instead of typing /con, you could also re-map considering to a key (details about how to re-map functions/commands can be found under "Hotkeys"). Check out the suggestion of Nusabrecat: "For example, I use my keypad to move around, and have my mouse in my other hand, so to keep actual hand movement to a minimum, I assigned /con to keypad 3. Now I just left click on a target, and hit 3, and up pops my chances. Another way to /con is simply right-click on the target. This works just as well and does the same thing, but there are a few reasons why I prefer to use my key.

1. Sometimes if lag is heavy, the server won't recognize your mouse's position because it is too busy at the moment, and will therefore disregard your click, as it can't tell what you are clicking on. This can be *frustrating*. But if you have something targeted already, the keystroke will go through and you will see if you're about to become monster bait or not.

2. If you are close to another PC and you want to get a general idea of his/her level via the /con, and you right click, you will inspect said PC as well. If you use the keystroke, you will not inspect them.

I killed a critter, what do I get for it?

You can get several things. First, you will get experience. But only for as long as the critter doesn't con green to you (meaning when you do a /con it should be blue or higher). There are a few exceptions (called "High-Green") where green will still give you experience. Then you might get a faction hit (see above). Normally animals don't give faction hits, but NPC's or critters like Goblins/Orcs/Gnolls and so on will. And you can loot your kill. Just right-click on it and you will see what they have on them.

I tried to loot the monster with a right click but it keeps telling me "It makes no sense to consider the dead" and doesn't show me the loot.

This message is sometimes displayed if you stand a bit too far from the NPC you are trying to loot. Move a bit closer or around it and try to loot it again.

What can I do with the stuff I looted?

Again, several things. You can sell it to a merchant or to a player to get money. Normally you will get higher prices by selling to players. (But beware: they might try to fool you. It's good to know about the value of an item.) Players won't buy anything and normally they like to buy in masses. Two good things to start with are Bat Wings and Bone Chips. The Wings are a spell ingredient for the spell "Levitate" and Necros or Shadow Knights need the Bone Chips to make their pets. Collect them until you have 20 of them (they are stackable, so you will only lose one slot in your inventory for 20 wings). Once you have 20 (the maximum for stackable items; after that you will need additional slots), try to sell them using the "auction channel." To use it, enter "/auct" followed by the thing you want to sell or buy. Maybe you want to ask for offers first or just sell to the first person that wants them. Always try to sell stacks (20) or multiple stacks. The chances of selling are much higher. The key is to find out what you can sell and what not. But in the beginning, sell everything (unless you can use it), either to players or merchants.

How can I carry more things around?

There are several "containers" which will allow you to carry more. Small bags can hold up to 4 items. Large Bags up to 6, Backpacks and some chests hold up to 8 items. There are even 10 slot backpacks out there (player made), but they are VERY expensive. So with 8 backpacks (maximum) you could carry 64 items. Stackable items use only one slot up to 20 pieces. You can tell which items are stackable because they have a small "1" in the lower right corner. You should also try to have 1 or 2 inventory slots without containers, as there are certain things which require a free inventory slot to work (e.g. to drink alcohol you have to put a bottle in the inventory slot and right click on it). Some say a backpack is the first thing a newbie should buy, as it allows you to carry around more loot stuff.

How do I drink/eat?

Eating and drinking is done automatically. In desert zones (like Ro), you will use more drinks than in other zones. You start off with 5 food and 5 drinks. Later you have to get more supplies.

Where do I get food/drinks?

You have several ways. One is to buy from merchants. Beware that alcohol does *not* count as drink. The cheapest food to buy are muffins, the cheapest drink is milk. You might have to search for a merchant that sells food and/or drink, or you can ask someone. Another way to get food and drink is to forage it. Some classes (e.g. Rangers and later Druids) and some races (e.g. Wood Elves) have the ability to search the ground for food. It's a skill (see section "Skills, Spells and Abilities") you have to *do*. It's not done automatically. If successful, you will find either food or water. A third way to get food is fishing. Fishing might be one of the most underestimated skills in *EverQuest*. It is fairly cheap to start. All you need is a pole (costs a few gold coins) and bait (can be foraged or bought for about 4 copper per bait). Then you put the pole in your primary hand and stand or sit next to some water (rivers, lakes or oceans) and start fishing. If you are successful, you will catch a fish (food or can be sold for about 4 silver), a fishscale (can be sold to other players in stacks (spell ingredient)), a rusty dagger (can be used or sold to other players (weapon for pets)) or an old shoe (can be weared as a minor armor or sold). From time to time you might lose your bait or you will lose one when you catch a fish. But all in all, it's a good skill. Needs some patience, but can save money. And there is nothing like sitting on a dock, fishing, and watching the sunset or sunrise. Another way to get food or drink is to summon it. There are 2 spells called "Summon Food" and "Summon Drink" which will magically create food or drink. These items are *no rent*, which means they will vanish 30 minutes after you log out of *EverQuest*. They cannot be sold to merchants. One last way is the "suicide" way. From level 1 to 4 you will not lose experience when you die (more about dying later). So you can put all your belongings in the bank (even weapons and equipment) and then attack a guard. The guard will kill you and you will start again with 5 food items and 5 drink items. Then you can get your items from the bank and continue your hunt. But it's not quite an honorable way and works only in the first 3 levels (it doesn't work at level 4; you don't lose XP, but you don't get your new food and drink, either).

Can I die when I'm out of food or drink?

Not directly. But you will no longer regenerate health or mana. And the effect is cumulative. So if you're out of food for a longer period, you will eat more than one "portion" when you finally have found food. So always keep an eye on the food/drink.

How long does the food/drink last?

It depends on what it is. A "snack" lasts only a short time, whereas a "banquet size meal" lasts much longer.

What happens when I die?

That depends on your level. From level 1 to 4 you will not lose experience. Later, it can be pretty significant (even risking to lose a level). But your corpse, with all the belongings you had on you, will lie where it was killed. You will start again at your Bind point (that point can later be changed with the spell "Bind Affinity"). The bind point is most likely in your newbie zone close to some guards. So you have to go to the same spot and loot your own corpse to get your things back.

How long will my corpse be there?

That depends on your level:

Characters All Levels: If you have no items on your corpse, it will disappear within 3 minutes.

Characters Level 1-5: Corpse will disappear within 30 minutes (real time) whether you are online or offline. Those of you wondering why this rule is in place? There would be WAY too many bodies if we didn't do it this way.

Characters Level 6 and above: Corpse will disappear within 24 hours if the player is online (being at the Character Select screen STILL counts as online). Corpses will disappear within 1 week if the player is offline. Note: the amount of time you spend online, while a corpse is decaying, will be proportionally subtracted from the amount of offline time available. For example, if you are online for 12 of the 24 hours, your corpse will have 3 days and 12 hours of offline time (half of one week) available to it.

What happens when the corpse disappears?

It will no longer be there. Also, all the items, money and belongings you were carrying will be lost. So it's a good idea to store some things you don't want to lose in the bank. Maybe even with a spare weapon or armor.

How can I find my corpse?

Best thing would be, not to lose it first hand. Knowing where you are makes it easier to collect a corpse. If you have to flee, you can enter "/loc" to see coordinates of your whereabouts. You can even create a hotkey for that purpose (see Hotkeys). If you know the coordinates or some close one, it will be easier to find your body. For more information about how to use "/loc" and the coordinate system, visit www.eqatlas.com.

Who can help me find my corpse?

Basically every player. But they have to search around like you would have to. The more information you have (things you've seen, coordinates etc.) the easier it is. Bards and Necromancers have special spells/skills to locate corpses. Try asking one of them for help. But always remember that they have to interrupt what they are doing to help you. So be thankful and if you can afford it, you can offer a donation. Some will not accept it, some will. The point is to show your gratitude.

I can see my corpse, but there is a tough enemy next to it.

Try /corpse. This summons the corpse to your location if you're close to it. Keep at it. By walking and entering /corpse (or using a hotkey) constantly, you can pull your corpse to a safe spot to loot (e.g. next to some guards).

I still can't get my corpse as it is too dangerous.

Then you have another chance, namely to get another player to pull the corpse to you. By using the command "/consent" followed by the players name, you give him the right to pull your corpse around. Earlier in *EverQuest* he was able to loot the corpse with /consent, but that is no longer the case, so it's more or less secure. I say more or less as he still could pull your corpse even farther away or put it next to a more dangerous critter. Be warned to do it only to players you fully trust.

What happens when I gain a level?

When you receive enough experience, you will gain a level. You will see a message on your screen stating "Welcome to Level X" together with a great sound (it sounds like a "*ding*", therefore a lot of people shout "DING" around the zone to tell that they leveled). You will have more health and mana (if you're a caster) and can continue to increase your skills/spells/abilities (see section "Skills, Spells and Abilities"). You will also be able to hunt tougher critters, whereas you might no longer get exp for others. You will also get 5 skill points to spend (see section "Skills, Spells and Abilities"). In the beginning, you will level fairly often; later on, it will be much tougher.

I can't find some of my abilities (like Fish or Kick)?

Check out the section about Hotkeys.

How can I prevent to lose my possessions by accident?

There are certain moments in the life in Norrath where the danger of dropping an item is very high. For example Bards switching their instruments, during the initial start of a trade and so on. When an item is dropped there is a risk that it gets lost. Another player (or even an NPC) might pick it up or it can fall into a tree or wall and make it unavailable. This danger has been reduced with the announce of a command called /fastdrop. The client now allows players to set "Item Dropping" preferences on the "General" options tab. The three options that can be set are:

Fast Drop. Items are dropped without confirmation.

Confirm. A confirmation box will be displayed whenever you try to drop an item.

Never. You are not allowed to drop items on the ground.

Alternatively, you can also set these options using the /fastdrop command. The arguments are:

On. Same as option "Fast Drop" on the General Tab.

Off. Same as option "Confirm" on the General Tab.

Never. Same as above.

Please note that whatever your setting, coin will always be dropped without confirmation. Additionally, the FastDrop option only applies to items being dropped upon the ground. Handing items directly to NPCs will still work regardless of your FastDrop setting. It is highly recommended that you use option "CONFIRM", as GMs will not reimburse any items that are accidentally dropped.

Equipment

How do I know what items I can use?

There are thousands of items in *EverQuest*. The best thing is to ask around. Look out for a higher level player of your race/class and politely ask if he has a few minutes for you. If he has, ask him about tips what to get for your level and budget. Also various websites offer lists of items. When buying/trading from another player, make sure to right click on the item before you accept the trade. It will show under RACE: and CLASS: who can use it. All/All means everyone can use it.

Q:What is a lore item?

Lore means you can have only one of that item on you (including the bank). If you try to loot a 2nd one it will not work and a msg pops up saying that you can't have more than one of that item.

What is a No Rent item?

No Rent means that the item will vanish 30 minutes after you camp out. This is always the case for summoned items (see below) as well as for specific other items that can be looted. In a recent patch it got changed that if you get disconnected, the item will continue to be on your character for 30 minutes. However, if it takes longer than that time the items will be gone (and in case of summoned bags everything within the bag). Such items (or items lost because they were inside a summoned bag) will not be reimbursed.

What is a No Drop item?

No Drop means you can't trade, sell or drop the item. Once you looted it, it will stick on your character unless you destroy it or hand it to an NPC as a "gift."

What is a Magic item?

If an item is *Magic* it can bring several advantages. Some of the items will raise (or lower) some of your stats. Other items have an effect (see below) or a proc (see below). You will also need a magic weapon to hit certain creatures (e.g. willowisps or ghouls). Magic Armor can also increase your stats or are just magic in the way that an Ogre as well as a Gnome can wear it.

What is a Summoned item?

Certain casters (especially Magicians) have the ability to summon items which you can use. These include water/food as well as weapons, bags, bandages or other usefull items. They offer some nice advantages (e.g. all summoned weapons are considered "magic", the bags offer a weight reduction), but also has a danger: all summoned items will vanish when you log out. This is also the case if you crash or go Linkdead. In case of bags the bag will vanish and destroy everything that was in the bag. These items are *gone*. There was a change that will hold the items up to 30 minutes if you come back right after a crash. However, this is an aid, and not guaranteed. They might be gone even if you return after 5 minutes. The best is to not count on it. There is no way to get them reimbursed. So use summoned items at your own risk.

What is an Effect on a weapon?

An *Effect* is a spell that is bound on a weapon or armor. To use it, right click on it in your inventory screen. Every use will use one "charge." You can see on the number next to *Charges*: how many there are left.

What is a Proc on a weapon?

The *Proc* is an *Effect* (see above) but without charges. It means the effect is randomized and will go of while you fight with the weapon. These effects are unlimited, but you can't decide when to use it.

What does the size of an item mean?

The information next to SIZE: does tell you what size of container you need to store it. For example: a wurmslayer is a big weapon and will not fit in a container, that can only hold tiny items. What size a container can hold can be checked by right clicking on the container. In case of armor this should not be mistaken as the size of the actual armor.

What does PRIMARY, SECONDARY, RANGE mean?

It shows in what hand the weapon goes. You can't equip two items at the same time if both of them only fit in your primary hand.

What does item xxx cost?

Prices vary a lot from server to server and from item to item. There are certain web sites that offer a price check, but you should not blindly follow them. If you want to buy a specific item it's worth asking around (especially trusted friends) and watch several auctions for that item to get the general idea of the price.

Skills, Spells and Abilities

What does the spell XXX do?

There are many, many spells in *EverQuest*. Some are DD (Direct Damage, the spell inflicts a damage directly), some are DoT's (Damage Over Time, the spell does lesser damage, but over and over again), some are heals, some for information, and some are Buffs (enhancement spells). If you can't figure out what the spell does, either ask a higher player of your class, or check out the various sites on the internet. Some sites are even dedicated to specific classes (like www.eqdruids.com).

What skills and abilities do I have?

Same as with spells, the skills and abilities vary from race to race and class to class. If you can't figure out what a skill does (like Taunt), then ask a higher player of your class/race or check out the various sites on the internet.

What is the max/cap on a specific skill?

The skill max varies. Most of the skills have the cap of (5*Level)+5, that means if you are at level 8, the max would be 45: (5* +5. Also the skills have a skill cap, where it will no longer go up. For example, Druids can have Tracking starting at Level 20 and the cap is at 50.

What do these things like "Feeble" or "Awful" mean?

When you click on Skills under the Persona menu, you'll see a long list of the various skills you now possess. Each skill will have a description underneath it. When you first start out, usually every skill will be listed as Awful, with the exception of your racial language and Common, which will both be Excellent. What do these mean?

Awful	Skill level from 0-10
Feeble	11-20
Very Bad	21-30
Bad	31-40
Below Average	41-50
Average	51-60
Above Average	61-70
Good	71-80
Very Good	81-90
Excellent	91-100
Master	101+

How high is my skill/ability?

You can check it by clicking on "Persona" and then on "Skills." But it will only give you a summary like "Feeble" or "Awful." If you want to know the value itself, you have to carefully watch your screen. Every time you increase a skill or ability it will tell you and give a number (like "You have become better at swimming! (14)"). You note down that value. Another way is to turn on logging ("/log"), which stores a logfile in your EQ directory (eqlog.txt). You can then either search through it manually or use a log-file parser. You can find some of these tools on www.eqvault.com under "Files."

How do I learn XXX?

You have two ways to learn skills or abilities. One is to put skill points into it. Every time you level up, you get 5 skill points to distribute. Search your guild trainer and right click on him. You will then see what you can learn. Some skills require a specific level (like "Back stabbing" at level 8 for Rogues), others require you to not only put skill points in it, but also money. Points you don't spend will stay and you can accumulate them. The second and IMHO better way is to just use the skill over and over again. That doesn't work for things like Offense or 1H Slash, but for a lot of others like Swimming, Sense Heading, Spell Abilities (Conjuration, Abjuration, Alteration, Evocation and Divination), Fishing and so on. Example: Every time I level up, I wait for the next pause I take (either meditating or healing up) and then I just click on Sense Heading over and over again, until it's maxed for my level (see about max/caps above). I also often spend about an hour or two into training the 5 spell abilities by casting the same spells over and over again (e.g. *Skin like Wood* for Alteration). I call this "Training Session." The big advantage is, that I don't depend on using the spells in "real" but I have all of them maxed at any time. That's important especially for spell abilities you don't need often (e.g. conjuration). The skill points can be saved to quickly increase a skill later to a certain level.

Any more tips on training?

Sure! Training starts costing money after level 20. Any skill that has a level minimum needs to have one point invested in it before it can start growing on its own (like "Back stabbing" at level 8 for Rogues). It is this writer's opinion that training points are precious, and should be used wisely. Don't waste them on things that will go up quickly, like melee skill, spell categories, or especially meditate. These will all go up on their own fairly quickly, and you can save your training points for skills later in life. They'll never disappear, so why 'impulse spend' them? Warriors, wouldn't you like to have 10 or 15 extra points to put into Dual Wield or Double Attack as soon as you get it? This is not to say that you should never use training for weapons; as you get to higher levels, it becomes harder and harder to up your skills. If you've been neglecting your piercing ability, it probably isn't a good idea to start practicing on a Sand Giant! Many veterans also advise putting 3 or so training points into sense heading to get it going, as it takes *forever* on its own. Also, giving any trade skills (Baking, Sewing, Pottery, etc . ...) a 5 point jump can save you a lot of time and money when you start them, although trade skills can only be trained up to 20, after which you can only up your skill by doing.

What do the different colors of spell symbols mean?

Some spells are "Self-only." Minor shielding is one of them. Note that the icon is yellow.

Here's a reminder of icon colors:

Yellow	Self-only
Red	an be cast on self and others
Purple	Area of Effect
Blue	Heals, cure, clarity
Green	non-damage spell

When will "Sense Heading" tell me the correct direction instead of "you think you are facing ..."?

Always. That's just the way the message pops up. If you see a direction, then it *is* the direction. Either you sense it, or you don't sense it. But you never sense a wrong direction.

GMs and Guides

(Note: information taken from official posts and FAQs. Procedures might change at any time and without warning.)

What is a GM?

A GM (Game Master) is an employee of Sony. He is helping players with problems due to bugs or problems at Sony's side. Every server has a designated GM with defined working hours. In addition there is mostly a GM available in CHAT as well as floating GM's without an assigned server.

What is a Guide?

A Guide is a volunteer player. A Guide is NO employee of Sony and does not get payed for his work (except he/she doesn't have to pay the monthly fee for one account). The Guide can help in certain specific problems (see below). However, Guides are bound within policies they have to follow.

What can a GM/Guide do for me?

They can aid in problems due to verifiable bugs, help with stuck corpses (e.g. corpses in a wall) or answer game-play related questions (no spoiler information about equipment, NPC's or quests). For a complete list check out the FAQ at www.*EverQuestlive*.com / Game Policies / "Game Masters and Guide FAQ"!

What can a GM/Guide not do for me?

They can't help if you die due to going Linkdead, give out spoiler information about quests or NPC's, summon you to a spot where you want to go, recover your corpse that is not stuck or with other incidents which the policies state. Again, for a complete list check out the FAQ at www.*EverQuestlive*.com = Game Policies = "Game Masters and Guide FAQ"!

How do I get the help from a GM/Guide?

You have to use the /petition command, followed by a description of your problem. Include as much details as possible. For example: "/petition I died in Blackburrow right at the zone line to Qeynos Hills. I searched for my corpse but can't find it. A passing Bard told me it might be stuck in the wall." This would be a good example whereas "/petition help" is a bad one. Also remember that the Guides/GM's are a) real persons with feelings and b) are not responsible for whatever happened. Try to stay calm and polite. Cursing, threatening or being rude will not help and much more likely lower the will of them to help you. Remember that Guides are volunteers and not paid employees of Sony, they are there to try to help you. So return the favor and treat them with dignity and respect, it is thankless work.

How can I become a Guide myself?

First, read the FAQ at www.*EverQuestlive*.com / Game Policies / "Game Masters and Guide FAQ" to ensure that it's really something you want to do. Remember that you are not allowed to tell anyone if you are a guide. So if you want to become one to "brag" around you may want to reconsider it. Otherwise go to the application form at: guideapp.*EverQuest*.com.

The Dangers of EverQuest

This section handles some basic scams you can run into. We have to be honest. *EverQuest* is played by Humans and like everywhere else some are nice and some just want to take advantage of the kindness of strangers. By knowing about some of these dangers you will have no problems in this game ....

This section is dedicated to the wisdom and teachings of our very own NakedNewbie.

Secret Information Scam

NEVER reveal your account name and/or password to *anyone* for any reason! You may now be thinking, "Well duh! Who would?" You'd be surprised at who would. The people behind *EverQuest* like Sony, and 989studios will *never* ask you while playing online for your password, account info, or credit card info. Be very careful of players posing as GMs (GameMasters). A REAL GM will have "GM" or "Guide" in their title when you do a /who. A real GM also has neutral faction for every mob in the game, meaning they will never be attacked by a MOB (monster) unless they attack first.

Trade Window Scam

This scam has unfortunately victimized literally hundreds of players to date. Thanks to Sony through a patch, this scam has been eliminated substantially, but not completely. To prevent this scam from happening to you is *very easy* to do. Simply *never* press the "trade" button unless you are 100 percent *positive* that you are ready to give the money or item(s) to the other player you are conducting the trade with. Always *carefully* look at both sections of the trade window when performing a trade with another player. The left section is the other player's, the right section is yours. For example, if you are buying a Shiny Brass Halberd and a Barbed Leather Whip from another player, make sure that *both* items are in the other player's section of the trade window *before* you press the "trade" button with your money in it. Also make sure to right-click on each item to verify that it IS the item you truly want *before* you press the "trade" button. Also make sure you can use the item with both race AND class.

In an opposite example, if you are the seller of the items, make sure that all the money is exact and in full before you press the "trade" button. Get it? And don't worry about someone removing items or money before you hit the "trade" button to get cheated. Sony fixed that making it impossible to complete a trade that way. You'll have to cancel it causing no loss to both parties.

False Promises Scam

This has happened to *hundreds* of players and it *still* happens every day! I cannot believe how naive and trustworthy many players are. *no offense to anyone*, here's my point. A player may try to sell you something that you wish to buy. They ask for the money first in advance and then tell you that the item you are buying is actually on a different character of theirs. They tell you to give them the money first, then they will log off and log back on as the other character to give you the item you are buying. *never* give your money to *anyone* without the goods being delivered to you *simultaneously* in the trade window!! There are unfortunately *many* players who will try their best to cheat you and deceive you! I'm sorry, but this IS a *true* fact. Of course, not all players are like this, but the bad ones are out there.

Drag Your Corpse For You Scam

Sometimes a player is quick to offer to drag your corpse to a safe spot when YOU cannot get it yourself. In theory, how do they do this? Once again, "/consent . After giving consent, they are able to drag your corpse using the /corpse command to a safe spot for you to retrieve it yourself. However, if you do not *fully* trust this person, that person may drag it to an even more dangerous spot.

I'll Show You a Perfect Place To Hunt Scam

This is a very rare scam, but it could happen to you. A veteran player may approach you and ask you to go with them to a really great place to hunt. A place that comes to mind is the dungeon Befallen. If you are a newbie, you should not enter Befallen or any place that you have not yet learned or are not yet high enough in level. The player takes you there, sets you at a dangerous spot, then *leaves you* coldly. What does the bad player get out of this? Nothing of yours, but their own evil satisfaction that you are gonna die in a place where you may not get your corpse again. Once again, this is a very rare scam. Be cautious anyway before you go somewhere with someone. That player may actually be a good person who only wants to hunt with someone, but that player may also be too brave and foolish. There are *many* players who think they can take on *big* risks which only causes themselves and *you* to die in a place that may be difficult to retrieve your corpse.

May I Try On Your Armor or Weapon Scam

Some players may approach you and tell you their "dream" of how they would look like in the armor you are wearing or how the weapon you are wielding would look on them. They then ask you if they could borrow the weapon or armor for "just a moment" to try it on themselves and check it out. *never* lend someone your weapon or armor!! What are you going to do if they do not return it?? A "petition" will *not* work because you gave them the item on your own free will!

Begging Because I Lost My Corpse Scam

From time to time, you will see a player using shout or ooc to beg everyone if someone would be kind to give them money and items because they lost their corpse and they have to start out fresh. Some of these players may even send you a tell directly. Whenever I get a shout, ooc, or a tell from one of these players, I immediately grill them thoroughly on how the hell they lost their corpse. The answers have varied greatly and most of them are outright ridiculous! One "Creative" story was someone came up to me wearing full bronze and wielding a BIBS. He begged me for money! I looked at him up and down and said, "Bud, you look like *you* could give me some money!" He told me that "somehow" when he logged on, all of his money in the bank *vanished*!!! Yeah right. I told him to petition it and he said the GMs could do nothing. There are some players out there that will be anonymous. They take off all their armor and goods so that nothing will appear on them in view. They then go out and beg while telling a fictional story of how they lost their corpse and Sony won't do anything about it.

Now let's look at the flip side of this coin. It *is* possible for *many* players to genuinely lose their corpse, which causes them to start over fresh with nothing. My point is that there are also many players that will try to deceive everyone just to get free gifts and money. It is your own judgment call.

Because I'm Evil, I Can't Buy Scam

Some, not all, "evil" player characters will tell you that because their character is "evil", they cannot buy from any of the local vendors food, drink, etc. They ask you to either buy the stuff for them or give it to them now and they will pay you later. They end up never paying you back. This may be no big deal to an established character, but to a newbie, this could be a great loss. *no offense* to anyone. I am just presenting a true action that *some* evil player characters will do to a newbie.

How to Prevent Losing an Item Accidentally

This is not a scam, but rather a tip on how to not accidentally lose an item. There are times when you may accidentally drop an item on the ground. This item may be very valuable to you. If you are not quick enough, anyone nearby you who is quicker will successfully pick up the item and they do not have to return it. How can you prevent this? By focusing on the *tip* of your *mouse-pointer*, *not* the item itself. When placing an item in any particular slot, do not aim the *item itself* to try to equip or store it. Instead, use the tip of your mouse-pointer on your screen to aim the item into the center of the open slot that you wish to place it in. Do this slowly and with precision. Avoid doing this while under stress or rushing, like in the heat of battle for example. Because if the tip of the mouse-pointer misses the center or near the center of the open slot that you want to place the item in, it will most likely fall to the ground.

Also *always* remember that if an item is *too big* to fit in any container you are carrying, and there are no more open available inventory slots, the item will automatically fall to the ground. *And*, if you have *no* open available inventory slots in the first place, any new container that you try to pick up or trade will also immediately fall to the ground.

In plain English, if something ever falls to the ground by accident, anyone nearby you can quickly pick it up before you can.

Buying and Selling Outside the Luclin Bazaar

These tips were provided by Sysop-Elbrop

Buying:

Abbreviations. Don't know what a GWC is? Then ask the person who is auctioning it. Nobody minds, sure they might make a sale out of you!

Prices. Someone's selling for a price out of your range? Then consider haggling. Worst case he says no.

Race/class. Ask the seller to confirm that your race/class can use the item.

Security: When you are buying the item a trade window opens. If you right click on the item it will bring up a description of the item (stats, race/class restrictions etc). Check that the item is everything you were told it was.

Change. If the item is 10pp and you have 100 gold then ask if they will accept it. While 100 gold is worth 10pp a lot of people might not want the extra weight. It's impolite to dump all your loose change on another player!

Selling

Price. Not sure how much the item is worth? Then ask around in one zone to get a rough idea then sell in another zone.

Description. Ok, there are a lot of items that are so well known that abbreviations are used when selling such as GLS (Giant light stone) or RTS (ruined totem staff). But remember even if you know what these are, not everyone does. Be prepared to get tells from people who want to know what a BIBS is.

Stats. If you are selling weapons or armor, then including the stats can help the sale. Not everyone knows the AC of bronze amour. You might just get a few extra sales by informing them.

Race/class. A lot of items are restricted to certain races or classes. Some can be used by all races and all classes. Try and make sure your customer is able to use the item before you waste too much time selling to them. If the customer can't use it, then tell him so; maybe he wants it for a friend or another character so he won't mind.

Bids. Instead of saying it costs 10pp, say bids start at 10pp. Recently, I started at 5pp for a pair of gloves and by the end I got 11pp! Some people use the /auction command to bid, others send you tells. Make sure you keep everyone alerted with /auction statements (/auction last bid 11pp on gloves).

Notes

Two terms WTB (want to buy) and WTS (want to sell). Often you will see these at the start of an auction. A simple and quick way of letting everyone know if you are looking to buy or sell the item.

Always make sure you have room in your inventory for what you are buying. If you don't, they fall to the ground and anyone can pick them up. I once dropped a banded helm and boots because of this.

Summoned items will vanish when you log off the game. Remember this if you see someone auctioning summoned items.

General Tips

Where can I enter a brief history about my character?

Change the view mode until you see yourself in the screen [F9], then right click on yourself. In the lower right corner of the screen you can see a text window where you can put information about yourself. This can be viewed by other players inspecting you.

How can I take a screenshot?

By pressing the [-] (minus) key on your Numpad. The screenshots are called EQ00000x.bmp with x as an increasing number. They are stored in your *EverQuest* directory.

What are the green bars and numbers on my screen?

That is the lag meter. It works like this:

- Left number: Your ping to the server (avg time to send a packet and get a reply)
- Middle Left: % of packets sent by your client lost (known as PL)
- Middle Right: % of packets sent by the server lost (known as PL)
- Right: Quantity of data received from server (don't know exactly how this is quantified).

If the right number falls to zero, you will find yourself starting a "reverse countdown to disconnection" where the PL numbers will climb steadily. Once you reach a hundred (if the connection cannot be recovered before the countdown reaches the number), you are disconnected.

What's the deal with the screen configurations? When do you typically use each of them?

Those are selected based on your own taste, your machine performance and what you're doing at the moment. Switch from one to the other by pressing [F10].

- Half-screen / Console view: The most cluttered screen set up with all the buttons and only 1/4 screen display. Often used when checking your char stats, inventory, ... but not really when playing the game (unless your hardware is borderline for the game requirements).

  [Press [F10] to move to...]

- HUD Mode: Full screen plus hotkeys, basic info (HP, mana), chat window and spell slots. That's the view you'll probably play in most of the time. Gives you better visibility. Make sure to learn how to switch between hotkey button banks ([Shift]+number) and where which hotkey is. This will make you a lot more efficient.

[Press [F10] to move to...]

- Full screen mode: Good for screenshots (numeric [-]) but useless when actually playing.

Can changing the camera angle ([F9]) actually be good for something other than taking screenshots?

Actually, this can be very useful when you fight in the open and want to switch to 3rd person view and move the camera a bit farther from your char. This way, you can see whether any wandering monster is about to join the fight. Makes it a bit more difficult to time your spellcasting, ...

though. This becomes useful after a couple of levels when your fights take more than 2 slashes or 1 spell to resolve. On some views, you can even zoom in and out with Ins/Del and rotate with Alt and arrow keys.

This is a collection of useful tips. Most are taken from the site *EverQuest*.allakhazam.com and only changed to fit the context. Kudos to the makers of this great site. Some tips you already read about, but are so important, that I left them in there. Credits go to the submitters of the tips (if known).

† While hunting low level mobs, remember that decaying skeletons, kobolds, spiders and beetles will gang up on you (if one sees you attacking another monster of its species). No problem for skeletons and kobolds who are very weak but the other 2 are harder to dispatch. Snakes, skunks, rats, ... will ignore you even if you attack another one next to them.

† It might be worth (once you reach level 2) to put 2 or 3 points in the "Sense Heading" skill. Then hotkey the sense heading button and click on it when you're running outside of a fight (for instance going through town). It is a skill that raises very slowly (atrociously slowly if you don't put a few starting points in it) but it will allow you to know in which direction you're headed once it reaches a certain level). There are other tricks to find your way but a good direction skill can come in very handy.

† If you're a spellcaster, timing is everything. Start casting your spells when whatever the monster (tried to) hit you with is moving back in its initial position (for instance, you see a skeleton arm moving back). That should give you the maximum spellcasting time before it hits again and thus less chance of being interrupted. With a bit of practice, you can get your timing right. Note that some mobs have 2 attacks per round so getting your timing right can sometimes be a bit tricky.

† You can fish while sitting down and meditating. So if you are near water and have to med or heal anyway, you can fish and make a little extra money.

† Summoned items disappear when you log out. So be careful about buying anything that was summoned such as food and drink.

† Looking for a sack or other container to store items with your newbie character, but don't want to purchase one? Most of the quests that involve getting multiple items for an NPC involve him giving you a container in which to collect the items. These can usually be used to store anything, and are essentially free containers which you can get often right at level 1.

† For classes with the ability to "sneak", when an NPC merchant regards you less than indifferently, enable sneak before selling or buying from the merchant to get better prices. (You'll know it's working when you /con the merchant and they are "indifferent" to you). This also allows players who couldn't normally deal with an NPC merchant (i.e., Aviak Merchant in South Karana) to buy and sell from them.

† If you hold the right-mouse button down

or the control key and press either the left or right movement keys, you slide to the left or right (normally you would pivot in place). This can provide a safer way to approach a blind corner.

† Program a social button to say /corpse. If you ever have your body in a bad spot and are afraid to go get it, hotkey that button. Then as you inch toward your body trying hard not to awake the nasties who have spawned on your body, press the hot key continually and your body will move toward you from a pretty good distance. When it comes to you, run to a safe place all the way pressing the hotkey and you will "drag" your corpse with you. This also works good for underwater corpse recovery. Also, summoning a corpse (/corpse) will not make invisibility drop, but looting it will. If you die in a dangerous place (say the west side of oasis) you may want to find someone to cast invisibility on you (caster and target must be in same group). You can then hot key /corpse to drag your corpse to a safe place to get your gear back. Added bonus, a corpse bouncing along the ground looks cool (anyone without see invisibility will only see the corpse dragging). (Submitted by Onyxx and Oglug)

† Here is a tip for maximizing profits while hunting with a group: This will take a lot of trust, so if you do not know your party members well do not do it.

1. Get a lot of backpacks, sacks or chests and distribute them to all party members.

2. Have one person loot the corpse until he is full, then the next person loots, and so on.

3. Do not go sell until everyone is full.

4. Have the person with the highest charisma sell all the items at a shop that will give him/her the best prices (most likely his/her home city).

5. Then split the gold between all members as the party sees fit (we always do an even split).

6. Now if there is an item that a person wants the party can have them buy it and split the money between the group or the group can give it to the person. This works very well with a group that hunts very often together. We have employed this tactic to our advantage very often but everyone needs to remember that people get dropped from the server. They will come back with the stuff or your share of the gold(if they are honorable). (Submitted by Brambo the Barbarian)

† Use of small boats (By Tothis) You get IN the boat and right click on it. You will get a message that says "You have the helm" and your movement keys now control the boat. Not only was I able to use this boat, but Rexan (my Dwarven friend) was able to stand in the back of the boat and keep lookout as I paddled us about. The advantage was that he could click on things and con them while my view was pretty much limited to the direction I was rowing us.

Some notes on using the boats to travel about:

1. The boats have a definite "front" and "back." If you get in and take control while facing the wrong way your controls will be reversed. Simple solution: right click to give up control of the boat, turn yourself around and resume control of the boat with another right click.

2. The boat is *not* zippy. This is *not* a shortcut. If you are tempted to do what we did (Travel from one side to the other) take a look at the map link on this site for the Ocean of Tears (the first one is better). *Each* little square is 1000X1000. This map is *huge*. We went from 8000(near the human Island) to -9000 (sisterhood's Island). The top speed of this boat is about the same as if you were running. By comparison, the Butcher Block Zone is about 6000X6000... and that's a pretty good sized zone. The big boat travels *much* faster...

3. No spells. Just like riding the big boat, something about these romantic ocean canoe trips just stuns your spellcasting.

4. If you fall out most races can't get back on unless you try to do so from dry land. (Humans seem to be able to get back on by going to the long sides and swimming forward) Also, we have managed to 'Lock' two boats together. Neither of us could move and had to swim to shore (so don't get too close to each other if you are each in separate boats).

5. The boat has hit points. This leads to the disturbing idea that it could be sunk.

† As soon as you start your character, go into options and reprogram your hotkeys to change auto attack from the default "A" key to something you will never accidentally hit, such as "~." This will prevent you from accidentally attacking a NPC you are talking to because you forgot to hit the enter key to bring up the talk screen.

If you hold down the numberlock key you will continue to run forward without having to keep a hand on the arrow key. This can free your hands to type messages to you group and friends. Just keep an eye on where you are going.

† If you are new to a zone, play close to the zone border while you check out the mobs in the area. This will give you a chance to run for cover if you get in over your head.

† Practice, practice, practice. If you find yourself standing around waiting for someone, use your time to work on a skill. Cast magic. Sense direction. Doesn't matter which skill you practice, you'll thank yourself later.

† Every action has a repercussion. Pay attention to the faction adjustments you are given. When you go to a new area, try to kill things the locals dislike to gain faction with them. You can readily build up either good will or ill will with almost every action. Start killing kobalds, and not only will every kobald in the area start to single you out for attack, but all of the kobald's allies will start to dislike

you as well. This is important, because the developers have seen fit to include high level killer NPC's in otherwise low level zones that will run up and whack you if they start to dislike you (or sometimes just because they can). Also, that kobald runt you have no problem smacking around probably has bigger siblings who will knock your socks off when they see you.

† Learn which monsters give good gold, and which give good experience. It does you no good to power game your Wizard to level 8 where you have a whole new set of spells to use if you can't afford to buy any of them.

† Consult with the maps section before starting into a new area. The cities and zones in this game are huge, and it is hard to memorize every piece of them. You should at least get familiar with where to run if you get in trouble.

† Please use /ooc for out of character statements. Also try and limit the use of /shout. It is a role playing game. This doesn't mean saying thee and thou, but it does mean that your character shouldn't know or talk about the real world, at least not on /shout.

† Before you sell to or buy from a shop keeper, /con him. The more he likes you the better the prices. An apprehensive shop keeper will quote you bad prices just because he doesn't like the looks of you. There can be a 15 to 20% difference in rates. If he isn't at least indifferent, you should try and find another shop keeper to sell to. Attitudes will vary even within a city. Buying and selling from the right person can save you a lot of gold in the long run.

† Don't play in one view. Get used to the other camera views (F9 and F10) and use them when appropriate. Most people will prefer to stay in the first person view most of the game. I know this is how I play. However, when in a battle, you may want to switch to one of the wider views where you can see what is happening all around you. The other views can also help you scout the terrain around you for friends or foes.

† I was amazed to find out that some newbies are playing in windowed mode. You are missing out on the glory of the game's graphics that way. Of course if your computer has limitations, then so be it. Otherwise this mode is strictly for inventory and other temporary things. Program all of your useful commands onto your hot keys (you have 36 of them after all). Then hit F10 once to go to partial full screen mode. You can move around and fight in this mode and still have access to all of your commands. There simply is no comparison to experiencing the game through Full Screen and Windowed modes. Along those lines, you should optimize your screen size by going to options and setting your screen size as high as your video card will allow. You will not believe the difference between the default setting and the higher settings. Get the most out of the game.

Some Last Thoughts

EverQuest is a great game. I'd say it's even more than a game. It's a community and a world of it's own, where a lot of great people from all over the world meet. *EverQuest* is also very addictive. Once you know the basic facts, it is a great place to be. You don't have to know all the things in this file by heart. In fact, many of the things mentioned in here are unknown to a lot of players. Use the file as a first source for questions you might encounter.

Created by Ellegon (aka TheRealEllegon or BalthusDire) with help from his friends below.

Credits (in alphabetic order and with the knowledge that I forgot many):

Ashara, DwWarrior, Balkor_Ironfist, CorwinH, Cyranith, Lost-INNer, Mara, Naked-Newbie, Nevat, Nusabrecat, Pand, Sinda, Sysop-Vinria, Sysop-Wendelius, Sysop-Elbrop, Tielle, T. Henmant, Wadin, Zandar, Zernan and all the others on the Newbie Board

A big thank you goes to Nusabrecat and to Balkin for his inspirational posts called "I made a mistake..."

Don't forget for updates and to have your questions answered come to the Newbie Zone!:

http://pub57.ezboard.com/
bthe*EverQuest*newbiezone

Equipment

There are hundreds of new items in *Shadows of Luclin*, far too many to list in the next eight pages. What we've got here is a collection of the most common useful items found in and near Shar Vahl.

Location (by zone) is listed beside each category name for armor, and in the "Loc." column for weapons and other items. **SVC**: Shar Vahl city, **GRIM:** Grimling Forest, **PAL:** Paludal Cavern, and **SWT:** Shadeweaver's Thicket. **BLT** indicates it's a "basic Luclin tailoring" item, for which instruction books are available in Shar Vahl.

Size ranges from 0 (very small) to 4 (very large).

Value is so misleading we almost omitted it. This column gives an *approximation* of how much an NPC merchant thinks the item is worth. Of course, he'll pay you less on average, and charge more, than the listed value in this column. Factors such as your Faction and Charisma will affect the price he sets. It quickly becomes obvious that an NPC merchant is often not the best judge of an item's value. In particular, he rarely values magical properties. (If a merchant is likely to impose a greater-than-normal difference between his buying and selling price, there's an "MM" note at the end of the line. The higher the "MM" value, the greater his buy/sell difference.)

Prices are given in the standard P G S C (platinum, gold, silver, copper) format.

Weight (Wt) is obvious.

Class and Race Restrictions. Which classes can wield each weapon, or type of weapon, are listed at the beginning of each category and in the Class column. For example, Clerics, Druids, Monks, Shadow Knights, Shamans and Warriors can all wield any 2H Blunt weapon, as listed at the beginning of that category (p. 234). In addition, a Beastlord can wield an iron two handed hammer, so "BL" is separately listed in its Class column.

There are both racial and class restrictions on armor. For each type of armor, the first line after the category name lists which classes and races can wear it, separated by "/".

Class abbreviations: **B**ar**d**, **B**east**L**ord, **Cl**eric, **Dr**uid, **En**chanter, **M**a**g**ician, **M**on**k**, **N**e**c**romancer, **P**a**l**adin, **R**a**n**ger, **Ro**gue, **S**hadow **K**night, **S**ha**m**an, **W**a**r**rior, and **W**i**z**ard. Racial abbreviations: **B**a**r**barian, **D**ark **E**lf, **Dw**arf, **Er**udite, **Gn**ome, **H**al**f**ling, **1/2** (Half Elf), **H**igh **E**lf, **H**u**m**an, **Ik**sar, **Og**re, **Tr**oll, **V**ah **S**hir, and **W**ood **E**lf.

Damage (Dmg) lists the maximum base damage for each weapon. An average strike will inflict up to this many points of damage (although the defender's AC and other factors can reduce the damage). **Delay** (Del) lists how many seconds it takes between strikes with this weapon (for an average character). Your own abilities and current condition might buff or debuff these numbers.

AC (Armor Class) lists armor's defensive protection. The higher the AC, the better the protection.

Each piece of armor protects a different part of your body, indicated by the abbreviation in parentheses immediately after its name: **H**ea**d**, **F**a**c**e, **N**e**ck**, **Sh**oulders, **B**a**ck**, **Ch**est, **W**ai**st**, **Arm**s, **Wri**sts, **H**a**nd**, **L**e**g**s, and **F**ee**t**.

Weapons

1H Blunt

Bard, Cleric, Druid, Monk, Paladin, Ranger, Rogue, Shadow Knight, Shaman and Warrior can use all these 1H Blunt weapons

Weapon	Loc.	Value	Size	Wt.	Del.	Dam.	Classes	Notes
Bone Shafted Warclub	GRIM	1700	2	6.0	3.5	5	Non-Casters	Throwable
Crude Bone Flail	SWT	190	2	9.0	3.7	5	Non-Casters	
Crude Bone Flail	GRIM	190	2	9.0	3.7	5	Non-Casters	
Crude Shell Crusher	GRIM	100	2	8.0	3.8	5	Non-Casters	Throwable
Crude Stone Flail	SWT	240	2	10.0	4.4	6	Non-Casters	Throwable
Crude Stone Morning Star	GRIM	240	2	10.0	4.4	6	Non-Casters	Throwable
Driftwood Club	GRIM	2000	2	5.0	2.7	4	Non-Casters	Throwable
Driftwood Staff	GRIM	4300	3	6.5	2.8	5	All	
Heavy Stone Warhammer	GRIM	1700	2	22.0	4.7	9	Non-Casters	Throwable
Iron Flail	SVC	380	2	10.8	3.7	6		
Iron Mace	SVC	200	2	9.6	3.8	6	Non-Casters	Throwable
Iron Warhammer	SVC	360	2	9.0	3.0	5	Non-Casters	Throwable
Jagged Stone Mace	GRIM	3500	2	9.0	3.8	6	Non-Casters	Throwable
Jagged Stone Morning Star	GRIM	4800	2	11.0	4.3	7	Non-Casters	Throwable
Marcescent Mace	SWT	120	2	7.0	3.5	5	Non-Casters	MM 0
Patonk	SWT	1000	2	5.0	2.9	5	Non-Casters	MM 1.5
Pitch Coated Battle Staff	GRIM	1200	3	8.5	3.2	5	All	
Pitch Coated Warclub	GRIM	6000	2	5.0	3.2	6	Non-Casters	Throwable
Polished Bone Flail	GRIM	3500	2	10.0	3.7	6	Non-Casters	
Shiny Stone Hammer	GRIM	5600	2	7.3	3.0	6	Non-Casters	MM 9
Sullied Mace	PAL	100	2	8.0	3.6	5	Non-Casters	Throwable
Waterlogged Driftwood Club	GRIM	2000	2	10.0	4.0	7	Non-Casters	Throwable
Wooden Practice Flail	SVC	95	2	7.2	3.6	3		
Wooden Practice Mace	SVC	50	2	6.4	3.7	3	Non-Casters	Throwable
Wooden Practice Warhammer	SVC	90	2	6.0	2.9	2	Non-Casters	Throwable

1H Projectile

Weapon	Loc.	Value	Size	Wt.	Del.	Dam.	Classes	Notes
Gor	SWT	100	1	1.0	3.0	5	All	MM 1.5

1H Slash

Bard, Paladin, Ranger, Rogue, Shadow Knight and Warrior can use all these 1H Slash weapons

Weapon	Loc.	Value	Size	Wt.	Del.	Dam.	Classes	Notes
Acrylia Edged Long Sword	SVC	50000	2	8.5	2.5	6		MM 4.2
Acrylia Edged Scimitar	SVC	50000	2	8.5	2.1	5	Dr	MM 4.2
Bone Handled Machete	GRIM	2300	2	8.5	3.2	5	Dr	
Crude Chitin Wingblade	GRIM	240	2	5.0	4.2	6		
Crude Fishing Cleaver	GRIM	50	2	6.5	3.6	5	Sm	Throwable

Weapon	Loc.	Value	Size	Wt.	Del.	Dam.	Classes	Notes
Iron Battle Axe	SVC	380	2	12.8	4.2	7		Throwable
Iron Broad Sword	SVC	120	2	9.0	3.6	6		
Iron Long Sword	SVC	400	2	9.0	3.5	6		
Iron Short Sword	SVC	100	2	6.0	2.8	5		
Jagged Stone Axe	GRIM		2	7.5	3.3	5	Sm	Throwable
Jagged Stone Battle Axe	GRIM	2800	2	9.5	3.7	6		Throwable
Leather Handled Mandible Blade	GRIM	3200	2	8.5	3.2	5		
Marcescent Battle Axe	SWT	200	2	8.0	4.1	6		MM 0
Marcescent Broad Sword	SWT	210	2	7.0	3.5	5		MM 0
Marcescent Hatchet	SWT	60	2	5.0	2.8	4	Sm	MM 0
Marcescent Scimitar	SWT	200	2	6.5	3.5	5	Dr	MM 0
Marcescent Short Sword	SWT	60	2	4.0	2.8	4	BL	MM 0
Polished Chitin Blade	GRIM	280	2	6.0	2.7	4		
Polished Chitin Wingblade	GRIM	3500	2	10.0	4.2	7		
Serrated Needle Claw	SWT	30	2	0.5	3.0	5		STR +1, MM 1.5
Shiny Ore Machete	GRIM	5900	2	5.0	2.4	5	Dr	MM 9
Shlis	SWT	1000	2	3.0	3.8	6		MM 1.5
Sullied Long Sword	PAL	200	2	7.5	3.3	5		
Sullied Short Sword	PAL	50	2	5.0	2.6	4		
Wooden Practice Broad Sword	SVC	30	2	6.0	3.5	3		
Wooden Practice Long Sword	SVC	100	2	6.0	3.4	3		
Wooden Practice Short Sword	SVC	25	2	4.0	2.7	2		

2H Blunt

Cleric, Druid, Monk, Shadow Knight, Shaman and Warrior can use all these 2H Blunt weapons

Weapon	Loc.	Value	Size	Wt.	Del.	Dam.	Classes	Notes
Aged Sapling Staff	GRIM	200	3	10.0	4.0	6	Casters	
Hardened Driftwood Great Staff	GRIM	6500	3	10.0	3.6	9	Rn, Casters	
Iron Two Handed Hammer	SVC	600	3	15.6	4.5	8	BL	
Sinew Wrapped Battle Staff	GRIM	6000	3	10.0	3.8	9	Casters	
Stone Two Handed Hammer	GRIM	7000	3	14.0	4.5	8		
Wooden Practice 2H Hammer	SVC	150	3	10.4	4.4	4	BL	

2H Slash

Paladin, Ranger, Shadow Knight and Warrior can use all these 2H Slash weapons

Weapon	Loc.	Value	Size	Wt.	Del.	Dam.	Classes	Notes
Acrylia Edged 2H Axe	SVC	100000	3	14.0	4.8	16		MM 4.2
Acrylia Edged 2H Sword	SVC	100000	3	13.0	4.2	14		MM 4.2
Chitin Bladed Harvester	GRIM	3700	3	13.0	4.8	8		
Crude Bone Halberd	SWT	320	4	13.0	5.6	10		
Crude Bone Halberd	GRIM	320	4	13.0	5.6	10		
Crude Stone Battle Axe	SWT	300	3	16.0	4.9	9		
Crude Stone Battle Axe	GRIM	300	3	16.0	4.9	9		
Hardened Bone Halberd	GRIM	4600	4	15.0	5.2	10		
Iron 2-H Battle Axe	SVC	600	3	19.5	4.9	10		
Iron Two Handed Sword	SVC	600	3	14.4	5.0	10		
Jagged Stone Battle Axe	GRIM	4200	3	14.0	4.6	9		

Weapon	Loc.	Value	Size	Wt.	Del.	Dam.	Classes	Notes
Marcescent Claymore	SWT	320	3	1.1	5.0	9		MM 0
Marcescent Halberd	SWT	340	4	13.0	5.5	10		MM 0
Sullied Two Handed Sword	PAL	300	3	12.0	4.8	9		
Wooden Practice 2H Sword	SVC	150	3	9.6	4.9	5		

Piercing

Bard, Ranger, Rogue, Shadow Knight and Warrior can use all these Piercing weapons (except where noted)

Weapon	Loc.	Value	Size	Wt.	Del.	Dam.	Classes	Notes
Acrylia Edged Rapier	SVC	50000	2	6.0	2.5	6		MM 4.2
Barbed Bone Fishing Spear	GRIM	3100	3	8.0	3.2	5	Sm	Throwable
Crude Bone Spear	SWT	130	2	5.0	3.2	4	BL, Sm	Throwable
Crude Bone Spear	GRIM	130	2	5.0	3.2	4	Sm	Throwable
Crude Flattened Ore Dagger	GRIM	30	1	3.0	2.4	3	Casters	Throwable
Crude Shell Dagger	GRIM	30	1	1.5	2.4	3	Casters	Throwable
Crude Stone Bladed Spear	SWT	200	3	7.0	3.8	5	BL, Sm	Throwable
Crude Stone Bladed Spear	GRIM	200	3	7.0	3.8	5	Sm	Throwable
Crude Stone Dagger	SWT	30	1	2.5	2.4	3	BL, Casters	Throwable
Crude Stone Dagger	GRIM	30	1	2.5	2.4	3	Casters	Throwable
Iron Dagger	SVC	60	1	3.0	2.4	4	BL, Casters	Throwable
Iron Spear	SVC	400	3	10.5	3.8	6	BL, Sm	Throwable
Marcescent Dirk	SWT	60	2	2.0	2.3	3	BL, Sm, Casters	MM 0
Marcescent Foil	SWT	120	2	4.0	2.8	4	Pl,	MM 0
Marcescent Pike	SWT	180	2	5.0	3.5	5	Pl,	MM 0
Pitch Coated Wood Spear	GRIM	200	3	6.0	3.4	5	Sm	Throwable
Polished Chitin Dagger	GRIM	280	1	3.0	2.2	3	Casters	Throwable
Polished Stone Fishing Dagger	GRIM	280	1	3.0	2.2	3	Casters	Throwable
Polished Stone Spear	GRIM	2500	2	6.0	3.4	5	Sm	Throwable
Recondite Bandit Dirk	PAL	3900	1	2.0	2.2	4	BL, Casters	Throwable, DEX +3, AC 1, MM 20
Scorpialis	SVC	5000	1	1.0	2.5	4	BL; not Rn, SK	No or Drop, MM 20
Sharpened Wolf Femur	GRIM	1800	1	4.0	2.3	3	Sm, Casters	
Sharpened Wood Spear	GRIM	200	3	7.0	3.8	5	Sm	Throwable
Shiny Stone Dagger	GRIM	4500	1	2.4	1.9	3	Casters	Throwable, MM 9
Shiny Stone Tipped Spear	GRIM	6400	3	6.8	2.7	6	Sm	MM 9
Slook	SWT	1000	2	5.0	3.9	6	BL, Sm	MM 1.5
Smooth Ore Dagger	GRIM	280	1	3.0	2.2	3	Casters	Throwable
Sullied Dagger	PAL	30	1	2.5	2.2	3	BL, Casters	Throwable
Sullied Rapier	PAL	50	2	5.0	2.9	4		
Sullied Shortened Spear	PAL	130	2	5.0	3.0	4	BL, Sm	Throwable
Sullied Spear	PAL	200	3	7.0	3.6	5	BL, Sm	Throwable
Treated Bone Tipped Spear	GRIM	5900	2	5.0	2.3	5		MM 9
Twisted Dagger	SVC	5000	1	1.0	2.5	4	BL; not Rn, SK	No Rent, No Drop, MM 20
Wooden Practice Dagger	SVC	15	1	2.0	2.3	1	BL, Casters	Throwable
Wooden Practice Spear	SVC	100	3	7.0	3.7	3	BL, Sm	Throwable

Armor

Item	Value	Size	Wt	AC	Notes
BATTLE PLATE (SVC) *(Bd,Cl,Pl,SK,Wr / Br,Er,1/2,Hm,VS)*					
Helm (Hd)	81000	1	4.7	13	
Visor (Fc)	40500	1	1.6	6	
Collar (Nk)	33300	1	4.1	8	
Pauldron (Sh)	94500	1	4.7	11	
Cloak (Bk)	108000	3	5.9	12	
Girdle (Wst)	74250	1	4.3	9	
Vambraces (Arm)	78300	1	6.7	11	
Bracers (Wri)	41850	1	4.1	10	
Gauntlets (Hnd)	67500	1	5.1	12	
Greaves (Lg)	121500	3	7.9	13	
Boots (Ft)	81000	2	6.9	11	
CH'KTOK (PAL) *(Bd,Cl,Pl,SK,Wr / Br,DE,Er,1/2,HE,Hm,VS,WE)*					
Breastplate (Ch)	4000	3	12.5	17	+8 vs. Fire, MM 5
Armplates (Arm)	2100	1	8.5	8	+3 vs. Fire, MM 5
Legplates (Lg)	3800	3	9.6	10	+5 vs. Fire, MM 5
CURED SHADE SILK (BLT) *(BL,Mk / Br,Hm,Ik,Og,Tr,VS)*					
Headband (Hd)	1200	1	0.1	4	MM 4
Mask (Fc)	700	1	0.1	3	MM 4
Collar (Nk)	950	1	0.1	3	MM 4
Mantle (Sh)	1350	1	0.1	3	MM 5
Cloak (Bk)	1350	2	0.1	4	MM 5
Robe (Ch)	1750	2	0.1	8	MM 5
Sash (Wst)	950	1	0.1	3	MM 5
Sleeves (Arm)	1350	1	0.1	4	MM 5
Wristbands (Wri)	950	1	0.1	3	MM 5
Gloves (Hnd)	1350	1	0.1	4	MM 5
Leggings (Lg)	1600	2	0.1	5	MM 5
Sandals (Ft)	950	1	0.1	4	MM 2
DINGY (SWT) *(All Classes / All Races)*					
Cap (Hd)	110	1	0.1	3	MM 3
Gorget (Nk)	90	1	0.2	2	MM 3
Shawl (Sh)	100	1	0.3	2	MM 3
Cloak (Bk)	150	2	0.2	3	MM 3
Vest (Ch)	260	2	0.5	5	MM 3
Sash (Wst)	100	1	0.1	2	MM 3
Arm Bands (Arm)	130	1	0.2	3	MM 3
Veil (Wri)	100	1	0.2	2	MM 3
Gloves (Hnd)	150	1	0.2	3	MM 3
Trousers (Lg)	200	2	0.3	4	MM 3
Slippers (Ft)	150	1	0.3	3	MM 3

Item	Value	Size	Wt	AC	Notes
DRATHA MAK GOR (SWT) *(Non-Casters / All Races)*					
Maktik (Hd)	1600	1	0.9	5	HP +2, +1 v Magic
Foosh (Fc)	1000	1	0.7	3	HP +2, +1 v Magic
Gragl (Nk)	1200	1	0.8	4	HP +2, +1 v Magic
Khef (Sh)	1800	1	1.8	4	HP +2, +1 v Magic
Shulka (Bk)	1800	2	2.3	5	HP +2, +1 v Magic
Bopta (Ch)	2600	2	4.1	9	HP +2, +1 v Magic
Hok (Wst)	1400	1	1.3	4	HP +2, +1 v Magic
Tok Shvek (Arm)	1600	1	1.8	5	HP +2, +1 v Magic
Shvek (Wri)	1200	1	1.3	4	HP +2, +1 v Magic
Takund (Hnd)	1800	1	1.8	5	HP +2, +1 v Magic
Plakta (Lg)	2200	2	4.6	6	HP +2, +1 v Magic
Plik (Ft)	1800	1	2.8	5	HP +2, +1 v Magic
FUNGAL FIEND MEMBRANE (PAL) *(Non-Casters / All Races)*					
Helm (Hd)	800	1	0.2	4	MM 4
Mask (Fc)	500	1	0.1	2	MM 4
Gorget (Nk)	600	1	0.1	3	MM 4
Mantle (Sh)	900	1	0.2	3	MM 5
Cape (Bk)	900	2	0.4	4	MM 5
Tunic (Ch)	1300	2	0.5	8	MM 5
Girth (Wst)	700	1	0.1	3	MM 5
Armbands (Arm)	800	1	0.3	4	MM 5
Bracers (Wri)	600	1	0.2	3	MM 5
Gauntlets (Hnd)	900	1	0.3	4	MM 5
Gloves (Hnd)	600	1	0.3	4	
Leggings (Lg)	1050	2	0.4	5	MM 5
Boots (Ft)	900	1	0.4	4	MM 1.4
HOLPA MAK GOR (SWT) *(Non-Casters / All Races)*					
Maktik (Hd)	1600	1	1.1	5	HP +2
Foosh (Fc)	1000	1	0.9	3	HP +2
Gragl (Nk)	1200	1	1.0	4	HP +2
Khef (Sh)	1800	1	2.0	4	HP +2
Shulka (Bk)	1800	2	2.5	5	HP +2
Bopta (Ch)	2600	2	4.5	9	HP +2
Hok (Wst)	1400	1	1.5	4	HP +2
Tok Shvek (Arm)	1600	1	2.0	5	HP +2
Shvek (Wri)	1200	1	1.5	4	HP +2
Takund (Hnd)	1800	1	2.0	5	HP +2
Plakta (Lg)	2200	2	5.0	6	HP +2
Plik (Ft)	1800	1	3.0	5	HP +2

Item	Value	Size	Wt	AC	Notes
LODA KAI (SWT) *(Bd,Cl,Pl,Rn,Ro,SK,Sm,Wr / Br,DE,Er,1/2,HE,Hm,Ik,VS,WE)*					
Helm (Hd)	1400	1	5.0	8	MM 5
Mask (Fc)	1200	1	1.5	4	MM 5
Gorget (Nk)	700	1	2.5	5	MM 5
Mantle (Sh)	1600	1	4.0	6	MM 5
Cloak (Bk)	1800	3	5.0	7	MM 5
Mail (Ch)	2200	2	8.5	15	MM 5
Belt (Wst)	1400	1	3.0	6	MM 5
Sleeves (Arm)	1300	1	4.0	7	MM 5
Bracer (Wri)	700	1	2.5	6	MM 5
Gauntlets (Hnd)	1200	1	4.5	7	MM 5
Leggings (Lg)	2100	2	6.5	8	MM 5
Boots (Ft)	1400	2	5.5	6	MM 5
MAKILU (SWT) *(Bd,Cl,Pl,Rn,Ro,SK,Sm,Wr / Br,DE,Er,1/2,HE,Hm,Ik,VS,WE)*					
Noktik (Hd)	1400	1	10.0	9	MM 5
Foosh (Fc)	1200	1	3.0	8	MM 5
Gragl (Nk)	700	1	5.0	6	MM 5
Khef (Sh)	1600	1	8.0	7	MM 5
Shulka (Bk)	1800	3	10.0	8	MM 5
Bopta (Ch)	2200	2	17.0	16	MM 5
Hok (Wst)	1400	1	6.0	7	MM 5
Tok Shvek (Arm)	1300	1	8.0	8	MM 5
Shvek (Wri)	700	1	5.0	7	MM 5
Takund (Hnd)	1200	1	9.0	8	MM 5
Plakta (Lg)	2100	2	13.0	9	MM 5
Plik (Ft)	1400	2	11.0	7	MM 5
PADDED (SVC) *(All Classes / Br,DE,Er,1/2,HE,Hm,Ik,VS,WE)*					
Cap (Hd)	400	1	0.3	3	
Veil (Fc)	300	1	0.3	2	
Choker (Nk)	300	1	0.3	2	
Shawl (Sh)	350	1	0.3	2	
Cape (Bk)	500	2	0.5	3	
Shirt (Ch)	1000	2	1.0	5	
Cord (Wst)	350	1	0.3	2	
Sleeves (Arm)	500	1	0.2	3	
Wristband (Wri)	300	1	0.4	2	
Gloves (Hnd)	500	1	0.5	3	
Pants (Lg)	700	2	0.9	4	
Sandals (Ft)	600	1	0.6	3	

Item	Value	Size	Wt	AC	Notes
PADDED LEATHER (SVC) *(Non-Casters / Br,DE,Er,1/2,HE,Hm,Ik,VS,WE)*					
Skullcap (Hd)	1600	1	0.6	4	
Mask (Fc)	1000	1	0.4	2	
Gorget (Nk)	1200	1	0.5	3	
Shoulderpads (Sh)	2000	1	2.0	4	
Cloak (Bk)	1800	2	2.0	4	
Tunic (Ch)	2800	2	4.0	9	
Belt (Wst)	1400	1	1.0	3	
Sleeves (Arm)	1600	1	1.5	4	
Wristbands (Wri)	1200	1	1.0	3	
Gloves (Hnd)	1800	1	1.5	4	
Leggings (Lg)	2400	2	4.5	6	
Boots (Ft)	2000	1	3.0	5	
REINFORCED HOPPERHIDE (BLT) *(Non-Casters / Br,DE,Er,1/2,HE,Hm,Ik,VS,WE)*					
Skullcap (Hd)	1600	1	0.6	6	
Mask (Fc)	1000	1	0.4	4	
Gorget (Nk)	1200	1	0.5	5	
Mantle (Sh)	1800	1	1.5	5	
Cloak (Bk)	1800	2	2.0	6	
Tunic (Ch)	2600	2	3.5	11	
Belt (Wst)	1400	1	1.0	5	
Sleeves (Arm)	1600	1	1.5	6	
Wristbands (Wri)	1200	1	1.0	5	
Gloves (Hnd)	1800	1	1.5	6	
Leggings (Lg)	2200	2	4.0	7	
Boots (Ft)	1800	1	2.5	6	
SHADE SILK (BLT) *(All Classes / All Races)*					
Headband (Hd)	450	1	0.4	3	INT +1, MM 2
Mask (Fc)	325	1	0.4	2	CHA +1, MM 2
Collar (Nk)	390	1	0.4	2	CHA +1, MM 2
Mantle (Sh)	450	1	0.4	2	WIS +1, MM 2
Cloak (Bk)	450	2	0.4	3	AGI +1, MM 2
Robe (Ch)	850	2	0.4	6	AGI +1, MM 2
Sash (Wst)	455	1	0.4	2	STR +1, MM 2
Sleeves (Arm)	450	1	0.4	3	STR +1, MM 2
Wristbands (Wri)	390	1	0.4	2	DEX +1, MM 2
Gloves (Hnd)	450	1	0.4	3	DEX +1, MM 2
Leggings (Lg)	450	2	0.4	4	STA +1, MM 2
Sandals (Ft)	450	1	0.4	3	STA +1, MM 2

SHADED HOPPERHIDE (SWT)
(All Classes / Br,DE,Er,1/2,HE,Hm,Ik,VS,WE)

Item	Value	Size	Wt	AC	Notes
Skullcap (Hd)	200	1	0.5	4	+1 vs. Magic
Mask (Fc)	160	1	0.3	2	+1 vs. Magic
Gorget (Nk)	160	1	0.4	2	+1 vs. Magic
Shoulderpads (Sh)	180	1	1.4	2	+1 vs. Magic
Cloak (Bk)	260	2	1.9	4	+1 vs. Magic
Tunic (Ch)	500	2	3.4	8	+1 vs. Magic
Belt (Wst)	180	1	0.9	2	+1 vs. Magic
Sleeves (Arm)	220	1	1.4	4	+1 vs. Magic
Wristbands (Wri)	180	1	0.9	2	+1 vs. Magic
Gloves (Hnd)	260	1	1.4	4	+1 vs. Magic
Pants (Lg)	340	2	3.9	6	+1 vs. Magic
Boots (Ft)	260	1	2.4	4	+1 vs. Magic

STEEL SPLINT MAIL (SVC)
(Bd,Cl,Pl,Rn,Ro,SK,Sm,Wr / Br,DE,Er,1/2,HE,Hm,Ik,VS,WE)

Item	Value	Size	Wt	AC	Notes
Coif (Hd)	15000	1	7.2	7	MM 3.5
Neckguard (Nk)	8000	1	3.3	5	MM 3.5
Mantle (Sh)	28000	1	5.6	5	MM 3.5
Cape (Bk)	30000	3	6.4	6	MM 3.5
Coat (Ch)	35000	2	12.0	12	MM 3.5
Skirt (Wst)	11000	1	4.0	5	MM 3.5
Sleeves (Arm)	10000	1	5.6	6	MM 3.5
Bracelet (Wri)	7000	1	3.2	5	MM 3.5
Gloves (Hnd)	15000	1	6.3	6	MM 3.5
Pants (Lg)	32000	2	8.7	7	MM 3.5
Boots (Ft)	25000	2	8.0	5	MM 3.5

STUDDED HOPPERHIDE (BLT)
(Non-Casters / Br,DE,Er,1/2,HE,Hm,Ik,VS,WE)

Item	Value	Size	Wt	AC	Notes
Skullcap (Hd)	1200	1	0.6	5	
Mask (Fc)	750	1	0.4	3	
Gorget (Nk)	900	1	0.5	4	
Shoulderpads (Sh)	1300	1	1.5	4	
Cloak (Bk)	1400	2	2.0	5	
Tunic (Ch)	1900	2	3.5	9	
Belt (Wst)	1000	1	1.0	4	
Sleeves (Arm)	1200	1	1.5	5	
Wristbands (Wri)	900	1	1.0	4	
Gloves (Hnd)	1400	1	1.5	5	
Leggings (Lg)	1600	2	4.0	6	
Boots (Ft)	1400	1	2.5	5	

TATTERED HOPPERHIDE (BLT)
(Non-Casters / Br,DE,Er,1/2,HE,Hm,Ik,VS,WE)

Item	Value	Size	Wt	AC	Notes
Skullcap (Hd)	150	1	0.6	3	
Mask (Fc)	150	1	0.4	2	
Gorget (Nk)	150	1	0.5	2	
Shoulderpads (Sh)	150	1	1.5	2	
Cloak (Bk)	150	2	2.0	3	
Tunic (Ch)	150	2	3.5	6	
Belt (Wst)	150	1	1.0	2	
Sleeves (Arm)	150	1	1.5	3	
Wristbnd (Wri)	150	1	1.0	2	
Gloves (Hnd)	150	1	1.5	3	
Pants (Lg)	150	2	4.0	4	
Boots (Ft)	150	1	2.5	3	

XAKRA DAT (SWT) *(All Classes / All Races)*

Item	Value	Size	Wt	AC	Notes
Helm (Hd)	2700	1	4.0	7	No Rent, +1 v Mag, MM 5
Mask (Fc)	2400	1	0.5	3	No Rent, +1 v Mag, MM 5
Gorget (Nk)	1100	1	1.5	4	No Rent, +1 v Mag, MM 5
Mantle (Sh)	3200	1	3.0	5	No Rent, +1 v Mag, MM 5
Cloak (Bk)	3600	3	3.5	6	No Rent, +1 v Mag, MM 5
Mail (Ch)	4400	2	7.0	14	No Rent, +1 v Mag, MM 5
Belt (Wst)	2800	1	2.0	5	No Rent, +1 v Mag, MM 5
Sleeves (Arm)	2600	1	3.0	6	No Rent, +1 v Mag, MM 5
Bracer (Wri)	1400	1	1.5	5	No Rent, +1 v Mag, MM 5
Gauntlets (Hnd)	2300	1	3.5	6	No Rent, +1 v Mag, MM 5
Leggings (Lg)	4200	2	5.0	7	No Rent, +1 v Mag, MM 5
Boots (Ft)	2700	2	4.5	5	No Rent, +1 v Mag, MM 5

XAKRA KEL (SWT)
(All Classes / Br,DE,Er,1/2,HE,Hm,Ik,VS,WE)

Item	Value	Size	Wt	AC	Notes
Cap (Hd)	200	1	0.1	4	No Rent
Veil (Fc)	160	1	0.1	2	No Rent
Choker (Nk)	160	1	0.1	2	No Rent
Shawl (Sh)	180	1	0.1	2	No Rent
Cape (Bk)	260	2	0.2	4	No Rent
Shirt (Ch)	500	2	0.4	8	No Rent
Cord (Wst)	180	1	0.1	2	No Rent
Sleeves (Arm)	220	1	0.1	4	No Rent
Wristband (Wri)	180	1	0.2	2	No Rent
Gloves (Hnd)	260	1	0.2	4	No Rent
Pants (Lg)	340	2	0.4	6	No Rent
Sandals (Ft)	260	1	0.3	4	No Rent

Item	Value	Size	Wt	AC	Notes
GOR BOPTA (CH) (SWT) *(Non-Casters / All Races)*	3000	2	6.0	5	MM 1.5
GOR PLAKTA (SWT) *(All Classes / All Races)*	3000	2	8.0	5	MM 1.5
PALOCHT (SWT) *(Non-Casters / All Races)*	2000	2	5.0	10	MM 1.5
RECONDITE BANDIT BRACER (WRI) (PAL) *(Non-Casters / All Races)*	900	1	3.0	3	AGI +2, DEX +2, MM 15

Food, Drink and Other Items

NR = No Rent, ND = No Drop

Item	Loc	Value	Size	Wt	Notes
Jewelry					
Recondite Insignia Ring	PAL	215	0	0.1	AGI +2,AC 1, MM 10
Loda Kai Earring	SWT	1	0	0	ND, HP +10, MM 0
Alcohol					
Birthday Beer	SVC	300	1	0.4	
Blugha	SWT	30	1	0.2	MM 1.5
Bold Beastlord Bock	SVC	60	1	0.4	MM 1.75
Brides Promise	SVC	5000	1	0.4	
Curled Whisker Whiskey	SVC	75	1	0.4	
Dloog	SWT	30	1	0.2	MM 1.5
Feral Furry Vodka (3)	SVC	55	1	0.2	
Ferocious Feline Cider	SVC	60	1	0.4	
Gladiator Choice Ale	SVC	100	1	0.4	
Grand Palace Sparkling Wine	SVC	1000	1	0.4	
Grooms Promise	SVC	5000	1	0.4	
Pawprint Porter (3)	SVC	55	1	0.5	
Payala Nectar Wine	SWT	10	2	1.0	MM 4
Placht	SWT	30	1	0.2	MM 1.5
Royal Rebirth Rum	SVC	2000	1	0.4	
Select Celebration Port	SVC	1500	1	0.4	
Shar Vahl Almond Liqueur	SVC	200	1	0.4	
Shar Vahl Cream Liqueur	SVC	150	1	0.4	
Victory Toast Whiskey	SVC	100	1	0.4	
Crate of Broote's Burly Bock	SVC	20	3	5.0	ND
Crate of Dawnshroud Dunkel	SVC	20	3	5.0	ND
Crate of Deep Cavern Bourbon	SVC	20	3	5.0	ND
Drink					
Nepeta Oil Extract	SVC	150	1	1.0	
Sweet Payala Nectar	SWT	30	2	1.0	MM 3
Food					
Almonds	SVC	5	1	1.0	
Blackened Pepper Snake	SVC	400	0	0.1	NR
Dried Payala Chips	SWT	10	2	1.0	MM 1.5
Dried Payala Trail Mix	SWT	10	2	1.0	MM 1.5
Dried Wolf Ear	SVC	8	1	1.0	
Festive Birthday Cake Slice	SVC	50	0	0.1	No Rent
Festive Wedding Cake Slice	SVC	100	0	0.1	No Rent
Freshly Baked Payala Tart	SWT	20	2	1.0	MM 1.5
Glazed Payala Pie	SWT	10	2	1.0	MM 2
Holpa Glub	SWT	10	1	0.2	MM 1.5
Holpa Mlech	SWT	10	1	0.2	MM 1.5
Honeyed Payala Jam	SWT	8	2	1.0	MM 1.5
Marinated Mushroom Bits	SVC	50	0	0.1	
Marinated Owlbear Kabob	SVC	500	0	0.1	NR
Moor Fish Pie	SVC	150	0	0.1	
Mushroom Bread	SVC	100	0	0.1	
Nepeta Cataria Mint	SVC	25	1	1.0	
Nepeta Mint Chocolate	SVC	30	0	0.1	NR
Owlbear Bone Chew	SVC	20	0	0.1	
Owlbear Marrow Meatcakes	SVC	10	1	1.0	
Owlbear Stuffed Mushroom	SVC	150	0	0.1	
Payala Fruit	SWT	5	2	1.0	MM 2.5
Saffron Spiced Mussels	SVC	550	0	0.1	NR
Salted Fish	SVC	150	1	1.0	
Seared Sea Bass	SVC	300	0	0.1	NR
Shawerma Sandwich	SVC	25	1	1.0	
Steamed Vegetable Feast	SVC	200	0	0.1	NR
Victory Cake Slice	SVC	50	0	0.1	NR
Woodwinds					
A Flawless Ivory Horn	SWT	300	2	1.0	CHA +2, MM 1.5
Ivory Horn	SWT	200	2	1.0	MM 1.5
Miscellaneous					
A Bloodling Carapace	SWT	20	1	1.0	MM 1.5
Broken Brigand Skull	SWT	1	1	0.1	NDMM 0
Carapace Shield Frame	SVC	550	3	3.0	NR, ND, STR +5, INT +8, AGI +1
A Claw Needle	SWT	30	2	0.2	MM 1.5
Cracked Ivory Horn	SWT	100	2	1.0	MM 1.5
Cracked Rhino Beetle Carapace	SWT	200	2	5.0	
Drop of Loda Kai Blood	SWT	1	0	0.1	ND, MM high
Letter of Credit	SVC	20	3	0.5	ND
Loda Kai Insignia	SWT	1	0	0	NDMM 0
A Needle Thin Claw	SWT	5	0	0.2	MM 1.5
Pristine Rhino Beetle Carapace	SWT	1000	2	5.0	
Rhino Beetle Carapace	SWT	450	2	5.0	MM 1.5
A Scorpion Tail	SVC	1000	0	3.0	NR, ND
Sharp Bloodling Pincer	SVC	1	0	0.1	ND, HP +5, MM high
Shattered Rhino Beetle Carapace	SWT	30	2	5.0	
A Stinking Pile of Refuse	SWT	30	2	5.0	NR, MM 1.5
A Whiptail Poison Gland	SVC	500	0	0.1	NR, ND

WIN MORE, PAY LESS
WHEN YOU SUBSCRIBE TO
INQUEST GAMER
EVERY MONTH, THE BEST GAMING COVERAGE ANYWHERE!
• EXCLUSIVE GAME NEWS AND PREVIEWS!
• THE BEST CARD GAME PRICE GUIDE!
• SAVE OVER $31 PER YEAR OFF THE NEWSSTAND PRICE!
I WANNA SAVE!
INQUEST GAMER
❑ 12 ISSUES FOR $28
❑ 24 ISSUES FOR $56
Clip out or photocopy this coupon and send it to:
WIZARD
P.O. Box 656
Yorktown Heights, NY 10598
❑ Payment enclosed ❑ Bill me /or bill my ❑ Visa ❑ MasterCard ❑ Discover
Credit Card #
Expiration
Name
Street
City
State
Please allow 7 to 10 weeks for delivery of first issue. Canadian orders: 1 year for $55.00 U.S.. All other foreign orders: 1 year for $80.00 U.S..
Savings based on cover price of $4.99.
SUBSCRIBE ONLINE AT www.wizardworld.com
ISG01